A
JOURNAL
OF THE
PLAGUE
YEARS

D1400325

A
JOURNAL
OF THE
PLAGUE
YEARS

STEFAN KANFER

ATHENEUM　1973　NEW YORK

Pittsburgh Filmmakers
477 Melwood Avenue
Pittsburgh, PA 15213

We are grateful for permission to reprint the following lines:

From "To Posterity" in Selected Poems of Bertolt Brecht, translated by H. R. Hays, copyright, 1947, by Bertolt Brecht and H. R. Hays. Reprinted by permission of Harcourt Brace Jovanovich, Inc.

From "Old Man Atom" or "The Talking Atom Blues." Reprinted by permission of T. B. Harms Company.

From "Don't Bite the Hand That's Feeding You." Words: Thomas Hoier; Music: Jimmy Morgan. Copyright 1915; Renewed 1942 Leo Feist Inc. Used by Permission.

*For Lilian and Ethan
and especially for May*

Thus week by week the prisoners of the plague put up what fight they could. Some, like Rambert, even contrived to fancy they were still behaving as free men and had the power of choice. But actually it would have been truer to say at this time, mid-August, the plague had swallowed up everything and everyone. No longer were there individual destinies; only a collective destiny, made of plague and the emotions shared by all. Strongest of these emotions was the sense of exile and deprivation, with all the cross-currents of revolt and fear set up by these. That is why the narrator thinks this moment, registering the climax of the summer heat and the disease, the best for describing, on general lines and by way of illustration, the excesses of the living, burials of the dead, and the plight of parted lovers.

ALBERT CAMUS,
The Plague

"Is there any other point to which you would wish to draw my attention?"

"To the curious incident of the dog in the night-time."

"The dog did nothing in the night-time."

"That was the curious incident," remarked Sherlock Holmes.

SIR ARTHUR CONAN DOYLE,
"Silver Blaze"

Acknowledgments

PERHAPS THE SADDEST ASPECT of the blacklist is its residue. A decade after the Faulk trial there are still scores of people who would be interviewed only upon the guarantee of anonymity. This guarantee I have regretfully honored.

The kindnesses I *can* acknowledge are listed in rough historical order; they are of equal importance:

Daniel S. Aaron allowed me to examine many unpublished documents and letters, particularly those of Joseph Freeman.

Peter Davis very kindly permitted me to read and quote from the private papers of his mother, Tess Slesinger.

Lillian Hellman, with characteristic candor, recalled some crucial moments of personal history.

Ring Lardner, Jr., remembered the Hollywood of the thirties and forties with his patented amalgam of honesty and salinity.

Abe Polonsky offered considerable insight into the early manipulations of the blacklisters, as did Walter Bernstein, Eliot Asinov and Conrad Bromberg.

For a lively account of the Hollywood Ten, I am indebted to Dalton Trumbo, whose interviews are legendary, and to the frank and vigorous correspondence of Albert Maltz. Alvah Bessie has also been kind enough to criticize certain of my writings on Hollywood Past.

For his total recall of the early fifties, Merle Miller deserves special gratitude. He took many hours away from what must have been a draining schedule in order to get the record clear and the details precise.

David Susskind and Daniel Melnik, formerly of Talent Associates, furnished me with certain anecdotes and leads.

Robert Cenedella and Sam Moore were particularly helpful with their accounts of early blacklisting in radio and television.

For legal as well as personal aspects of the epoch, I am particularly grateful for the patience and help of George Berger of Philips, Nizer, Benjamin, Krim and Ballon. I abused his firm's patience, indulgence and real estate many times, examining and reexamining items of the Faulk trial.

Sidney Cohn, another acute legal mind, recalled some acrid moments from the lives of his clients, Carl Foreman and John Garfield. Arnold Foreman also contributed some memories of Garfield's final days.

For their personal recollections of the blacklist, I am in the debt of Jack Gilford, Joshua Shelley, John Randolph, Zero Mostel, Maurice Rapf, Millard Lampell, Woody Allen, Les Brown, Walter Goodman, Josh Greenfeld, as well as all those who answered my questionnaires.

For a detailed overview, and for a memory which allowed no lapses, the phenomenal Madeline Lee Gilford is owed special gratitude. Only one other eyewitness allowed me so much time and diligence: the late Stanley Prager, whose screen, broadcasting and stage experiences were shared openly, without rancor or regret. His life was a model of grace under pressure.

I am sorry to say that most members of the right were deliberately elusive; if they were invincible in the fifties, they were invisible in the seventies. A notable exception was Thomas Bolan, who consented to a lengthy interview and to panel discussions with me, without the expectation of privilege.

I am particularly grateful for the editorial exactitude and patience of Herman Gollob, as well as the counsel of Lynn Nesbit.

I want to salute as well the Job-like librarians of *Time* and

Life and to thank Henry Anatole Grunwald, Managing Editor of *Time* magazine, for his many instructions, perceptions and indulgences.

Louise N. Fisher was my amanuensis for this book; Leah S. Gordon was responsible for unearthing sources that were assumed to be lost or hidden. Even with such an assiduous researcher, however, I must assume the primary responsibility for all conclusions or errata.

Finally, I thank the people to whom this book is dedicated, my wife and children, who may now have the answer to the mystery of my peculiar schedule these past three years.

A
JOURNAL
OF THE
PLAGUE
YEARS

PROLOGUE

1

FARCE IS TRAGEDY out for a good time. Its characters miss catastrophe by a pulse beat (What if the husband had peeked behind the door? What if the policeman had knocked a minute earlier?). Its situations are always improbabilities made tantalizingly possible.

Philip Loeb was an expert farceur; he knew how close laughter could edge to a shriek. And he was aware that, somewhere, history had lost its timing. New York, which had rewarded him, given him good roles, made him prominent, now merely stank. (They were going to do a study on air pollution, the *Times* said. Typical. A study, when you could inhale and know what was wrong.) His wife was dead; his son, the bright and promising boy turned irreversibly schizoid, cowered in a public institution. His own name seemed diseased. Even now, September 1, 1955, checking into the Hotel Taft, he gave the false name of Fred Lang. At least it meant something in German: Long Peace. What did Philip Loeb mean any more? Nothing in the theater. Less than that in television. He closed the door behind the bellboy, carefully changed into pajamas and lay down. He shook the capsules into his palm.

A ridiculous place to finish, room 507 of the Hotel Taft under an assumed name. But no more absurd than the beginning, if there was a beginning. To where are such things traced? Back to the thirties, probably, when he was cavorting in the *Garrick Gaieties* or caroming off the walls in *Room Service.* "Dancing on moonbeams with skill, charm and frenzy," said Brooks Atkinson in the *Times.* That was onstage, where he would engender only love. Offstage was another matter. In 1936, in *New Masses,* he had signed an apology for the indefensible: Stalin's Moscow Trials. Later there were the backstage political harangues at Actors' Equity when the organization was searching for a political identity. By 1945 Loeb had created enough acrimony to find cloaked and seething opposition in his own union, the union for which he had helped to win such niceties as rehearsal pay and a minimum weekly salary of $57.50. At first it was a whispering campaign. But very soon the attacks grew strident and personal. So low were the blows that an elderly actor, a brass-collar Republican who had voted for Coolidge, Hoover, Landon and Willkie, defended the accused in *Equity Magazine:* "The charges against you, Mr. Loeb," he wrote, "seem to be four in number. 1. That you are a Jew. 2. That you are a Communist. 3. That you are a troublemaker, a rabble-rouser. 4. That you are personally ambitious. I will have no truck with these charges."

Personally ambitious. That was the biggest laugh. "Personally ambitious for what?" Loeb had asked his friends. For the starring role in a Western? For the office of Secretary of State? Mayor? Commissar? But after 1950 it was the second charge that seemed the most farcical. In June of that year the little paperback *Red Channels* was published, describing "Communist influence in radio and television." There were seventeen listings for Loeb; somebody had done a lot of thumbing through yellowed papers. The *New Masses* thing was there, the End Jim Crow in Baseball Committee, the membership in the Council for Pan-American Democracy, as well as other organizations the Attorney General had designated as Communist-front groups.

Now the farce teetered. Before the appearance of *Red Channels*, Loeb was the burbling, warm Papa in *The Goldbergs*, a television show of mounting popularity. Its owner, writer, star was Gertrude Berg, creator of Molly Goldberg, the Bronx Malaprop. ("Maybe he got himself run over by a cabsitac, they run around like cackaroachers.") She had seen in Loeb the permanent Jewish father who could suffer as Jewish fathers were supposed to suffer, *mit shmeck*. The audience found him admirable; so did the network and the sponsor. But after *Red Channels'* revelations General Foods felt that Loeb was not quite the same actor he once had been. Not funny enough. Too—controversial. Gertrude Berg refused to fire him. CBS dropped the show. NBC picked it up. But no sponsor wanted its name associated with controversy. Miserably, Mrs. Berg came to Loeb with a provisional settlement of $85,000. It was a choice, she said, of losing one man or a whole show—that meant forty employees out of work. "No," the actor told her, "I'm sorry. I have no price." He appealed to the unions for aid. But they had little time to hear him and no understanding of his dire condition. After all, the labor officers reasoned, unemployment is a permanent risk of the profession. Loeb was a fine, an experienced professional. If he lost one network job, another would soon turn up. But none did. In 1951, after his funds had evaporated, Loeb surrendered. By then the Goldbergs were on harder times and lower ratings. The payoff had dipped to $40,000. Sam Jaffe, his little wizened face framed by an aureole of wiry hair, offered his shocked fellow actors a Talmudic riddle: "It was the old question: if you are in a fire, do you save a baby or a priceless manuscript?" It had cost $12,000 a year to keep Philip Loeb's boy in a private institution. The father had saved his baby—for a time.

He auditioned for replacement parts in the theater. Even there he was not allowed to function. The June 1953 issue of the *American Mercury* carried an article entitled "New York's Great Red Way." A professional anti-Communist named Vincent Hartnett had carefully charted Loeb's affiliations. Hartnett

Prologue

was a solo Christian crusader, a professional Red-hunter. In appearance, he resembled Inspector Lestrade, the bright-eyed, incompetent terrier of the Sherlock Holmes canon. In spirit, however, he resembled another policeman: Javert, the pitiless tracker of *Les Misérables*. In Loeb, Hartnett had found his Jean Valjean.

The actor examined his little yellow magazine with new dread; he was prominently featured. "As the purge of Communists and notable Communist-fronters continues in Hollywood and TV," Hartnett wrote, "Broadway is fast emerging as the last stronghold of show-business Marxists and their supporters. . . . Philip Loeb for years was one of the loudest noises on the 'popular front.' A year ago he appeared before the Senate Internal Security Subcommittee, admitted past affiliation with a score of Communist-front organizations but denied party membership, and swore he thought Communists were a 'menace' to our country. This, however, did not prevent him from running with a number of the 'menaces' on a left-wing ticket in a TV actors' election some months later, nor from speaking (with several 'menaces') at a fund-raising rally for the ticket."

Broadway soon had nothing for Loeb. His last job was downtown in a revival of *The Three Sisters* for $87.50 a week. The money had vanished months before. The boy was now in a state home in Massachusetts. There he had written an agonized letter, a terminal plea to be returned to a place where he might be cured.

Long Peace. At sixty-one a man had earned the right to lie down. Loeb swallowed the capsules. The water tasted of chlorine. He lay back, waiting.

Before the funeral, Loeb's sister wept. "He's been hurt so terribly. Now see what they did to him. They took his living away. They took his life away. A person can only stand so much."

Sam Jaffe was more succinct after the services. "I think we know what killed Phil," he said. The knot of mourners nodded, but no one articulated the word. Nor did the newspapers. In 1955, the blacklist, like cancer, was omitted from obituaries.

2

The term and practice of blacklisting has an ancient, aristocratic past. Amherst, in his *Terrae Filius, or The Secret History of the Universities of Oxford*, speaks of the Proctor's black book, and tells us that no one can proceed to a degree whose name is found there. On the blacklist in the black book were gentlemen who had contracted bad debts, or who had made tactical blunders. Later, says Brewer's Dictionary, it came to mean a list of persons in disgrace, or who have incurred censure or punishment—a list of bankrupts for the private guidance of the mercantile community. The Random House Dictionary gives an acutely modern definition: "n. A list of persons under suspicion, disfavor, censure, etc.: His record as an anarchist put him on the government's blacklist. . . . —v.t. to put (a person) on a blacklist. [BLACK + LIST; orig. political]."

It is in this modern context that Philip Loeb rises from casualty to exemplar. Fusing entertainment and politics, he was at once frightfully naïve and wholly committed. Bewildered, he found himself in collision with his better impulses and his society's worst. Through a series of mounting personal catastrophes he came to be killed by the list which proscribed him. It is true that Loeb's circumstances were uniquely miserable; most other blacklistees did not suffer physical death. But Loeb was not the only one to commit suicide because of "suspicion, disfavor, censure, etc." And there were other varieties of extinction—professional, political, financial, social. In that sense, nearly everyone on the blacklist died along with Loeb.

In recent times, several books have attempted to chronicle the causes and career of the blacklist. Most, it seems to me, have mistakenly concentrated their focus on the scrimmage of government investigators and their witnesses. This encourages a myth that has already ossified into text- and reference-book form. Thus we read in Leslie Halliwell's widely respected library work *The Filmgoer's Companion*, "Dalton Trumbo, one of the Hollywood Ten, blacklisted by McCarthy." This is doubly misleading. Trumbo and many other Hollywood *personae* were blacklisted long before Senator Joe McCarthy forged the handwriting on the wall, before he broke, let alone mounted, the Red issue. Of course Halliwell also uses the Senator's name as mere shorthand; he means, as well, the McCarthy era. Here, too, the book is mistaken. The blacklist officially began before that epoch and flourished long after the censure vote. In fact, McCarthy never displayed much interest in show business—very likely because he *was* show business, in a malign but recognizable form: the insult comic given feature billing.

No, to represent the blacklist solely by hearings is like telling the story of the Terror solely from a bench at the tribunal. The true play of vengeance took place *after* the lawyers and legislators had packed their briefcases, when the press had vanished. Quotations from the Hollywood hearings are of course irresistible; it is proper that the stage be given over to a revival of the drama and that the leads and walk-ons be allowed to strut and fret: Bertolt Brecht, the Hollywood Ten, Senator Rankin, Representative Nixon, J. Parnell Thomas, Francis Walter, and the cavalcade of performers and writers are too fascinating to be excluded from any chronicle of their time. But of equal fascination are the secular blacklisters, the offstage collaborators and the progress of the walking wounded, injured by actual misdeed or—far more often—by pernicious innuendo.

Dalton Trumbo, that most durable of the Hollywood Ten, has written that there were in that dark time "neither saints nor devils . . . there were only victims." This strikes me as highly disingenuous. It is true that we are all scorched when history comes too close, that hangman and prisoner frequently exchange roles when the biographies are written. Nevertheless, as we shall see, there are at all times men who manufacture misery and men who profit from it. Sometimes they are the same men. There are also those who suffer with the great and who, having escaped, tend to exaggerate their roles in a kind of nobility by association. Perhaps they are entitled. Kafka wrote, "One must cheat no one, not even the world of its triumph." Most of the loud survivors did not cheat the world; their ostentatious martyrdom must be heard.

In *Rosencrantz and Guildenstern Are Dead* Tom Stoppard made a saline observation which outlasts his absurdist exercise: If you are Rosencrantz or Guildenstern, Hamlet is only a walk-on. In the historical play of the blacklist the large names of Truman, Churchill, Stalin, Joe McCarthy, Julius and Ethel Rosenberg, George Marshall, Alger Hiss are Hamletic figures. For years they have been posed like fists against the sun, eclipsing figures of equal inhumanity or grace. Those figures are the engineers and *blessés* of the blacklist, individuals largely ignored by historians who regard show business as a footnote, not a text. It is the purpose of this book to raise them all from the bottom of the page. I have done so at the expense of the Hamlets who are barely visible in the background. They have held the stage long enough.

The scope of this history is the entertainment profession, principally cinema and broadcasting, two areas with which I have had some acquaintance. Show business is not hermetically separated from its national environment. But it does obey laws and bend to pressures that exist in no other stratum of American life, and I believe that performers and writers are frequently more accurate seismographs of their era than politicians and statesmen.

Though the harsh concourse proceeds from the forties, I have begun with brief accounts of the early stirrings of the partisans, right first, then left. For those who wish more expanded fever charts of the thirties, two books are especially recommended. Daniel Aaron's towering *Writers on the Left* remains a model of distinction and forbearance, a lucid comprehension of the encounter of Marxism and the creative intellect in America. Another vision, more pained and subjective, is contained in Murray Kempton's moving valedictory, *Part of Our Time*, with its November prose frosted over with the chill of death. The sound that both books leave behind is muffled and final, the echo of a metal door. Yet even rusted locks may be reopened. When he published *Part of Our Time* in 1957, Murray Kempton wrote of the blacklisted film writers: "Their story is a failure of promise; first of the promise in themselves, and last, of the promise of the Hollywood which was so kind to them until they became an embarrassment and then turned them out. The promise at the beginnings of most of them appears now to have been largely smoke and thunder; the promise which vanished at the end appears now to have been tinsel, as Hollywood is tinsel. They were entombed, most of them, not for being true to themselves, but for sitting up too long with their own press releases."

This lofty disdain was quoted with approval by Walter Goodman in his great history of the HUAC, *The Committee*. When the book was reviewed in 1968, the *New Republic* reversed the verdict of the Kempton court: "[Kempton's] tone . . . is no longer adequate for our history. It can never be more than the refined expression of the very crude and philistine notion that the victim is usually guilty of something. . . . The rhetoric of the Hollywood Ten may have been inferior to their cause, as the rhetoric of victims quite often is. It ought to be said for [the writers] that, in their test, they did what they could with the remaining resources of language and dignity, and that they did better than we. They earned the respect which irony excludes, and their country needs more than anything else that passionate indignation which irony refuses to provide."

The writer: Murray Kempton. The reason for the revision is now painfully manifest. What seemed concluded in the early sixties had been renewed in a decade. Kempton foresaw that the spirit of the blacklist was always to be welcomed in its ancestral home, Washington, D.C.

ONE

"ALL RIGHT, we are two nations," John Dos Passos had written after the execution of Sacco and Vanzetti. The phrase is at once immortal and insufficient. Even under Dos Passos' simplistic general surgery we were, in the thirties, not two but three nations. At the center was a vast body, inactive, opaque, capable of twitching galvanically only when voltage was applied at its terminals. At one extreme gathered the progressives, a misty coalition of parties and individuals who coated the twentieth century with a gloss of optimism so strong that it admitted no scrutiny. For them the time was, variously, the era of the common man, the moment of total revolution, the arrival of the Marxist express. "If only we knew, if only we knew," are the last words of Olga, the most poignant of Chekhov's *Three Sisters*, longing for a sense of the steadily receding future. The progressives knew. The future was Now.

At the other terminal were the resistants, citizens possessed of Gothic certainty, who regarded the second hand as regrettable, the minute hand as a mistake, the hour hand as catastrophe. For them the evidence of the century was an affront. In *Anti-Intellectualism in American Life*, Richard Hofstadter encapsulated their anti-movement:

"The fundamentalist mind . . . looks upon the world as an arena for conflict between absolute good and absolute evil, and accordingly it scorns compromises (who would compromise with Satan?) and can tolerate no ambiguities. It cannot find serious importance in what it believes to be trifling degrees of difference: liberals support measures that are for all practical purposes socialistic, and socialism is nothing more than a variant of Communism, which everyone knows is atheism."

From the beginning the fundamentalist mind regarded the film industry—the century's sole claimant to a synthetic art form—as a microcosm of bad absolutes, a drop of water choked with bacilli. By 1907 the *Chicago Tribune* wrote that nickelodeons ministered "to the lowest passions of childhood." "Wholly vicious, they should be censored and suppressed," said the editorial. There could be "no voice raised to defend the majority of five-cent theatres because they cannot be defended."

Two years later the complaints of cinema immorality grew so strident that the Mayor of New York closed the nickelodeons until a group of unimpeachable citizens agreed to pre-examine the fare. The film scandals of the twenties, notably the Fatty Arbuckle murder trial and the Chaplin divorces, plus the ostentatious self-regulation of the Hays Office, merely ratified the fundamentalist's assumptions. He knew what the gossip columns merely hinted: film was a moral solvent. The shadow play was caused by the gestures of free-thinkers, atheists, revolutionaries. In his study of American film during the Jurassic era, *A Million and One Nights*, Terry Ramsaye reported: "It is not an accident but rather a phase of screen evolution which finds the American motion picture industry, and therefore the screens of the world, administered rather largely by our best and most facile internationalists, the Jews, with those of Russian extraction slightly prominent over the Germans."

Those facile internationalists represented, to Manichaean thinking, the Beelzebubs and Belials sent to destroy the work of the Creator: America. In Washington, December 10, 1920, the lobby of the International Reform Bureau, Rev. Dr. Wilbur Crafts presiding, gave out a tautological press release. The IRB would "rescue the motion pictures from the hands of the Devil and 500 un-Christian Jews." As the first step in removing the menace of the movies, Dr. Crafts told the reformers that he would "appeal to the Catholic Church and . . . crash into Congress backed by the Christian Churches and reform organizations, which was the only way to defeat the $40,000,000 slush fund the movie men had come to Washington with."

Such capital adventures provided Mencken and his followers with "unceasing delight [in] the pursuit of witches and heretics, the desperate struggles of inferior men to claw their way into heaven." The self-righteous pursuers were seen not as a pack of hounds but as a group of poodles, clipped and trained for the circus, at which Mencken was at once ringmaster and boxholder. When the totalitarian sweep began in the thirties, the Menckenian amusement continued but the mirth became forced—a shield pretending to be a lance. That "unceasing delight," that cackling at fools, was soon to grow sickly and contemptuous. Still, in the early thirties the parasitic art of satire was as robust as its host.

Untroubled by the speculative or artistic itch, the far right constructed elaborate fantasies of xenophobia. In them, Russians of transparent intent sent messages, sometimes through paraphysical means, to agents in the United States. These agents, unlike the Bolsheviks, could assume normal American appearances with two-piece suits and shaves. They had manuals of instructions but only one order: bring down the edifice. They acted through (1) labor unions, which conspired to stop the machine, (2) Negroes who wished to vote in the South, and (3) liberals subdivided into descending categories: Communists, fellow-travelers, opportunists and dupes. These groups acted as if they were separate entities, as if they would not recognize each other on the street. But it was known that the leaders met frequently in "cells," modules of discontent and revolution. The meetings were at night, usually under a naked light bulb dangling from the ceiling, like the illumination in cheap hotels. In the daytime these leaders returned to their customary stations to undo the American character. They were at once rattlingly imbecilic—they gave themselves away by using such code words as "bosses," "anti-fascism" and "counter-revolutionary." Yet they were simultaneously as clever as Professor Moriarty; they were already at the center of the communications business, publishing, radio and, most important, movies. There they could bend public opinion—a term that the Manichaean defined as every man's opinion except his own. Disguised as entertainment, propaganda could be sent forth until adults were tainted and children gutted. At last, at a given signal, the audience would rise as one and destroy God's American apparatus until red flags fluttered on the town square and the *Saturday Evening Post* was printed in the Cyrillic alphabet.

Perhaps the most kinetic of the early fantasists was Mrs. Elizabeth Dilling, a rare amalgam of Madame Defarge and Ko-Ko. In 1934, after an exhaustive ransacking of organization letterheads, leftist periodicals and the Protocols of Zion, Mrs. Dilling published (at her own expense) modern America's first comprehensive blacklist. Like the great brontosaurus, *The Red Network* was grotesque and doomed, but it was a potent ancestor. More perfect examples would follow.

Clothbound in the color of its title, *The Red Network* contained a tight *précis* of the Union of Soviet Socialist Republics: "'Mother of harlots and abominations of the earth' (Rev. 17:5), is the world's first government to raise the flag of absolute hatred and enmity to God Almighty. It not only makes no secret of its satanic Marxian atheism but finances and boastfully backs immoral sex and militant atheistic movements the world over." In alphabetical order *The Red Network* listed organizations which included, along with the *Daily Worker*, the *Letters of Sacco and Vanzetti*; the National Association for the Advancement of Colored People; the *New Republic*; the New School for Social Research; the YMCA and YWCA. ("An ex-Communist tells me that Eleanor Copenhaver, National Industrial Secretary of the Y.W.C.A., has recently married Sherwood Anderson, prominent Communist worker. There should be a thorough investigation made of the whole personnel and program of the Y.W.C.A. and either a change of name or a change of National Board policy made. Why should *Christians* support those who 'wave scarlet banner triumphantly for Communism and Liberty?' ")

After the organizations came Mrs. Dilling's "Who Is Who in Radicalism," an alphabetical file of individuals who "contributed in some measure to one or more phases of the Red movement in the United States."

Among the blacklistees: "BOURKE-WHITE, MARGARET: a Communist-Recommended Author; pub. book of photos of Russia. DARROW, CLARENCE: Roosevelt appointee, chmn. NRA review bd. 1934. DEWEY, JOHN: contrib. "New Republic." FREUD, SIGMUND: sex psychoanalyst, says 'Religious ideas are illusions,' etc. ROOSEVELT, MRS. FRANKLIN D.: pacifist; vice pres. N.Y. Lg. Women Voters. WILDER, THORNTON N.: Amer. Com. World Congress Against War."

The very universality of her catalogue defeated Mrs. Dilling. *The Red Network* was openly referred to as the Red Nutwork. At a Philadelphia rally Mr. Dilling, a sanitary engineer, heard his wife referred to as Mrs. Dillinger. He addressed the speaker as "you dirty little Jew" and belted him in the nose. Gilbert Seldes in the first of his brisk surveys of pop ideologies, *Witch Hunt*, chortled, "I know many writers who, having seen the names of Theodore Dreiser, Sinclair Lewis, Upton Sinclair and other leading intellectuals, including practically all the younger writers, in the Dilling Network, felt it a slight to their *amour propre* to have been omitted, and one at least wrote a request to be included in a new edition."

Seldes' amusement was tempered by the knowledge that the book had been endorsed by William Randolph Hearst and Colonel Robert R. McCormick, publisher of the *Chicago Tribune*. "I trust," wrote the Colonel, "that the book will have a large sale so that Americans will know who are the enemies of society within our gate."

The trust was misplaced; the time was not propitious and the editions were not large. With the re-election of Roosevelt and the dissolution of Europe, the domestic blacklist grew so long that it could not function. A billion subversives were now grossly perceptible to their opponents: they were the members of organized labor, the devisers of the New Deal and the interventionists who were wickedly edging the U.S. into war.

F.D.R.'s administration proved invulnerable—returned to office by twenty-seven million dupes, it had a residuum of power which no organization in or out of Congress could hope to invalidate. The assault would have to be made on the periphery. No other aspect of American life had the undertow of the entertainment business, with its proliferating audience, its manufactured and authentic scandals and daily gossip columnists. Here the Thirty Years' War on the century began.

It was not a frivolous business, this removal of Satan from Washington. But those who battled for the Restoration were so lacking in culture and literary or theatrical background that they continually provided their own parodies.

J. B. Matthews, for example, had moved from Methodist missionarying to liberal reform to pacifism to socialism to Communism—to uni-dimensioned political conservatism. By 1936 he had thrown all his associations into the garbage. But by 1938 the double apostate had begun to sift through the rubbish; perhaps, he thought, something could be salvaged from the invalidated past. Something could—a career. Matthews, thickening with the years, growing, perhaps consciously, to resemble the vested, paunchy robber barons he suddenly admired, began to sell his old acquaintances. "To me," he liked to say, "the letterhead of a communist front is a nugget." On service for the House Un-American Activities Committee, the self-anointed expert on American Marxism testified that Shirley Temple (then nine) had performed a great service for the

Communist Party by sending greetings to the French Communist paper *Ce Soir*. Harold Ickes hooted, "They've gone to Hollywood and discovered a great Red plot. They have found dangerous radicals there, led by little Shirley Temple. Imagine the great committee raiding her nursery and seizing her dolls in evidence." Very amusing about the dolls; still Matthews had made his point. He had never said that Shirley was a Communist; only that she was a dupe. Only that even the truly innocent could be made to serve the Devil's will.

Martin Dies' celebrated investigation of the Federal Theatre provided the right with its first real showcase. Chairman Dies liked to affect a hill-country good-ol'-boy manner, and his chunky, unlined face rarely betrayed a hint of connivance or despair. But Dies was in fact a second-generation Texas Congressman, and, like his father, Martin seemed to suspect any American darker than white, or one whose accent betrayed an origin east or north of the Lone Star State. He lived for an investigation of "the extent, character and object of un-American propaganda activities in the United States." Dies made passing swipes at fascists, but his animal passion was saved for the atheistic godless communistic left—or, as he saw it, Franklin D. Roosevelt's entire New Deal. Congressman Dies was sharply aware of the President's Bolshevik bias: had not WPA administrator Harry Hopkins himself rejoiced at the play *Power*, which dared to celebrate the TVA? Had not Hopkins stepped backstage to exhort the cast: "The big power companies have spent millions on propaganda for the utilities. It's about time the consumer had a mouthpiece. I say more plays like *Power* and more power to you." And *Prologue to Glory*—that was a more pernicious offender. It showed the young Lincoln battling with government functionaries. Representative J. Parnell Thomas called it "a propaganda play to prove that all politicians are crooked." And *Lysistrata—that* play was shut down in the state of Washington after the Mayor of Seattle received complaints about Aristophanes' "spicy show."

The objections were not solely from know-nothings. Theater critic George Jean Nathan found the WPA's younger performers "spongers and grafters and no more deserving of charity from this particular source than they were deserving of Civil War pensions or Congressional dispensations of pâté de foie gras." The *New York Times* agreed: "They must not starve, but need they act?"

They need not. As historians love to recount, Congressman Joe Starnes of Alabama, who sat to the right of Chariman Dies, let go the master howler of the thirties. When he heard the Federal Theatre's directress, Hallie Flanagan, quote Christopher Marlowe, he demanded, "You are quoting from this Marlowe. Is he a Communist?" When enlightened, Mr. Starnes plowed on: "Of course, we had what some people call Communists back in the days of the Greek theater. . . . So we cannot say when it began." For the rest of the committee, however, it was certain that it began on Inauguration Day, 1933, and that it was time to go into reverse. Congressman Thomas condensed the Committee's findings to an essence: "Practically every play presented under the auspices of the Project is sheer propaganda for Communism or the New Deal."

In the end, immediately before a Congressional vote to save the Federal Theatre, Illinois' junior Senator, Everett Dirksen, gave an unconscious imitation of the King in *Huckleberry Finn*, all full of tears and flapdoodle, as he ran down some Federal Theatre productions: "*A New Kind of Love*. I wonder what that can be. It smacks somewhat of the Soviet. . . . Then there is *Cheating Husbands*. That would be well for the front page of some Washington daily. Next we have *Compassionate Maggie*, and this great rhetorical and intriguing question *Did Adam Sin?* . . . And then this very happy title *Love 'Em and Leave 'Em*. Also we have *Mary's Other Husband*. Now if you want that kind of salacious tripe [Dirksen had seen none of the plays], well then, vote for it, but if anybody has an interest in decency on the stage, if anyone has an interest in real cultural values, you will not find it in this kind of junk. . . ." The amendment was readily defeated, 192 to 56.

A far more premonitory investigation of show business has been ignored by historians who regard the House Un-American Activities Committee alternately as the funhouse and the outer circle of hell. In 1941 only the naïve or deluded doubted that war was imminent. But, on the right, several Senators still stood on the beach, commanding the ocean to roll back. It was useless, they decided, to attack the President. Instead, they would embarrass his administration by exposing the vicious, warmongering movies that the New Deal had secretly sponsored in California. With the lunatic timing characteristic of the pre-war isolationists, Senator Burton K. Wheeler of Idaho chose September 1941 for his probe of Hollywood. Shrewdly maneuvering his coterie of similarly outraged Senators, Wheeler held a preliminary investigation "to determine if an investigation should be held." The *ad hoc* subcommittee made four charges against Celluloid City:

1. Though movie houses were losing money on war films, an industry controlled by "foreign-born" producers persisted in making pictures calculated to drag the U.S. into a European conflict.

2. New Dealers had asked the film-makers to do this.

3. Hollywood had a stake in a British victory because British rental fees often made the difference between profit and loss on American movies.

4. The movies were a tightly controlled monopoly exercising a rigid censorship that turned 17,000 theaters into daily and nightly mass meetings for war.

It was apparent from opening day that "foreign-born" meant Jewish. The prim, vigorous isolationist Senator Gerald P. Nye met the whispers with a loud retort: "If anti-Semitism exists in America, the Jews have themselves to blame." Nye's statement harmonized with those of his friend Charles A. Lindbergh, who the same month told an America First rally: "The three most important groups pressing the country toward war are the British, the Jewish and the Roosevelt administration." The Jews in particular, he said, were dangerous because of "their large ownership and influence in our motion pictures, our press, our radio and our Government."

Boos and titters greeted the investigation that *Life* Magazine called "the funniest political circus of the year." It was self-interest rather than national interest that caused *Life* to give Wheeler such derisive coverage; among the Senator's condemned properties were the internationalist *March of Time* newsreels. The Senate Committee was used to mockery from the press and the gallery: what distressed it was the counsel engaged by the foreign-born. He was a lawyer, ex-Presidential candidate, Republican and forensic stylist named Wendell Willkie, who immediately characterized the investigators as a kangaroo court. Their purpose, he said, was to accuse, judge and condemn the administration's foreign policy, Along the way, they aimed to pressure Hollywood into avoiding "accurate and factual" pictures of Nazism, to block national defense and to "divide the American people into discordant racial and religious groups."

The subcommittee resentfully pushed on, offering seventeen movies as evidence of war-mongering. The best of them was made by that perennial butt of moral scourges, Charlie Chaplin. Adenoid Hynkel, *The Great Dictator*, was a mockery of the Chancellor of Germany, they said. Of course Chaplin disliked Hitler, Senator Wheeler argued; the tramp was a British subject. *That Hamilton Woman* was, to Senator Bennett Champ Clark, "a perversion of history." Admiral Nelson's impassioned plea to the King of Naples for aid against Napoleon was quite accurately labeled "bald interventionist propaganda." As for *Sergeant York*, Gary Cooper was attempting to drive an unwilling people to war.

Willkie countered with the movie *Escape*, starring Robert Taylor searching encampments behind barbed wire for his aged mother. The film, claimed the defense, showed "a portrait of the concentration camp system; it reveals the incredible cruelties of the Nazis. We are prepared to prove that this is an accurate presentation." Nonsense, said Nye, "the moviemakers, born abroad and animated by the hatreds of the Old World," were injecting into American films "the most vicious propaganda I've ever seen"—all this a year after William L. Shirer's *Berlin Diary* had become a national best-seller.

It was event, not argument, that invalidated the subcommittee and its findings. On December 7 isolationism was caught without a costume. History closed the doors to the show. It would reopen six years later with a different cast and new lyrics.

In *Life,* Willkie was given space to editorialize about the investigation of film content. Willkie, not previously celebrated for his championship of civil liberties, composed a premonitory catalogue of dangers:

"The entire proceeding is extrajudicial," he maintained.

The individual under investigation is placed on the witness stand and the committee is the sole judge of everything that happens thereafter. There are no rules of evidence, and other witnesses may be called to spread any kind of gossip and innuendo. In fact, that often appears to be the kind of testimony sought.

What is the object of investigations of this nature? Ostensibly they are to guide Congress in shaping new legislation. Actually they are to focus the spotlight of publicity upon some Representative or Senator and his victim . . . often the witnesses are men of high reputation whereas the examining Senator or Representative is not known widely outside his state. What better opportunity for national prominence? At times an inferiority complex possessed by the inquisitor is involved, and he finds great satisfaction in holding up a well-known figure to scorn and obloquy, whose lawyer must sit by unable to protect him. . . . The challenge to freedom of expression never comes openly or through obvious measures, but begins with pressure and covert intimidation. The agencies of public opinion, upon which independent and enlightened people depend, must be kept continuously free from government domination, whether it be by a bureau, a commission, or by the skillful chairman of a powerful Congressional committee. And the time to stand out against the threat of domination is at the start.

Willkie barked in a void. In the rush of war and necessary coalitions, both the enemies and guards of civil liberties were unheard. Because the Axis so openly espoused it, anti-Semitism temporarily became unfashionable. As for intimidation of entertainers, Congress had other, better things to do than look at pictures. Besides, movies were no longer disseminating propaganda, they were boosting morale. E for Effort flags fluttered over Warner Bros. and MGM. The right could afford to wait. It had patience; it was not going anywhere.

Its quarry—the show-business left—was another matter; another theater, really. It was young in personnel, in outlook, in energy. That group claimed for itself what the right could not—an abiding humanity and tolerance. It also claimed the gift of clairvoyance. The American body was moribund. Of that the left was certain. The loud stertorian breaths, the patriotic rumbles and Congressional investigations were the throes of a dying giant. The vast spectrum of progressives—many of whom could not abide each other—stood by the bedside, listening for the death rattle, awaiting the reading of the will, seeing the whole process in the historical present. . . .

TWO

THEY CONSUME all the oxygen in the room when they arrive in thirties Hollywood; the town has seen nothing like the Eastern leftists. Monroe Stahr, Fitzgerald's Jewish tycoon, cares so much about Communism that he investigates the phenomenon as closely as any film executive of his period—he has the script department work up a two-page treatment of the Manifesto. His secretary, Cecilia, does better; she finds that Party member, a man named Brimmer, "a little on the order of Spencer Tracy, but with a stronger face." Fitzgerald, for the last time, defines an epoch with local insights. When Brimmer asks Stahr why the producers refused to support the Anti-Nazi League, Stahr tells him, "Because of you people. It's your way of getting at the writers."

"The writers are the farmers in this business," returns Brimmer pleasantly. "They grow the grain but they're not in at the feast. Their feeling toward the producer is like the farmers' resentment of the city fellow." . . .

"You don't really think you're going to overthrow the government."

"No, Mr. Stahr. But we think perhaps you are."

So the palaver goes in High Hollywood, where it is plausible —even fashionable—for collectivists and millionaires to argue and booze away an afternoon together. Movie radicalism is shortly to become a caricature, the red bleached out in the insipid California sun. But just now the caricature seems to verge on portrait.

In the spring of 1931 Joseph Freeman, the ubiquitous chronicler and theorist of thirties radicalism, goes West. Freeman begins his American life as a Yiddish-speaking immigrant in a Brooklyn ghetto. The first novel he reads is *The Last of the Mohicans*—in a Hebrew translation. His angry radicalism starts early and never totally fades. Throughout his life he is to remain affected by James Fenimore Cooper's gilded fictions. Freeman calls his autobiography *An American Testament: A Narrative of Rebels and Romantics,* and his view of old Hollywood is not that of a social critic but of a wide-eyed outsider mystified by capital and process. "MGM thinks they have an idea so brilliant that their rivals will steal it as soon as they hear about it," he writes a comrade. "They do not want anyone to know even that they intend to make a film around Soviet Russia . . . the sixth or seventh or eighth version of the scenario (I've forgotten which) must be written now. I don't quite see the use of it, since Napoleon's line must prevail in the end. . . ." Napoleon is Irving Thalberg, the original for Monroe Stahr.

Later, when Freeman becomes editor of the Communist

New Masses, he returns to the West, not as a futile scenarist but as a collector of cash for the Party. By then the *Daily Worker* has declared Hollywood "the West Coast center of progressivism," but the Bosses are still wary of the Brimmers. Freeman is told to make his harangue *sotto voce.* His part is rewritten; he is no longer a Red fund-raiser. He is, instead, an "anti-fascist editor." J. Edward Bromberg, an associate from the old Group Theatre, drives Freeman to a party. The actor prepares to move on; he has not been invited. "I only make a thousand dollars a week," he explains. "There won't be anyone there who makes less than fifteen hundred. They'd resent it if I came in."

Freeman dismisses this as negative snobbery, insists that Bromberg join him, and then watches the actor silently attack his drink, ostracized by the corporate elite. If this is the kind of anti-fascist Hollywood is manufacturing, Freeman decides, the hell with them all, and he zeros in on the help, two blacks and two European refugees. He grows eloquent; the refugees begin to weep. The guests, shattered, contribute $20,000 to the Cause. Witnesses, who continue to see everything as through a 35-mm. lens, later characterize it as a beautifully directed scene, a "brilliant bit of stage business."

No American playwright scrambles out of urban obscurity faster than Clifford Odets—nor tumbles back as tragically. Odets, who writes *Waiting for Lefty* and *Paradise Lost* as if with a baseball bat, Odets, spiny-tempered, spiky-haired hope of New York, the phosphor of that collection of romantic talent that calls itself the Group Theatre—what does he want with the movies? He is about as comfortable in Hollywood as a tarantula on a wedding cake. He admits to an old Manhattan friend that for him Hollywood is Sin, yet he will not leave it. It is a peccadillo for which there will be neither forgiveness nor recovery. As a shield for the sneers, Odets assumes a bristling pugnacity. Still he cannot escape the cheap shots from great kidders like Moss Hart, who tells the young author that the Odets experience has persuaded many scenarists to turn left and go West. "You mean," asks Odets, "my plays convert them?" "No," replies Hart, "your salary."

Early in the thirties, two kids with a similar curse—famous fathers—decide that the solution to the American agony lies in Soviet history. Ring Lardner, Jr., and Budd Schulberg, son of the anti-labor studio chief B. P. Schulberg, decide to see the U.S.S.R. for themselves. Budd, who hides an exquisite sensitivity in a blunt-nosed pugilistic stance, inhales the latest Communist doctrine and finds it bracing. Lardner, as saturnine and skeptical as his old man, is not so sure. Budd calls him rightwing when Ring writes a satire of a Russian newspaper and pastes it upon a wall like an impudent poster. A certain Soviet Professor Pinkavitch, adviser to the boys, examines the Lardner wallpaper and demands an explanation. "It's parody," explains the young author and, when Pinkavitch frowns, broadens his definition: "*You* know, Professor, humor for humor's sake." But Pinkavitch does not know. "We don't have that in the Soviet Union," he grumbles.

There is a use for it Stateside. The U.S. Communist Party never bothers to know its enemy (who will redouble the ignorance). What it will not learn, it invents. America is edging toward totalitarianism, the Hollywood branch decides, as evidenced by Martin Dies' noodleheaded effort to expose Reds in show business.

At a rally against the Dies Committee, Dorothy Parker suddenly seems to dwell in the place she dreaded, Wit's End, as she recites, "The people want democracy—real democracy, Mr. Dies, and they look toward Hollywood to give it to them because they don't get it any more in their newspapers. And that's why you're out here, Mr. Dies—that's why you want to destroy the Hollywood progressive organizations—because you've got to control this medium if you want to bring fascism to this country. . . . We're grateful for our jobs and we're grateful for the opportunity it gives us to speak for American democracy. . . ."

Edmund Wilson later sends his regrets: Miss Parker, he concludes, had "succumbed to the expiatory mania that has become epidemic with film writers . . . making appeals on behalf of those organizations which talked about being 'progressive' and succeeded in convincing their followers that they were working for the social revolution, though they had really no other purpose than to promote the foreign policy of the Soviet Union. She ought, of course, to have been satirizing Hollywood and sticking pins into fellow-travelers but she has not, as far as I know, ever written a word about either."

That "expiatory mania" is the masochistic ritual of humiliation experienced by many fellow-traveling intellectuals who take out their motivations, sand and buff them and then put them back inside, hoping to emerge one day with a perfect doctrine. John Howard Lawson, another adamantine New York playwright softening in Hollywood, speaks for all of them: "We all know that many intellectuals are so confused . . . that they waver idiotically between Communism and various manifestations of social fascism. . . . I am a fellow-traveler because I have not demonstrated any ability to serve the revolutionary working class either in my writing or my practical activity."

Clifton Fadiman, a critic who is to become Average America's favorite MC on the radio quiz *Information Please,* confesses his professional inadequacies: "A person born in the middle class as I was, educated in bourgeois institutions, more or less professionally interested in literature, is poorly prepared to take a leading part [in revolutionary activity]."

If the writers suffer the sensations of political impotence, performers are sometimes basket cases. The Caliban of the left theater, Lionel Stander, whistles the Communist rallying song, "The Internationale," in a scene which requires him to wait for an elevator. "Even in Brazil they'll know where I stand," he croaks happily. But Party officials are horrified. John Howard Lawson points to Stander as a textbook example of how a progressive should not behave. What the Communists of the period want is secrecy, not declaration; it is dangerous, they announce, to expose "progressive" beliefs.

S. J. Perelman sums up the surrealistic and clandestine quality of the Hollywood left in "Waiting for Santy," a skit lampooning Odets. As Santa Claus, the boss, holds up a tear-gas bomb, "the gnomes utter cries of joy, join hands and dance around him shouting exultantly. All except Riskin and Briskin, that is, who exchange a quick glance and go underground."

In stations underground the leftists find a shortage of air and no room to turn around. The peculiar oscillations of the Party line exact unique penalties. It is one thing, after all, to have a producer change his mind in the middle of a conference, or to have an audience reject your last picture. It is quite another to reverse your political tides like a Baltic estuary. After a brief period of solidarity the dissolution of Hollywood radicalism begins with the Moscow Trials, which have about them the indecipherable quality of bad foreign cinema. (Take the case, for instance, of Krestinsky, the former Deputy Foreign Minister, who thinks so little of saving the Revolution that he announces in open court that he retracts his confession, obtained under torture. The astonished judge adjourns the trial until the following day, when Krestinsky retracts his retraction.) Yet there are many who find six thousand miles a sufficient ethical barrier. In the May 3, 1938, issue of *New Masses* there appears an announcement: THE MOSCOW TRAILS: A *statement by American Progressives.* "Though the reports of the trials have appeared in only fragmentary form in most American newspapers," it states, "they have by sheer weight of evidence established a clear presumption of guilt of the defendants . . . for twenty years the opponents of the Soviet Union have . . . been forced to resort to covert means. They have disseminated reactionary propaganda and financial patronage to disaffected elements within the Soviet Union through special agents. Drastic attack must be met by drastic defense: it is in this light that we regard the trials. . . . We call on [American liberals] to support the efforts of the Soviet Union to free itself from insidious internal dangers, and to rally support from the international fight against fascism—the principal menace to peace and democracy." Among the signers: Harold Clurman of the Group Theatre, scenarists Lester Cole, Irwin Shaw, John Howard Lawson, Samuel Ornitz, Albert Maltz, Dorothy Parker, actors Morris Carnovsky, Jules (later John) Garfield, Lionel Stander.

The trials are merely a forecourt of moral confusion. The Spanish Civil War exerts a great undertow of valid indignation, a sense that the fascism of Europe could, at last, be exposed and tested. Some, like the pugilistic *New Masses* drama critic Alvah Bessie and Ring Lardner, Jr.'s, promising brother Jim, go to Spain to align themselves with the Loyalist side. Bessie will come back angrier but still blindly romantic. Lardner will not return. Most of the radicals, however, are content to man battle stations along the cocktail-party circuit, where they contrive to hear nothing of the Stanlinist betrayal.

The *Daily Worker* exuberantly reports that every Spanish Loyalist meeting in Hollywood grosses from $5,000 to $8,000— "Think of that, you New York Provincials." A bulletin is issued on how to raise funds in an entertaining fashion: Have a "guest book" to register names and addresses. "For beer parties, comrades, remember that pouring in the middle gives more foam and less liquid. . . ." (Those crowded little guest books will not be lost; they will become, like the pages of the *Daily Worker* and the *New Masses*, the fundamental articles of faith for Congressional investigators.)

The show-business comrades perform in a vanity production in which reality gets second billing. John Howard Lawson, head of the Screen Writers' Guild, encourages partisans not to write an entire Communist picture—a statement tantamount to ordering an ice cube not to freeze the entire stove. The actors are even more delirious. Back East, Whitford Kane, playing the gravedigger to Maurice Evans' Hamlet, gives the anti-fascist salute in Act V, Scene I. "Here's how I feel in my part," Kane tells the *Daily Worker*. "The rich girl, Ophelia, drowns herself, and by all that is right a suicide is not allowed to have a Christian burial. When she gets one I resent it. 'Shall great folk who drown or hang themselves get privileges not given a suicide of the poor class?' I ask. And there I raise my hand."

The same organ reports that the 1938 Party convention had polled its delegates and found that "the favorite movie actress is Claudette Colbert, while tall, dark and handsome Gary Cooper wins the honors in the male division." And finally comes the jewel of left entertainment: "It's gone and happened. People everywhere in the progressive, audacious and outspoken theatre have talked about it for so long. . . . But it's here—the social-minded night club."

The mix of fatuity, authentic rage at the fascist tide and earnest regard for the workingman is proved unstable in 1939. Mid-August, three hundred intellectuals and artists sign a statement denouncing "the fantastic falsehood that the USSR and totalitarian states are basically alike." Among the signers: Clifford Odets, Dashiell Hammett, S. J. Perelman, James Thurber.

A week later the Nazi-Soviet Pact is announced.

William Bledsoe, former editor of the Screen Writers' Guild magazine, declares with vulgar accuracy, "Certain glamor boys and girls, famous writers and directors, were on their knees at the shrine of the crossed hammer-and-sickle when the bombshell fell. It hit them like a dropped option."

Many slink from the barricades; a few have breakdowns, a diminution of the imaginative faculty, a drying-up of expression that will last two decades. Others are adjustable. The Hollywood Anti-Nazi League, organized by the hard and soft left to "combat fascist aggression," goes into a cocoon during the Pact. It emerges, fluttering, as the Hollywood League for Democratic Action. "It was suggested to the board," recalls actress Florence Eldridge (Mrs. Fredric March), "that to be *for* something was more dynamic than to be against something." And what is it for? A different New Year's card for 1940—one which denounces "the war to lead America to war."

Dalton Trumbo's chronicle of a faceless, limbless soldier, *Johnny Got His Gun*, is serialized in the *Daily Worker*. The harrowing little novel abruptly drops out for three decades—a period beginning on June 21, 1941. On that day, at a Guild meeting, a scenarist appears, her face ashen. "The Motherland has been attacked!" she wails. Russia has been invaded by Hitler's troops.

An era of good feeling, like all eras of good feeling, is engendered by common loathing. The Soviets, according to *Life's* 1943 Russian Issue, "are one hell of a people. . . ." As for the NKVD, that is only "a national police similar to the FBI" whose job is "tracking traitors." Ambassador Joseph Davies' democratic apologia for Stalin, *Mission to Moscow*, is condensed in the *Reader's Digest*, then made into a Warner Bros. film that James Agee calls "almost describable as the first Soviet production to come from a major American studio . . . a great, glad two-million-dollar bowl of canned borscht."

Harrison Salisbury makes Russia John Wayne's kind of turf. A boss of the Urals is "tough as one of Zane Grey's Texas gunmen" who could "stand up and slug it out toe to toe with such American pioneers as Jim Hill, Jay Gould or Jim Fiske." But the arsenal of suspicion and hostility is never really defused.

At the war's conclusion, the Party reawakens the appetite for its own farrow. Perhaps the most talented of the Hollywood left, novelist Albert Maltz, assays the thought of his comrades and publishes a will of rights, "What Shall We Ask of Writers?" The errors of writers and critics, he says, flow from a central source: "the vulgarization of the theory . . . that art is a weapon." The slogan, he goes on, has lost its definition; it has come to mean that unless art is a "leaflet serving immediate political ends, necessities and programs, it is worthless, or escapist or vicious." For support, he cites Engels, who praised the work of Balzac despite his "vicious political position." Maltz asks for a fairness doctrine for such unclassifiable non-Communist progressives as James T. Farrell and John Steinbeck. He exposes the casuistry of the Party critics who could praise Lillian Hellman's *Watch on the Rhine* in 1940, then attack the film adaptation of it in 1942 "because the events that transpired in the two years called for a different political program. The work of art was not viewed on either occasion as to its real quality . . . but primarily as to whether or not it was the proper 'leaflet' for the moment."

The sniper cannot hold the position. Samuel Sillen, editor of the *New Masses*, skies from N.Y. to L.A. and calls a special meeting to denounce the lethal heresies. Witnesses to that meeting are to remember Alvah Bessie's dictum: "We need writers who will joyfully impose upon themselves the discipline of understanding and acting upon working-class theory," and director Herbert Biberman's diatribe against his old comrade, his "every accent dripping with hatred." Like an election poster, Maltz's article is crayoned with graffiti: "liquidationist," "anti-progressive." Howard Fast delivers the *coup de grâce*. Maltz's declaration is, "in its final form, reactionary." Two months later Maltz recants. His argument, he announces, "was one-sided, non-dialectical treatment of complex issues. . . . I see now that my characterization of [the Trotskyite James T. Farrell] was decidedly lax. . . . My critics were entirely right in writing that certain fundamental ideas in my article would, if pursued to their conclusion, result in the dissolution of the left-wing cultural movement."

In the end, it is not Maltz, nor his critics, nor Roosevelt, nor Stalin, nor bourgeois decadence, nor Communist malaise that forces the dissolution of the left-wing cultural movement. It is the movement itself. Flaubert's *Sentimental Education* charts the distance between the revolutionary theory and its actual practice. But that novel's roots are in another century, and the thirties revolutionaries drive with no rear-view mirror. In *U.S.A.* John Dos Passos gives a merciless, cubistic view of the radical delirium and its negative analogue, experience. But Dos Passos is out of favor. So the personae of the left drama, deaf to their own signals, forget the identity of the enemy and go for each other's throats. They seldom miss. The journey through the depression, the theater and Hollywood have made them jealous siblings who, in Logan Smith's phrase, would never know their mother.

Richard Rovere has written, "The American intellectuals who fell hardest for Communism were men, not of aristocratic tastes in art but of tastes at once conventional and execrable. Many of them, of course, had no literary tastes of any sort. The reading (and sadder, the writing) matter of Communists was the dreariest kind of journalism. If they read poetry at all, it was likely to be Whittier and Sandburg, not Rimbaud and Ezra Pound . . . the cultural tone they set in the thirties was . . . deplorable because it was metallic and strident. Communist culture was not aristocratic; it was cheap and vulgar and corny."

This argument was sarcastically countered by Maxwell Geismar, onetime editor of the *New Masses:* "I had always thought of the Thirties as a brilliant, lively, exciting and hopeful period: in my later thinking I saw it as the last true outburst of our social and literary creativity before the somnolence of the 1940s, the silence of the 1950s. But I was wrong, it seemed. I had been deceived. The Thirties had been a period of deceit and disenchantment, of failure and frustration, of political conspiracy and agit-prop."

How pleasant it would be to give either side the argument. But both are tragically correct. It must not be forgotten that the old left, particularly the strident, metallic show-business left, never truly comprehended the nature of the enemy. Early, its supporters caught the injustices of fascist Europe—but they were willing to agree with Vishinsky that "fascism is a matter of taste" when the Russian ox was gored. They fought, often at great personal risk, for the rights of the enslaved black American—but when the government's racist policies herded the Japanese-Americans into detention camps, the Party offered no cogent objections. When a group of Minnesota Trotskyites was convicted under the Smith Act, no cry of unconstitutionality was heard from the left entertainers. For them, free speech was variable. When a very loud, not overly clubbable anti-Communist submitted an article to the *Screen Writer* he received a rejection slip of consummate sophistry: "It is difficult to support your belief in 'the inalienable right of man's mind to be exposed to any thought whatever, however intolerable that thought might be to anyone else.' Frequently such a right encroaches upon the right of others to their lives. It was this 'inalienable right' in Fascist countries which directly resulted in the slaughter of five million Jews."

Later Dalton Trumbo wrote a negative defense of censorship in the *Daily Worker:* "If you tell me Hollywood, in contrast with the novel and the theatre, has produced nothing so provocative or so progressive as *Freedom Road* or *Deep Are the Roots,* I will grant you the point, but I may also add that neither does . . . Hollywood's forthcoming schedule include such tempting items as the so-called biography of Stalin by Leon Trotsky."

Hypocrisy, self-deceit, factionalism—on all counts the show-business left stands legitimately charged. It is impossible to disagree with Ring Lardner's Shavian characterization of them: "Revolutionaries are always composed of the best and the worst in people," or to refute Lillian Hellman's *précis:* "There were a few wonderful people. But most of them struck me as utter damn fools."

It is tempting, especially in the light of contemporary social insight, to wish a plague on both houses, the lunatic, turreted mansion of the right and the windowless frame dwelling of the left. But the plague fell upon only one house, and that one the best dwelling, the one that held so much of the era's human potential. For there was far more to the movement than hypocrisy and babbling self-deceit. Its members were not attracted to the Party for the aesthetics and policies of Josef Stalin. Save for the most dogged and banal of hacks, they became Communists and fellow-travelers because they found in Marxism a contagious impatience with circumstances. Often they came from sooty, airless places where even the light was poor. (Years later Clifford Odets would speak for all of them when he told a HUAC investigator, "I did not learn my hatred of poverty, sir, out of Communism.")

In the theater and especially in Hollywood, they found simplistic villainies that could have been composed by a *Worker* cartoonist. All of the studio workers knew, for example, that producer Walter Wanger used to hang an 8x10 glossy of Mussolini in his office. Columbia's Harry Cohn went further: just before the war he produced a benign short entitled *Mussolini Speaks*. Il Duce's young son joined, for a while, with Hal Roach in order to learn the movie business. Not many years before, Samuel Goldwyn had tithed every member of his studio a day's pay to be spent against the dreaded gubernatorial candidate Upton Sinclair. There was no shortage of rightist anti-Semitic literature in Hollywood: Lillian Hellman found a proclamation of hate folded into her edition of the *Los Angeles Times*. Union opposition was everywhere: strikes were assumed without question to be Communist-supported. Jack Warner watched from studio rooftops as Hollywood policemen beat Warner Bros. strikers into bloody, faceless martyrs. Walt Disney's studios were similarly afflicted. Willie Bioff, a Chicagoan by habit and a goon by choice, was Hollywood representative of the International Alliance of Theatrical Stage Employees. Revealed as an extortionist and common thief, Bioff was ceremoniously packed off to jail, protesting his innocence all the way. He was framed, he insisted, by Reds.

Given the absolute rule of the studio chieftains, given the global and local conditions of the thirties, it is astonishing not that so many were Marxists but that so few were political at all. And even in the unflattering light of recall, what is the worst that can be said of those few? Essentially, that they failed themselves. In a 1937 entry in her journal, the scenarist Tess Slesinger, half-joking at her fellow-travelers, wrote in her journal, "Are We History Or Are We Mice?" History, that was the Grail. Trotsky had dumped many of his enemies in "the dustbin of history." That dustbin was to the thirties radicals, in Kempton's felicitous phrase, what hell was to the Maine farmer. To them the future was arriving by airmail special. They were so busy unwrapping it they never bothered to look at the country of origin. Thirty years later, asked for a location, many of them give their address as History. That is indeed where they *tried* to march. But for all the revisionist claims, the political paleontologist will find the showfolk of the old left, every one, in the dustbin.

It would be comforting to regard this procession with Audenesque indulgence—"You were silly like us/your gift survived it all." But they were not geniuses; their gifts did not survive. No extravagant reappraisals of the Art of the Thirties can truly reclaim their work. In the drama that follows we will see them commit many errors and fatuities. It will be easy at any time to stop and mock them, as it is easy at any time to freeze the frame of a movie and make the participants appear ridiculous.

But, in the end, they deserve more. At their worst they were blind visionaries who believed that by walking forward they ascended into the air. They were furtive when they should have been open, romantic in an era that needed social realism, molten when they should have been crystalline. But at their meanest, they did subscribe to a faith in, and not against, the human potential. They did attempt an elevation of the poor, enfranchisement of the damaged and despairing, an awakening of conscience in a world they saw narcoticized. If they were strident or philistine, they have paid their dues, paid them at usurious rates. It is well, I think, to remember that even the putative scenarist who remained Stalinist to the end of his life, Bertolt Brecht, could distort his view and still preserve his vision.

> You who shall emerge from the flood
> In which we are sinking,
> Think—
> When you speak of our weaknesses,
> Also of the dark time
> That brought them forth. . . .
> When there was only injustice and no resistance.
> For we knew only too well:
> Even the hatred of squalor
> Makes the brow grow stern.
> Even anger against injustice
> Makes the voice grow harsh. Alas, we
> Who wished to lay the foundations of kindness
> Could not ourselves be kind.
>
> But you, when at last it comes to pass
> That man can help his fellow man,
> Do not judge us
> Too harshly.

THREE

"The inquiry into a dream is another dream."   HALIFAX

SELF-PARODY is the price of style. Like Franklin Delano Roosevelt and Ernest Hemingway, the House Un-American Activities Committee leaders were beginning to caricature themselves in the mid-forties. John Rankin had turned into a spoonbread cartoon. Untroubled by doubt or thought, his deeply bagged eyes opened inward on an attic of antique prejudices. Only occasionally did he break from the interior to ask the witness questions which had already been answered or which had nothing to do with the mainstream of investigation. Back in 1945 he had announced to the House that he was the recipient of reports concerning "one of the most dangerous plots ever instigated for the overthrow of this government. It has its headquarters in Hollywood. . . . We're on the trail of the tarantula now and we're going to follow through. The best people in California are helping us."

For his colleagues' edification Rankin prepared a detailed analysis of the Soviet: "Stalin is a gentile and Trotsky was a Jew. Stalin was educated for the priesthood. The Bible says, teach a child the way he should go and when he is old he will not depart therefrom. It was but natural therefore that when Stalin got into power he should open the churches. . . . Stalin broke up the Comintern. . . . He restored rank and discipline in his army and introduced the incentive payment plan among the men who work in his factories. Communism," he bombinated, "hounded and persecuted the Savior during his earthly ministry, inspired his crucifixion, derided him in his dying agony and then gambled for his garments at the foot of the cross." It was the un-Christian Communists, then, whom Rankin pursued; his loathing of Trotsky was equaled only by the Communists he yapped after.

As for Chairman J. Parnell Thomas, he was not known for ethnic slander. He aimed higher. Flashing his Pekinese dignity, pounding his gavel like a trap-drummer, the bald, choleric Thomas continued his ceaseless vendetta against anyone or anything associated with F.D.R. As long ago as 1938 he had made a mixed metaphorical pronouncement. "Wittingly or unwittingly, the New Deal masterminds have pawned themselves out to the Communist strategists until they are so far out on the limb it is practically impossible for them to get back."

By November 1947, despite the protests of the hellish government and its affiliate, Hollywood, Thomas had persuaded the HUAC to sit in judgment; the "Inquiry into Hollywood Communism" was given official sanction. Scores of screenwriters injected the Communist line into movies, Thomas told Congress. He had been furnished—during preliminary closed hearings—with a "complete list of all the pictures which have been produced in Hollywood in the past eight years which contain communist propaganda." Still, he wanted to be fair. He would take "Communist actors, writers, directors and producers and confront them in public session with the testimony and evidence against them."

Accordingly, he subpoenaed forty-one film-makers of varying political coloration. An indignant and vocal group immediately let it be known that they would not under any circumstances cooperate with the HUAC, which they called an inquisition. They became known as the "unfriendly nineteen" even before they got to Washington, and were, of course, Thomas' prime suspects.

Most of the nineteen* were writers. None of them were phlegmatic men; the rumors of the Committee's intentions assured their hackles new exercise. In a room at the Shoreham Hotel in Washington, D.C., they waited angrily for their drumhead court-martial. In another room of the hotel, manners were subdued and conversation was more sanguine. There, the lawyers for the nineteen were receiving reassurance from the studio men: bland, dignified Eric Johnston, ex-president of the U.S. Chamber of Commerce, now president of the Motion Picture Association, and attorneys Paul V. McNutt and Maurice Benjamin. In a preliminary hearing Johnston had assured the committee, "The Communists hate and fear the American motion picture. It is their number one hate." Now he leaped to the other side of the net to reassure the defense. Robert Kenny, former Attorney General of California, whose withered arm seemed to force the rest of his body into spasmodic energies, articulated his clients' prominent concern: "The subject with which we are chiefly concerned is the character of the statements attributed to J. Parnell Thomas by the newspapers. He was quoted as saying that the producers had agreed to establish a blacklist throughout the motion picture industry."

"Nonsense!" expostulated Johnston, in the prose style of an Alger hero. "As long as I live I will never be a party to anything as un-American as a blacklist, and any statement purporting to

---

* Alvah Bessie, scenarist; Herbert Biberman, director; Bertolt Brecht, scenarist; Lester Cole, scenarist; Richard Collins, scenarist; Edward Dmytryk, director; Gordon Kahn, scenarist; Howard Koch, producer; Ring Lardner, Jr., scenarist; John Howard Lawson, scenarist; Albert Maltz, scenarist; Lewis Milestone, director; Samuel Ornitz, scenarist; Larry Parks, actor; Irving Pichel, scenarist; Robert Rossen, director; Waldo Salt, scenarist; Adrian Scott, scenarist; Dalton Trumbo, scenarist.

quote me as agreeing to a blacklist is a libel upon me as a good American."

Kenny's associate, Bartley Crum, was the most humane and optimistic civil-liberties lawyer of his epoch. He rose, beaming, to shake Johnston's hand. "Eric, I knew you were being misquoted. I'd never believe that you'd go along with anything as vicious as a blacklist in a democracy."

"Tell the boys not to worry," Johnston soothed. "There will never be a blacklist. We're not going to go totalitarian to please this committee."

The Committee was pleased with other matters on the morning of opening day. In the rotunda of the House Office Building spectators stood in ranks similar in attitude and intent to the folks patiently lining 50th Street, awaiting the twelve-o'clock show at Radio City Music Hall. Thomas, who had rehearsed his entrance two days before for "our friends the photographers," entered at twenty minutes after ten o'clock, allowed a brief, delirious festival of flashbulbs, settled on a red plush cushion and then established the tone of the inquiry. He called as his first significant witness Mr. Jack Warner of Warner Bros. Warner was a perennial extemporaneous speaker at fund-raisings. Once, following a State Department tour of Europe, he gave his staff an after-work lecture of three hours' duration. It was said afterward by his sourest employees that Warner had attended so many banquets he would make a speech at the sight of a halved grapefruit.

Given a microphone and a benign jury, the executive found himself once more unable to stop. At first, as the Committee beamed tolerantly, Warner aimed his invective at "ideological termites" who burrowed into American business. "My brothers and I," he announced, "will be happy to subscribe generously to a pest removal fund. We are willing to establish such a fund to ship to Russia the people who don't like our American system of government and prefer the communistic system to ours."

It was true, he continued, that Warner Bros. *had* made *Mission to Moscow*. But that, he reminded his audience, was in 1942, "when our country was fighting for its existence with Russia as one of our allies."

When he concluded his righteous diatribe, Warner seemed astonished to find that he was not excused. Robert E. Stripling had a question. The Committee's chief investigator, Stripling had climbed slowly from Texas to heaven. He had begun as a clerk for Martin Dies, then, in time, become assistant sergeant-at-arms in the House. His incessant curiosity, coupled with a soft, benign manner, made him an ideal interrogator. When the Congressmen could think of nothing more to ask the studio chief, Stripling leaned his narrow, intelligent face forward to ask whether there had been a period during which Communists had infiltrated the studios.

"As I said in Los Angeles on May 16," Warner commented sourly, "I have never seen a Communist, and I wouldn't know one if I saw one."

The reply was precisely the trigger Stripling needed. He turned to Warner's previously secret testimony and had it read into the record. In May, Warner had said that the Communists injected "95 percent of their propaganda into films through the medium of writers."

What writers? the Committee wished to know. Well, Warner was not certain. "When I say these people are Communists, as I said before, it is hearsay." Nevertheless, there were some obvious cases: "Howard Koch, *In Our Time*. Ring Lardner was on several pictures. He didn't put any message in *The Kokomo Kid*. John Howard Lawson, *Action in the North Atlantic*. Albert Maltz in *Pride of the Marines*."

Chairman Thomas: "Did he get much into *Pride of the Marines?*"

Mr. Warner: "No. . . . Everything they endeavor to write in, if they photographed it, I cut it out." On the other hand, said Warner, there had been one little thing where the fellow on the train said, "My name isn't Jones, so I can't get a job." "It was this kid named Diamond, a Jewish boy, in the Marines, a hero at Guadalcanal . . . some of these lines gave innuendos and double meanings and things like that, and you have to take 8 or 10 Harvard Law courses to find out what they mean."

Mr. Stripling: "They are very subtle."

Mr. Warner: "Exceedingly so."

Now Representative Richard Nixon of California stirred himself. Nixon acknowledged Warner Bros.' arsenal of films against fascism: *Confessions of a Nazi Spy* was, to this new critic, "a very fine job." But that was a hundred years ago in 1940. He wanted to know "whether or not Warner Bros. has made, or is making at the present time, any pictures pointing out the methods and the evils of totalitarian communism, as you so effectively have pointed out the evils of the totalitarian Nazis."

"Well, not really," said Mr. Warner. "Not yet." But soon. Soon.

Mr. Nixon detected fresh evidence of conspiracy: "The reason you have not made pictures pointing out the evils of the totalitarian system on the left, as well as on the right is . . . that if you did so you would have tremendous objection from within the industry itself?"

No, Warner did not think so. With patriotic gusto the producer replied by introducing into the record a catalogue of pro-American short subjects produced by Warner Bros. And, like the sleight-of-hand worker that he was, Warner sought to draw the Committee's attention away from the table. East, he maintained, *there* was where your Red propaganda originated. In New York he had seen *All My Sons*, by Arthur Miller. . . . "They write about 21 cylinder heads that were broken. They can't write about the 500,000 good airplane motors produced. That play disgusted me. I almost got into a fist fight in the lobby. . . . It was directed by a chap named Elia Kazan who is now at 20th Century-Fox as a director. He directed *Boomerang* and is now going somewhere to make a picture for them."

Mr. Thomas: "What is the new one?"

Mr. Warner: *"Gentlemen's Agreement.* Can I say something off the record?"

Mr. Thomas: "Put it on the record."

Mr. Warner: "This fellow is also one of the mob. I know of him. I pass him by but won't talk to him."

Warner was no longer comfortable under the glare. Still the Committee would not relinquish him. Representative John McDowell of Pennsylvania asked about deportation procedures. "Actual fascist political figures from Germany and Italy; we have discovered some of them here in the United States. Would you agree with me they ought to be given back to Italy and Germany?"

Mr. Warner's reply was carefully measured. "Are they motion picture people?"

But all this was merely prologue. What Mr. Thomas wanted to know in May, and he really wanted to know now, was whether Roosevelt had forced Warner Bros. to film *Mission to Moscow.*

No, absolutely not, insisted Warner. "My brother contacted Mr. Davies after reading *Mission to Moscow* as a best-seller on the stands and in the newspapers. Mr. Davies stated, 'There are other companies wanting to produce this book and I would be very happy to do business with you if you want to make it,' or words to that effect. My brother made the deal." Mr. Stripling plowed on, reading Warner's secret testimony, growing so stupefied that once Warner had to remind him that he had skipped a page. At last, when the witness had given his final sales talk, he spoke, to the Committee's distress, against the formation of a blacklist even for Commies. "I can't, for the life of me, figure where men could get together and try in any form, shape or manner to deprive a man of a livelihood because of his political beliefs. It would be a conspiracy, my attorney tells me, and I know that myself." And, booming about uplifting moral standards at the studios—"sort of good public relations"—he stepped down.

During Warner's testimony, Ring Lardner, Jr., began to woolgather. Warner had reminded him, inescapably, of another mogul with similar political inclinations: Darryl Zanuck. "At 20th Century-Fox," Lardner recalled, "Zanuck flyspecked each script for a red taint—or so he said. When I was subpoenaed, he gave out the news that I had tried to sneak in propaganda in my pictures. But like Jack Warner, Zanuck had always smoked it out. 'Why,' he complained to the Hollywood reporters, 'Lardner even tried to get some stuff in *Forever Amber.*' *That* accusation was too much. I went back to consult my conference notes (at a Zanuck conference, a secretary took down his comments verbatim. When anybody else spoke, she rested.). Sure enough, Zanuck had expunged one subversive line. It was: 'Charles is every inch a king; he always seeks the devious solution.'"

It was 12:30 when Warner was dismissed; by resumption at 2:00 P.M. the Committee's method was established. The curtain-raiser was to be packed with celebrities, regarded by the Committee with awe and approval. They would be designated as "friendly," and they would be allowed to ramble at will, provided that along the way they gave vague instances of leftist infiltration. The Reds would get theirs in Act Two.

The second friendly witness was Samuel Grosvenor Wood, who had directed *Saratoga Trunk, Good-bye, Mr. Chips, For Whom the Bell Tolls, Kitty Foyle* and *Kings Row.* Wood was invited not because of his credits, but because of his activities off screen; he was a member and past president of the Motion Picture Alliance for the Preservation of American Ideals. Like most such organizations, the Alliance was a negative creation, a coalition formed of Hollywood personnel who, in a statement of principles, deplored and resented "the growing impression that this industry is made up of, and dominated by, Communists, radicals, and crackpots." (Wood was the League's most typical spokesman; with untroubled conscience he had directed the adaptation of Ernest Hemingway's novel of the Spanish Civil War. Moreover, he had worked with a script by the known leftist Dudley Nichols.) For the Committee, Wood named a few of his colleagues: Morrie Ryskind, Gary Cooper, Clark Gable, Bob Taylor and several labor leaders. "It is difficult," he complained, "to remember all the names. I don't know whether that is enough." He brightened suddenly: "Oh, there's Ginger Rogers."

Lallygagging replies like this made the *Nation*'s historian Carey McWilliams fulminate against the Alliance as "shot through with self-hatred, the blind, mole-like fear of change, the deep-seated social envy and sense of personal inadequacy, the cheap cynicism and pseudo hardboiled know-nothingness of those who cannot imagine the existence of values really worth defending and who traduce, by their very act and statement, the basic American ideals."

John Gunther was less vituperative. "Even in the most reactionary studio," he noticed, "nobody will be quicker than an MPA-sympathizer to grab off a Russian director, or a best-selling novel by a leading anti-fascist, if the prospect is lucrative enough, since the profit motive is the final arbiter in Hollywood, the ultimate and unanswerable determinant of all behavior."

Wood took this occasion to reply to these and other critics: "If you mention you are opposed to the Communist Party, then you are anti-labor, anti-Semitic, or anti-Negro, and you will end up being called a Fascist, but they never start that until they find out you are opposed to the Communist Party; but if you wanted to drop their rompers you would find the hammer and sickle on their rear ends, I think."

Hypnotized by Wood's rhetoric, Representative McDowell revealed more than he wished: "You said you had been termed anti-Semitic and Fascist. Trotsky named Stalin time after time after time, in his book, as being anti-Semitic, so on that point alone you and Stalin stand together."

Mr. Wood: "That doesn't stop there. There are personal matters and everything else. We are constantly being threatened, and so on." And so on. Mr. Wood stood down.

By now the aims of the HUAC had been apprehended by the most apolitical of naïfs. It was time, decided the Hollywood liberals, to Do Something. "Something" was that great leftover from the Roosevelt days, a *committee*. Hadn't they, liberals all, appeared at bond drives, rallied the troops, campaigned for Roosevelt? Here again were the same names, certain that their collective prestige could recall Chairman Thomas, repeal his Committee's mischief and bring the nation to itself. Hadn't the bonds been sold? Hadn't we won the war? Hadn't Roosevelt been re-elected—and re-re-elected?

Disturbed by a trend they labeled "ominous," directors William Wyler and John Huston and scenarist Philip Dunne organized the Committee for the First Amendment. The committee's press release declared that " . . . any investigation into the political beliefs of the individual is contrary to the basic principles of our democracy. Any attempt to curb freedom of expression and to set arbitrary standards of Americanism is in itself disloyal to both the spirit and the letter of the Constitution."

Daily Variety weighed the committee's dicta and discerned a somewhat less lofty purpose: to plan "a backfire against the House Un-American Activities Committee via a drive to battle the top headlines out of Washington each day."

The Bad Committee was rumbling and threatening to rip the bark off Hollywood to reveal the Bolshevism beneath. Well, said the showfolk, let them. The Good Committee would provide its own schedule (for what was acting but a good sense of timing?). It would enter Washington when the unfriendly witnesses got up to testify. With the Good Committeemen's declared beliefs in free speech, their unimpeachable backgrounds, their instant recognizability, they would shove Thomas off page one with four-star indignation.

As the liberals coalesced, Thomas continued his probe. Louis B. Mayer, the second M of MGM, was as fulsome as Warner, though briefer. His studio had also sinned: it had confected a film entitled *Song of Russia*, starring Robert Taylor. But, he reminded the chairman, MGM had made *Ninotchka* and *Comrade X.* "We kidded the pants off them in that picture," Mayer remembered wistfully; "but they were not our allies then."

The witness was also asked if MGM was making anti-Communist pictures at the present time.

Mr. Mayer: "I think the one we are going to start shooting promptly." (Laughter)

As for *Song of Russia*, Mayer wove a garland of quotes from the press. "The *New York Times* said, 'It is really a honey of a topical musical film, full of rare humor, rich vitality, and a proper respect for the Russians' fight in the war.' The *London Daily Sketch* says, ' . . . turned out to be strictly an American anthem.' "

Mayer's final excerpt was unassailable: "The *New York Herald-Tribune* said: 'Russia itself has all too little to do with *Song of Russia*.' "

Mr. Mayer had little else for the Committee. The writers whom he suspected of Communism were already known: Lester Cole, Dalton Trumbo, Donald Ogden Stewart. Still, the witness was a powerful executive, hence a dynamic thinker. Thus Representative Vail sought Mayer's advice: "Can you tell us just what motivates these writers and these actors, whose incomes are in astronomical figures, to embrace Communism?"

Mr. Mayer did not hesitate. He had given the Marxist dialectic years of rumination. "My opinion, Mr. Congressman," he replied, "which I have expressed many times in discussion, I think they are cracked."

Mayer was followed by Ayn Rand, a Russian *émigré*, author

of *The Fountainhead* and scenarist. In 1947 Miss Rand had barely begun to popularize her exquisite philosophy of Greed. But on the stand she gave transparent evidence that she was operating in a closed system to which only the speaker held the key. She had weighed *Song of Russia* and found it wanton. True, Rand had not returned to Russia since 1926, but she had read about it and learned of the disease of collectivism. She knew propaganda when she saw it. Perhaps the most flagrant of the film's distortions, in her view, was the evidence of not unmiserable people.

"Doesn't anybody smile in Russia any more?" Representative McDowell wanted to know.

"Well, pretty much no," replied the philosopher.

"They don't smile?"

"Not quite that way, no. If they do, it is privately and accidentally. Certainly it is not social. They don't smile in approval of their system."

Thus, with impenetrable sequiturs and rambling dialogues, the Committee ended its first day's revelations. After exposure to such exchanges the audience could have been warned not to drive or operate machinery for two hours; and there were more barbiturates on the shelf.

During the next week the HUAC dropped management and aimed for box office. Adolphe Menjou played a character lead, dressed to the nines in a $200 De Gaz brown pin-striped suit. Lillian Hellman called him with some justice "a haberdasher's gentleman." His haughty floorwalker mannerisms and his inflated *amour propre* made Menjou a favorite target of derision on the left; in fact he was better read than most of the Committee, and if he was possessed by an *idée fixe*, at least it was an *idée*. Few of his questioners had as much.

Mr. Menjou gave the Committee his list of Know Your Enemy books, including *The Dream We Lost* by Frieda Utley; *Towards Soviet America* by William Z. Foster, then head of the USCP; and *Pattern for World Revolution*, written anonymously. Menjou was against artistic control of the movie business: Red films met with his approval provided they were labeled as such. Menjou agreed with Nixon; censorship was a Russian notion, not an American one. What was needed was not a muzzle but a choke collar. "We have many Communist writers who are splendid writers," he explained. "They do not have to write Communistically at all, but they have to be watched." Of course, he dilated, the HUAC intended no such thing as censorship. "It is perfectly infantile to say that this Committee is trying to control the industry," said Menjou. "How could they possibly control the industry? They wouldn't know anything about it. You wouldn't know how to make a picture *or anything else.** I don't see how that could be said by any man with the intelligence of a louse."

Between the big acts a few jugglers appeared. *Esquire* critic John C. Moffitt had been a member of the Hollywood Anti-Nazi League; he remembered the Party line articulated by Lawson: "As a writer try to get 5 minutes of the Communist doctrine . . . in every script that you write. If you can, make the message come from the mouth of Gary Cooper or some other important star who is unaware of what he is saying; by the time it is discovered he is in New York and a great deal of expense will be involved to bring him back and reshoot the scene."

Actors were drilled by Lawson: "If you are nothing more than an extra wearing white flannels on a country club veranda, do your best to appear decadent, do your best to appear to be a snob; do your best to create class antagonism . . . if you are an extra on a tenement street do your best to look downtrodden, do your best to look a victim of existing society."

Moffitt saw the agit-prop most clearly in "picture after picture in which the banker is represented as an unsympathetic man, who hates to give the GI a loan." This was an oblique

* Italics mine. S.K.

reference to Robert E. Sherwood's *The Best Years of Our Lives*, which explored, with characters as large as Macy's parade floats, the experiences of soldiers returning home. In one case a friendly banker (Fredric March) was indeed bawled out by his frowning superior for advancing a loan to a veteran with no collateral.

Moffitt was to appear a study in moderation compared to the next witness, Rupert Hughes. Now seventy-five and hard of hearing, Hughes resembled the "dog heavy" in one of critic Moffitt's dreaded Red movies. He had once spoken against Roosevelt's Four Freedoms because "they would rob the American people of the stimulus of fear and poverty." Now he underlined the nuclear jitters: "Russia may be fighting us any minute—in fact, is fighting us now." This expert witness, like his fellows, could not certify who in Hollywood was a Communist but, like Huysmans, who claimed an ability to distinguish blonde, redhead or brunette by her musk, Hughes insisted, "You can't help smelling them, in a way."

Here the show and its audience flagged. At one point the gallery grew so restive that Thomas beat a constant staccato with his gavel. Then, with a metronomic sense of strategy, the chairman abruptly cut short the rhetoricians. In a great cause, a few innocent heads must fall: he brought on Robert Taylor. More than a thousand women, of varying age and stamina, crowded the caucus room for a scene with the real Bob Taylor in the flesh, overlaid with brown suit with faint blue line and maroon necktie. A sixty-five-year-old lady climbed a radiator for a better view of the star. She fell or was pushed and struck her head. Later the cleaning staff found pieces of torn dresses and coat buttons littering the floor. A middle-aged woman in a red hat kept shouting "Hurray for Robert Taylor," and the libidinous sighs, while Taylor testified, fell and broke like waves at Malibu.

The idol immediately dropped some names, among them

"Howard Da Silva [who] always seems to have something to say at the wrong time."

Would Mr. Taylor, asked the Committee, refuse to act in a picture in which a Communist was also cast?

"I most assuredly would, and I would not even have to know that he was a Communist. This may sound biased. However, if I were even suspicious of a person being a Communist with whom I was scheduled to work, I'm afraid it would have to be him or me, because life is a little too short to be around people who annoy me as much as these fellow travelers and Communists do."

In other ways, however, the star proved unsatisfactory to the Committee. In earlier testimony Taylor had given the impression that he was shoehorned into *Song of Russia* by efforts of the State Department. After brisk re-education by studio lawyers, he felt the need to issue a disclaimer: "If I ever gave the impression . . . that I was forced into making *Song of Russia,* I would like to say, in my own defense, lest I look a little silly by saying I was ever forced to do the picture, I was not forced, because nobody can force you to make any picture."

The *Daily Worker* could get no mileage out of this federal vaudeville, although it made a strained effort. When the witness was asked by Thomas, "How long have you been an actor?" the *Worker* said, "After the laughter died down Taylor claimed to have been an actor since 1934"—with the implication that the audience, contemptuous of Taylor, yocked at the notion of anyone mistaking him for a thespian. In fact, the audience was openly on the performer's—and thus the Committee's—side. It was yet another instance of the Party's lifelong inability to grasp the fundamentals of street theater.

Some of the lesser witnesses were not without interest: Howard Rushmore, ex-film critic for the *Worker,* remembered being canned for liking *Gone with the Wind.* He had called it "a magnificent bore"; the management wanted more calumny and he refused to supply it. He also stated that the Party had certain "sacred red cows," performers who could not give a bad performance. Chaplin was one; Edward G. Robinson was another. The next witness, scenarist Morrie Ryskind, who had won a Pulitzer Prize for *Of Thee I Sing,* had some more names: Gordon Kahn, editor of the Screen Writers' Guild magazine, the *Screen Writer;* and Lester Cole: "If he isn't a Communist, I don't think Mahatma Gandhi is an Indian." Evidently Gandhi was not; the biased Robert Taylor had accepted Cole as the scenarist of his new picture, *The High Wall.*

A few unrecognizable and cranky screenwriters brought their charges of Red conspiracy, reintroduced *l'affaire* Maltz and read Trumbo's old garrulities. Even the Hearst papers had begun to turn away by now; the *New York Journal-American* no longer used red ink when it made its eight-column announcement: ACTORS AND WRITERS CHARGE REDS INFEST SCREEN GUILDS. The people decided that Washington had advertised plums and was giving away pits. Thomas returned to the power of the marquee.

In elementary demonology, the Committee hearings of October 23, 1947, have a special essence. Here, in one room, are Ronald Reagan, George Murphy, Richard Nixon—all bit players soon to be elevated to major politicians. Unfortunately, upon inspection, these devils appear very tame and minor. Nixon's questioning was, throughout, restrained and almost shy. Entertainment was not his turf and he would always display an abashment before actors, a tribute that a trained performer pays a natural. It is true that he was an apologist for the Committee, that he was, in his pragmatic wariness, to prove a more formidable enemy than the quick, dangerous Thomas. But even here Nixon had larger issues in mind. He was on the Committee to learn, not to grandstand. Hiss was his making, not Hollywood. As for Reagan and Murphy, both men came as entertainers, not as politicos. Their tone was, to the Committeemen, distressingly moderate, and their politics extraneous. In fact Robert

Montgomery, George Murphy and Ronald Reagan, who had all been active in the actors' union Screen Actors' Guild, had a very minor glamour and a palpable distrust of the HUAC probe. Montgomery, past president of the Screen Actors' Guild, felt that the Guild's highly vocal Communist minority was minuscule, though ambitious and disciplined. "They appear at public meetings tremendously well organized and with a complete program for the evening," he observed.

"Mr. Montgomery," said the chairman, "they even appear at Congressional hearings." (Laughter)

George Murphy, Shirley Temple's hoofing and puffing father-figure, who told Committeemen he was only an actor-dancer, felt that there were indeed Communists in the union. When he became an officer of the SAG he had mysteriously received the *Daily Worker*, gratis, for a year. But he felt Hollywood was "very successful in keeping any attempts to propagandize off the screen." Ronald Reagan gave HUAC investigator Stripling a cogent instance of Communist tactics, the kind which were to provide the HUAC and private investigators with years of profitable employment: he was telephoned one afternoon by a woman who announced a Paul Robeson concert recital. The money for the tickets, she said, would all go to a charity hospital. Would Reagan lend his name to the cause? The actor hesitated, then "felt a little bit as if I had been stuffy for a minute, and I said, 'Certainly, you can use my name.' I left town for a couple of weeks and, when I returned, I was handed a newspaper story that said that this recital was held . . . under the auspices of the Joint Anti-Fascist Refugee Committee. . . . I did not . . . see one word about the hospital." Reagan, like his colleagues, would be duped no more. Yet he felt that the town could keep the Reds at arm's length simply by scrutinizing the evidence. "As Thomas Jefferson put it," he said, "if all the American people know all of the facts they will never make a mistake."

"That is just why this Committee was created by the House

of Representatives," returned Thomas hotly. "Once the American people are acquainted with the facts there is no question but what the American people will do . . . a job . . . that is, to make America just as pure as we can possibly make it."

The audience leaned forward. Thomas continued the box-office approach to purity.

The chairman's prize witness was Gary Cooper, who wore a white shirt and was against Communism because, "from what I hear, . . . it isn't on the level." Playing the lone cowpoke before the dudes from back East, Gary seemed bemused by his straight men. The Committee presented him with a Communist leaflet from abroad. "Gary Cooper," it read, "who took part in the fights for the independence of Spain, held a speech before a crowd of ninety thousand in Philadelphia . . . he said, 'In our days it is the greatest honor to be a Communist.' "

Stripling asked, "Have you any comment on that, Mr. Cooper?"

Cooper ran his finger around his collar and through stiff lips permitted himself a shucks. "Well, a ninety-thousand audience is a little tough to disregard, but it is not true." When he was asked whether Communism was on the increase or the decrease out in Hollywood, Cooper gave the show away. "It is very difficult to say right now, within these last few months, because it has become unpopular and a little risky to say too much. You notice the difference. People who were quite easy to express their thoughts before begin to clam up more than they used to."

Director Leo McCarey, the ostentatiously Catholic filmmaker, agreed: leftism was growing unpopular. As for himself, he had always loathed the Reds, and the enemy reciprocated; *Going My Way* and *The Bells of St. Mary's* had not produced one ruble from Russia. Stripling played interlocutor.

Mr. Stripling: "What is the trouble?"

Mr. McCarey: "Well, I think I have a character in there that they do not like."

Mr. Stripling: "Bing Crosby?"

Mr. McCarey: "No, God."

Lillian Hellman referred to that exchange as "the most blasphemous and irreligious I have ever heard in public." Even the unshakable A. J. Liebling admitted that "the announcement that the Deity was under contract to a movie company was perhaps to be expected sooner or later, but it jarred me nevertheless." Nevertheless, it drew "(laughter)" and the importance of boffs properly placed was as vital to the HUAC as to Bob Hope.

Mrs. Lela Rogers, mother of Ginger, added a new species of lunacy to the proceedings. At Howard Hughes' RKO film studio she had enjoyed a special assignment: security officer without portfolio. As unofficial story editor, the brass-collar Republican spent her hours examining scripts and stories for fitness. Cary Grant had found *None But the Lonely Heart* ideal despite Mrs. Rogers demur. "It was a story filled with despair and hopelessness," she reported, "and in my opinion it was not a Cary Grant vehicle." She also objected to the employment of Clifford Odets. "I have here a column of Mr. O. O. McIntyre . . . in which Mr. McIntyre says Mr. Clifford Odets, play writer, is a member of the Communist Party. I never saw that denied." Mrs. Rogers testified that, as her daughter's manageress, she felt compelled to spurn *Sister Carrie* because it was just as open propaganda as *None But the Lonely Heart*. She also fingered Trumbo's *Tender Comrade* (the title was lifted from Tennyson) because of Ginger's line "Share and share alike—that's democracy."

Mrs. Rogers' was an impossible act to top. Oliver Carlson, a minor political-science instructor at the University of California (extension division), was invited to testify so that he could provide the record with a catalogue of the People's Education Center. This was a typical far-left academy, a salad of frivolity and commitment. Its courses included: One World —the foreign policies of the Big Four; Radio Comedy Writing;

Russian I; What Is This Thing Called Jazz?; and Advertising Copywriting. The catalogue provided the Committee with even more names: Abe Burrows, who taught the class in Radio Comedy Writing; Alexander Knox (Cinema for the Layman); and Edward Dmytryk, Herbert Biberman and Adrian Scott (Motion Picture Direction).

Walt Disney was perhaps the friendliest witness of all. A Missouri *grand seigneur*, Disney, like Warner, was still wounded by memories of a strike at his studio. "A delegation of my boys, my artists," he recalled, had come to him with suspicions of a Communist takeover in the union. The head wrongo was Herbert Sorrell, who threatened to make "a dustbowl out of my plant." Disney was recalcitrant; Sorrell did call his men out. "When he pulled the strike," continued Disney, "the first people to smear me and put me on the unfair list were all the Commie front organizations. I can't recall them all, they change so often, but one that is clear in my mind is the League of Women Voters—and the *People's World*, the *Daily Worker* and the *PM Magazine* in New York."

When Disney completed his testimony and returned to his desk, he discovered a small error. The following week he wired J. Parnell Thomas. "I regret that I named the League of Women Voters," wrote Disney, "when I intended to name the League of Women Shoppers." It was the hearings' first incontrovertible case of mistaken identity; all that followed had a similar history: the accusation, given wide coverage, the discovery of error and, finally, the retraction, customarily ignored. The League of Women Voters survived Disney's error, but at the considerable cost of canceled contributions and darkened reputation.

Disney's statements closed the first week. At the intermission, Chairman Thomas announced the witness lineup for Monday: "Mr. Eric Johnston, Mr. Roy Brewer, Mr. John Howard Lawson, Dalton Trumbo, Mr. Alvah Bessie, and Mr. Emmett Lavery."

It was a lineup delightfully compatible to the strategy of the Good Committee. They began to counterattack—and, abruptly, the disappointments commenced. Their attorney, Bartley Crum —like J. Parnell Thomas—sought big names. On the long-distance phone from the Shoreham Hotel in Los Angeles, the nineteen heard Crum badgering David O. Selznick: "But, David, you've *got* to be the chairman of the Committee for the First Amendment . . . you couldn't be in more distinguished company." Selznick refused. Crum reddened. "I saw a man like you in Germany after the war. He was an independent producer. He was a Jew. He was a liberal too. He didn't want to be involved either. Are you listening, David? Do you know what became of that man because he wouldn't fight? I saw him, David! He was a cake of soap!" Selznick was not present at the radio broadcast "Hollywood Fights Back," or on the celebrity flight from Los Angeles to Washington, with stopoffs at Kansas City, St. Louis and Pittsburgh, where twenty-one notables signed autographs and released statements. Humphrey Bogart told reporters, "The Committee is not empowered to dictate what Americans shall think." Fredric March was more ominous: "Who do you think they're really after? They're after you." Danny Kaye echoed Roosevelt and Willkie: "Most fair-minded Americans hope the Committee will abandon the practice of merely providing a forum to those who for political purposes or otherwise seek headlines they could not otherwise obtain." Lucille Ball read a portion of the Bill of Rights, and Keenan Wynn and Henry Morgan lampooned the quotes from Committee witnesses: "I don't have any proof . . .," "I can't give you any specific examples, but everybody knows that . . .," "I don't know for sure but I heard from a reliable source that . . ."

Of all the radio speeches, the most ominous came from Thomas Mann, exile, who saw in the proceedings not a clown show but an inhuman preamble.

"I have the honor to expose myself as a hostile witness," he stated. "I testify that I am very much interested in the moving-picture industry and that, since my arrival in the United States nine years ago, I've seen a great many Hollywood films. If Communist propaganda had been smuggled into any of them, it must have been most thoroughly hidden. I, for one, never noticed anything of the sort.

"I testify, moreover, that to my mind the ignorant and superstitious persecution of the believers in a political and economic doctrine which is, after all, the creation of great minds and great thinkers—I testify that this persecution is not only degrading for the persecutors themselves but also very harmful to the cultural reputation of this country. As an American citizen of German birth, I finally testify that I am painfully familiar with certain political trends. Spiritual intolerance, political inquisitions, and declining legal security, and all this in the name of an alleged 'state of emergency' . . . that is how it started in Germany. What followed was fascism and what followed fascism was war."

To the Good Committee, moral fervor was building, aided by J. Parnell Thomas and his exemplars of ignorance and hypocrisy. It was a classic misreading of evidence, but in their solipsistic drive the performers could see only their own names in the paper.

Floating far above the stars, the banner headlines drifted into the public consciousness. The *Washington Post* had reported RED REPORTS TO SUBVERT VIA SCREEN DESCRIBED—PRODUCERS REPORT ANTI-PROPAGANDA GAINS: WOOD URGES PARTY BE OUTLAWED. The *New York Times* had stated MENJOU TESTIFIES COMMUNISTS TAINT THE FILM INDUSTRY. The *St. Louis Post-Dispatch* told its readers ROBERT TAYLOR TESTIFIES TO INCREASING SIGNS OF HOLLYWOOD RED ACTIVITY and added that Taylor told Congressional investigators he had seen "more indications" of Communist activity in filmland in the last four or five years than previously. The *New York Post* was livelier: BOBBY SOXERS AND MOTHERS: WOMEN CHEER ROBERT TAYLOR AS HE URGES BAN

ON REDS. The *Times* soberly reported Thomas' charges: 79 IN HOLLYWOOD FOUND SUBVERSIVE, INQUIRY HEAD SAYS—EVIDENCE OF COMMUNIST SPYING WILL BE OFFERED NEXT WEEK. And the *New York Herald Tribune* added: DISNEY TESTIFIES REDS TOOK OVER ARTISTS IN STRIKE—FAVORS OUTLAWING PARTY IF IT IS UN-AMERICAN.

The Good Committee, unaware of impending tragedy, progressed toward confrontation. Chairman Thomas heard of their petition for redress of grievances and smiled. Let them come, he told his colleagues. He welcomed the visit. Before the war, as a soldier in Martin Dies' meager crusade, Thomas had been an intruder in Hollywood; the artists would now know the unique sense of unease that is felt by juniors on professional turf.

Angrily, innocently, the representatives of the Committee for the First Amendment wheeled and then descended on the atrocious city.

FOUR

THOMAS' PLAN was not especially devious; it was only dazzling. He had announced to the public that Eric Johnston was to be the opening witness of Week Two, Scene One. Designed in sandblasted Federal style, Johnston would have given the Hollywood gallery a platform, however narrow, of dignity and hope. But the motion-picture executive was not the first guest. Instead, the chairman shuffled his cards of identity and called John Howard Lawson. Attorney Robert Kenny immediately moved to quash the subpoena addressed to his client on the grounds that the HUAC was illegal and unconstitutional. This was automatically dismissed: "No committee of Congress," observed the chairman, "has the right to establish its own legality or constitutionality."

Kenny's associate, Bartley Crum, tried another tactic. He asked to examine the dismissed witnesses Adolphe Menjou, Sam Wood, Ayn Rand, etc., "in order to show that these witnesses lied." The request was denied. The recall, as we will see, would have been disastrous to either side. Lawson proceeded to extinction. "Mr. Chairman," he began, producing papers, "I have a statement here which I wish to make—"

The chairman asked for the brief, examined it and barked, "I

62

don't care to read any more. . . . The statement will not be read. I read the first line."

The themes of Lawson's complaint could indeed be caught from his overture: "For a week, this Committee has conducted an illegal and indecent trial of American citizens, whom the Committee has selected to be publicly pilloried and smeared."

Since he was not allowed to read, Lawson extemporized: "You have spent one week vilifying me before the American public. . . . I wish to protest against the unwillingness of this Committee to read a statement, when you permitted Mr. Warner, Mr. Mayer, and others to read statements in this room."

The Committee *had* allowed the producers unlimited use of the hall as sales room; so far Lawson was ahead on points. But his voice was already strident; Stripling had only to act the picador and the witness would supply the blood. Lawson was asked if he was a member of the Screen Writers' Guild.

Lawson: "The raising of any question here in regard to membership, political beliefs, or affiliation—"

Stripling: "Mr. Chairman—"

Lawson: "—is absolutely beyond the powers of this Committee."

Stripling: "Mr. Chairman—"

Lawson: "But—"

Thomas banged his gavel over the ascending decibels of the audience. "I want to caution the people," he warned. "You are the guests of this Committee. . . . I do not care for any applause or any demonstrations of one kind or another."

"I am not on trial here, Mr. Chairman," continued Lawson. "This Committee is on trial here before the American people. Let us get that straight." From that point Lawson's script grew loftier and more outraged. Stripling asked him the great question, for which all these reporters, all these onlookers, friendly and hostile, had been assembled: "Are you now or have you ever been a member of the Communist Party of the United States?"

Lawson could answer in the affirmative and jettison his career. He could perform the prodigal-son act (Yes, I was a Communist but I sincerely regret this youthful indiscretion). Or he could answer that he was not and never had been a member of the Party—a tactic which would lead to perjury proceedings. The final course was evasion, doubling back on his tracks, baying and whuffing until the bloodhounds grew exhausted and gave up the hunt.

Lawson, his humorous Angus face grown suddenly outraged, tried the broken-field run. "The question of Communism is in no way related to this inquiry," he maintained. "[This] is an attempt to get control of the screen and to invade the basic rights of American citizens."

The witness then hawked Americanism like a Legionnaire, invoking the Bill of Rights, lamenting, "It is unfortunate and tragic that I have to teach this Committee the basic principles of American—" But that was as far as he got. Again the Committee asked whether or not Lawson was a member of the Party. He dodged and whirled, but when the chairman asked if he refused to answer the question, Lawson thundered that he would offer his beliefs, affiliations "and everything else to the American public, and they will know where I stand. . . . I have written Americanism for many years, and I shall continue to fight for the Bill of Rights, which you are trying to destroy."

Mr. Thomas, secretly pleased with Lawson's deportment, impersonated the high priest struck at the altar: "Officers," he called, gaveling furiously, "take this man away from the stand." (Applause and boos.)

When Lawson had been led away, Louis Russell, an ursine ex-FBI man, now prime investigator for the Committee, produced thirty-five articles of evidence proving Lawson's allegiance to the hard left, including his Communist Party registration num-

ber: 47275. Russell, whose last year had been spent "pursuin'
mah investigations," could not have taken more than a week
of intensive research to uncover Lawson's subversions. A decade
before, in *New Theatre Magazine,* the scenarist had obliged the
Committee by bluntly asserting, "As for myself, I do not hesitate to say that it is my aim to present the Communist position
and to do so in the most specific manner."

As Russell wound down his recital, Thomas stated the essential nature of the inquiry. "John Howard Lawson refused to
answer the question, 'Are you a member of the Communist
Party?' and other questions put to him. Therefore it is the
unanimous opinion of this Subcommittee that John Howard
Lawson is in contempt of Congress."

All else was epilogue. Eric Johnston, summoned at last, spoke
in fatigued metaphors: "I'm not here to try to whitewash
Hollywood, and I'm not here to help sling a tar brush at it
either." He challenged the investigators to name the films
which contained Communist propanganda, spoke of the power
of intimidation, and mentioned the world's "great hunger for
our wheat and our fuel to stave off hunger and off cold, but
hungry and cold as they may be, men always hunger for freedom. . . . Communists can hang out all the iron curtains they
like, but they'll never be able to shut out the story of a land
where free men walk without fear and live with abundance."
(Applause.)

After some cranky palaver, Stripling produced the kind of
skeleton beloved by hostile genealogists. Edward T. Cheyfitz,
one of Johnston's assistants, was a former member of the
Communist Party. True, he had left it, disillusioned, more than
six years before, but he had been a Red: that was enough. As a
Parthian shot Thomas informed Johnston that he topped him
in film-going. Johnston's schedule permitted him one or two
pictures a week. "Your average is not as good as mine," the
chairman boasted. Act Two, Day One was over.

The Good Committee was as disorganized as a cast at first rehearsal. No one knew his lines; press conferences were hastily summoned sans flacks. Audiences seemed indifferent and—this was the cruelest hurt—reporters mocked the notion of Salvation through Celebrity. The newsmen had not been trained by the gossip columnists Lolly and Hedda; they were tired Washington pros who had watched pressure groups burgeon and deflate in a night. Perhaps they were even a whit colder, a shade edgier, because the conferees were showfolk who kept pausing in their speeches as if they expected ovations. Canada Lee, the great black actor, seized a reporter by the arm and said, "How can they talk about Americanism when they still have segregation in Georgia?"

"What's that got to do with these hearings?" came the cold reply.

John Garfield boasted to another press man, "I fought for Roosevelt for four straight terms." The reporter answered, "So did I, but what the hell has Roosevelt got to do with whether these guys hold Communist Party cards or not?" Danny Kaye tried to dramatize injustice: "This whole procedure is as if I came out before an audience of five thousand people and before I'd said a word the audience shouted, 'You stink.' " He waited for the laugh, but all he heard was heavy breathing. From the back of the house rose a croak: "Tell a joke, Danny." Westbrook Pegler, who was more annoyed at the exercises offstage than on, was delighted to report that during World War II Kaye had been classified 4F because of his "mental attitude."

The Hearst papers by this time had become fully convinced that the Reds were raping the future through the medium of celluloid. FILM CENSORSHIP IS ONLY RECOURSE, they editorialized. The *Los Angeles Examiner* gave a detailed overview of Red Hollywood: "It is sheer poltroonery or worse for the motion picture magnates to provide a medium for Communism. . . . An industry which puts its box office returns above the flag and the nation's security deserves no consideration: For bad as it is to defile people's minds with filth, it is vastly worse to corrupt and debauch their patriotism."

The *New York Herald Tribune*, after examining the testimony of Lawson and Johnston, told its readers: MOVIE CHIEF ADMITS AIDE WAS COMMIE.

Against these notices the Committee for the First Amendment desperately tried to exhibit luster and integrity, but the structure was like the flat on a back lot: Georgian columns in front, two-by-fours off camera.

Back in the hearing room, witness Dalton Trumbo offered twenty scripts in evidence of his non-polluting talent. "Too many pages," Thomas fumed. Stripling asked a few low-key questions, then let go the big one. Trumbo boomed evasions until at last the chairman thundered, "The witness is excused!" Trumbo predicted, "This is the beginning of an American concentration camp." And Thomas riposted, "This is typical Communist tactics." (Applause.)

After each witness came up and went down swinging, investigator Louis Russell came to the stand and drawled into the record a series of Communist associations attached to the previous speaker. The investigator was like a prospector with no geological training. Diamonds and quartz glittered alike to him; Trumbo's CP number, 36802, was soberly listed alongside a photostat of the *Daily Worker* which showed the table of contents for the winter edition of *Mainstream*, which in turn showed a poem entitled "Confessional" by Dalton Trumbo.

Each unfriendly witness tried to offer a prepared statement to the Committee. It was spurned or tolerated with a great show of weariness. The boredom was not entirely theatrical; most of the statements were of the "You-can't-scare-the-*real*-Americans" variety. Trumbo added a *soupçon* of Louella Parsons: "I shall make no comment at all on the petty professional jealousies, the private feuds, the intra-studio conflicts which here have been elevated to the dignity of the record." Otherwise he, like his colleagues, accurately maintained that the HUAC violated "the most elementary principles of constitutional guarantees when you require anyone to parade for your approval his opinion upon race, religion, politics or any other matter."

Maltz was far more cogent, though ruder. He addressed Stripling by the traitorous title "Mr. Quisling," a reference to the Norwegian collaborator. He reminded the Committee that he supported a good deal of humane legislation opposed by Mr. Thomas and his predecessor Rankin, including the anti-lynching bill. Samuel Ornitz, an old-time radical who seemed tired and ill, had been listed in Elizabeth Dilling's *Red Network*. Now he inclined his bald head over his notes and said a *Kaddish* for democracy: "The Jew is the first to suffer. . . . In speaking as a Jew I speak in a deeper sense as an American, as the one who has to take the first blow for my fellow Americans."

The others, Alvah Bessie, Herbert Biberman, Edward Dmytryk, Adrian Scott, Ring Lardner, Jr., Lester Cole, gave *pro forma* declarations of solidarity and contempt. Only the bony, sardonic Lardner betrayed a sense of the ridiculous. But humor for humor's sake was now untranslatable even in English. His reply to the Big Question echoed a B-movie fallen woman: "I could answer it, but if I did, I would hate myself in the morning." As the sergeant-at-arms moved to lead the witness away, Lardner spoke to the court reporter: "I think I am leaving by force."

The Committee never failed to acknowledge its critics or its fans. Editorials in *PM*, the *Saturday Review of Literature* and *The New Yorker* had annoyed Thomas. "I am proud to say," he boasted in the middle of the week, "that this committee has not been swayed, intimidated or influenced by either Hollywood glamour, pressure groups, threats, ridicule, or high pressure tactics on the part of high-paid puppets and apologists for certain elements of the motion picture industry." Representative McDowell, however, had been swayed enough by glamour to read into the record the world's most anti-climatic telegram: "Congratulations on your splendid courage. Communist rattlesnakes are bent on inoculating the mind of our American youth. Clean out the rats. You are not injuring our industry. You are helping to keep them American. Bless you. LEO CARILLO."

As the week wound down, as the writers' leftist activities were exposed and detailed, the Good Committee was almost silent. Bogart was heard to grumble that it had all been a mistake. The energy had leaked from the protest; the testimonies had given onlookers a sense of ominous melancholy. It was justified. Of all the second-week witnesses, only two would maintain their film careers, one by venturing beyond the Committee's radius, the other by staying well within it. The latter, a vigorous, dark-haired boy on the order of Monroe Stahr, called himself Dore Schary. Dore (formerly Isadore) was a $100-a-week scriptwriter who had ascended into the six-figure category as executive in charge of production at RKO. Schary let the HUAC know that he would not be pushed around. Investigators had previously revealed that the composer Hanns Eisler was a Communist and driven him from the country. Schary, when asked, had the temerity to state that he would hire Eisler today if it was not proven that he was a foreign agent.

Thomas empurpled like an eggplant. "Have you ever heard of Rip Van Winkle?" he demanded. "If some people in the United States don't wake up and get out of the long sleep, we will find some of the difficulties here that they have encountered in France and Italy and Yugoslavia and Poland and Finland, and some of these South American countries. It is the Rip Van Winkle opinion that has been permitting Communism to grow throughout the world the way it has. That is all." (Loud applause.)

Thomas had been hinting to the press that an important new witness was shortly to be sprung on the public. Now Stripling gave a hint. "Have you employed at your studio," he asked Schary, "a person by the name of Bertolt Brecht?" Schary had not. The Committee was in no mood to buy the witness' feigned innocence. His studio, RKO, had purchased the short story "Rachel," by a known Red, Howard Fast, and Schary had displayed no objections. Clearly, this was a dupe to be watched. Still, the witness remained polite and allowed that the Committee knew more about the spread of Communism than he did. It was just that the labor groups, management, guilds could do their own policing in Hollywood. They—

"Thank you very much, Mr. Schary," concluded Thomas. "And don't forget what I said about Rip Van Winkle." (Laughter)

Bertolt Brecht's HUAC testimony has been recorded too often to need much reiteration here. In terms of talent alone, he was the Committee's last important witness, the eleventh of what came to be known as the Hollywood Ten. Here, finally, was a demonstrably impudent revolutionary, once number five on Hitler's most-wanted list, writer of incendiary tracts and poems. In theory, then, Brecht's genius before the pea-brained tribunal would seem to concentrate the qualities of the inquisition: know-nothing v. intellectual; decaying state v. its laughing mortician.

But no, the Committeemen were wholly flimflammed by this Marxist Til Eulenspiegel. Like Thomas Mann, the rumpled, unshaven Brecht was unamused by the hearings. Behind the idiot questions he saw flames. It had started this way in Germany; thereafter, in his phrase, he and his compatriots had changed countries more often than shoes. He half-expected the Committee investigators to forge an American Communist Party card in his name. And, against this event, he had come to Washington with a passport in his pocket. Martin Esslin, reviewing Brecht's performance, calls it "typical Schweikian subservience," but it has unique Brechtian brushstrokes familiar to the connoisseur. The playwright appeared at the hearing with a Mr. Baumgardt, a translator whose accent was even harsher than Brecht's. The playwright deliberately mixed the plots of two of his plays, *The Measures Taken* and *He Who Says Yes*, in order to confuse the Committee. The measures he took were in excess of the situation. None of the questioners knew who he was or what he had written. When, for example, Stripling cornered Brecht with an obviously militant marching number from a Communist songbook and asked, "Did you write that?" the answer came back, "No. I wrote a German poem, but that is very different from this." (Laughter) Whenever a questionable phrase was surgically removed from the canon, Brecht or Baumgardt blamed it on the English translation and the legislators sagely clucked. It was a shame what the Reds did to authors, they mused, twisting words and phrases, writing literary history, enlisting the innocent in their battle for the soul of mankind.

When the great question was asked, Brecht looked up with large eyes and answered in a Lear-like cascade, "No, no, no, no, no, never." There were those who later swore they had seen Brecht's Party card back in the thirties, but manifestly the Committee did not know of them. The Congressmen credulously accepted the witness's righteous dilations: "Mr. Chairman, I have heard my colleagues when they considered this question not as proper, but I am a guest in this country and do not want to enter into any legal arguments so I will answer your question fully as well as I can. I was not a member, or am not a member, of any Communist Party." And did people suggest to him that he join the Party? Yes. And who were they? "Oh," said Brecht airily, "readers." The panel, giving new meaning to the word naïveté, found these answers a model of decorum. "Thank you," said Thomas. "You are a good example to the witnesses of Mr. Kenny and Mr. Crum."

Several weeks later Brecht was in Paris explaining to an old friend why California no longer offered the good life. "When they accused me of wanting to steal the Empire State Building," he said, "it was high time for me to leave."

After the German playwright, interest plummeted. J. Parnell Thomas wrapped up his hearing with a tocsin: "I want to emphasize that the Committee is not adjourning sine die, but will resume hearings as soon as possible. . . . The industry should set about immediately to clean its own house and not wait for public opinion to force it to do so. . . ."

Thomas had promised to reveal the identities of seventy-nine prominent people associated with the Communist Party and its functions. Only eleven had been interviewed. As it turned out, wrote A. J. Liebling with mock disappointment, "Chairman Thomas announced the close of the hearings with sixty-eight termites to go."

Even to Robert E. Stripling, the hearings, in their final days, assumed "the overtones of a broken record." A Gallup Poll showed that while 37 percent of the people approved of the hearings, 36 percent did not. The centrist papers—the *New York Times* and *Herald Tribune,* the *Chicago Daily News* and the *Washington Post*—continued their attacks on the Committee's "publicity hunt." Samuel Goldwyn, visiting New York, told night-club reporters that he denounced the Committee. In Washington, Paul V. McNutt, as counsel for the studios, issued statements accusing the HUAC of attempting to intimidate the motion-picture industry.

Thomas, a Clausewitz in the guise of a corporal, rallied his forces for a flank charge. To a special session of Congress, calling for the appropriation of funds to resist Red infiltrations of Europe, the Chairman brought ten citations for contempt. He was immediately opposed. Representative Sadowski lectured his fellows: "There is another and a greater law than the laws of Michigan or of the Congress, and that is the law that Thou shalt not bear false witness against thy neighbor." Representative Eberharter agreed. "I say that the First Amendment has placed an invincible shield around all Americans—the ten witnesses now faced with contempt citations no less than any other Americans—that protects them from the kind of intrusion practiced in the so-called Hollywood hearings."

Thomas thought he saw several apertures in that shield. His forces sought admission. Representative McDowell, adopting a

fine military pose, solemnly recited the list of countries already
fallen to Communism, beginning with Russia, then issued a
lengthy diatribe against Albert Maltz, "a colonel in the conspiratorial, political army of Soviet Russia. This Maltz," continued McDowell, "addressed Robert Stripling as Mr. Quisling,
a world-wide synonym for traitor. . . . Sometimes, Mr.
Speaker, one wonders if public service and love of country, with
all of its great magnitude, is sufficient pull to retain a membership or employment on this difficult Congressional assignment."
Then, after labeling O. John Rogge, former special assistant to
the Attorney General of the United States, "an American
Vishinsky," he sat down.

Representative Rankin had studied the hearings and found
them lacking in follow-through. He waved a copy of the Good
Committee's petition to Congress. "I want to read you some of
the names," he said, lending legitimacy to Ornitz' plaint of anti-
Semitism. "One of the names is June Havoc. We found out
from the motion picture almanac that her real name is June
Hovick. Another one was Danny Kaye, and we found out that
his real name was David Daniel Kamirsky. Another one here is
John Beal, whose real name is J. Alexander Bliedung. Another
is Cy Bartlett, whose real name is Sacha Baraniev. Another
one is Eddie Cantor, whose real name is Edward Iskowitz.
There is one who calls himself Edward Robinson. His real name
is Emanuel Goldenberg. There is another one here who calls
himself Melvyn Douglas, whose real name is Melvyn Hessel-
berg. There are others too numerous to mention. They are
attacking the Committee for doing its duty to protect this
country and save the American people from the horrible fate
the Communists have meted out to the unfortunate Christian
people of Europe."

After the racist harangue, Representative Nixon's speech was
a model of composure and smug logic. There were but two questions at issue before the Congress, he maintained. Had the witnesses indeed refused to answer the Committee's questions? And,

more important, did the Committee have the power to ask these questions? Nixon voted yes, and yes again. So did most of his colleagues. In the case of Albert Maltz it was 346 for contempt and 17 against.

Until this ratification, it was possible for Hollywood management to resist the Committee, to discredit its corrupt "findings" and its attempts at censorship. But 346 Congressmen representing God knew how many constituents, each a potential filmgoer—that was a matter larger than conscience. After the vote, Representative Karl Mundt told the negative seventeen Congresssmen: "You find yourselves left alone, because in Hollywood [the witnesses'] employers today are stating publicly that they want no more to do with them until they can make up their minds whether they are proud to be Americans." Thus the news was leaked. The picture business was, despite the support of press and celebrities, at the edge of capitulation.

On the same day that the contempt citations were won, November 24, 1947, a group of incredibly well-groomed, extremely tense executives gathered in a public room at the Waldorf-Astoria Hotel in New York. (Mundt had erred in his geography, nothing more.) This was not the first time the movie executives had met to discuss the problem of Red infiltration. Shortly after the war, production-company heads had met *in camera* at the Hillcrest Country Club in California. They had gathered to listen to reports of Communist activities made by the Motion Picture Alliance for the Preservation of American Ideals. But no hard evidence was available. Name names, demanded the executives. One of the informants, pressed, produced the evidence against another of the leftist studio brats: Maurice Rapf, son of the MGM producer Harry Rapf. Samuel Goldwyn got to his feet. "If this snot-nosed baby is the Red boss in Hollywood, gentlemen, we've got nothing to fear. Let's go home."

But in 1947 political worries could not be so easily banished. For almost twenty-four hours, the gossip columnists reported, the studio toppers* harangued. For this time there were authentic terrors to consider. RKO figured its declining profits as two cents on the dollar. The enormous post-war attendance had begun its precipitous decline. Production and labor costs were escalating. Even without the HUAC the studios had received a blizzard of angry mail and dark publicity. The Legion of Decency was to condemn *Forever Amber*; Howard Hughes' *The Outlaw* was attacked as salacious, a clear instance of Hollywood's moral backslide. To aid their own economies, England and Western Europe restricted the import of American films. Cans of completed but politically vulnerable pictures rested on the shelves of the studios, provisionally listed as assets for fiscal '48.

There is but one story in the history of Hollywood: sin, scandal and self-regulation. The following afternoon the producers performed the freshest version. As reporters lined up at the Waldorf, they received two-page handouts which bespoke an agony of caution and revision:

> Members of the Association of Motion Picture Producers deplore the action of the ten Hollywood men who have been cited for contempt by the House of Representatives. We do not desire to prejudge their legal rights, but their actions have been a disservice to their employers and have impaired their usefulness to the industry.
>
> We will forthwith discharge or suspend without compensation those in our employ, and we will not re-employ any of the ten until such time as he is acquitted, or has purged himself of contempt, and declares under oath that he is not a Communist.

---

* Among them: F. Barnes and Paul V. McNutt, counsels; Eric Johnston, President MPAA; Barney Balaban, Nicholas M. Schenck, Harry Cohn, Joseph M. Schenk, J. Cheever Cowdin, Walter Wanger, Mendel Silberberg, Donald Nelson, Samuel Goldwyn, Y. Frank Freeman, Henry Ginsberg, Albert Warner, Louis B. Mayer, Dore Schary, Spyros Skouras, Nate Blumberg, William Goetz, Ned Depinet, producers.

On the broader issue of alleged subversive and disloyal elements in Hollywood, our members are likewise prepared to take positive action.

We will not knowingly employ a Communist or a member of any party or group which advocates the overthrow of the Government of the United States by force, or by any illegal or unconstitutional method.

Here came the mirror logic:

In pursuing this policy, we are not going to be swayed by any hysteria or intimidation from any source. *

We are frank to recognize that such a policy involves dangers and risks. There is the danger of hurting innocent people, there is the risk of creating an atmosphere of fear. We will guard against this danger, this risk, this fear. To this end we will invite the Hollywood talent guilds to work with us to eliminate any subversives; to protect the innocent, and to safeguard free speech and a free screen whenever threatened.

Having implied that Congress was too harsh toward the industry, the producers paradoxically sought to blame it for a lack of stringency.

The absence of a national policy, established by Congress, with respect to the employment of Communists in private industry makes our task difficult. Ours is a nation of laws. We request Congress to enact legislation to rid itself of subversive, disloyal elements.

And finally came the modest disclaimer:

Nothing subversive or un-American has appeared on the screen, nor can any number of Hollywood investigations obscure the patriotic service of the 30,000 Americans em-

* Italics mine. S.K.

ployed in Hollywood who have given our Government invaluable aid in war and peace.

For curious readers who wondered how the producers were forced so quickly to this nervous prostration, Ed Sullivan had an answer.

Even back in 1947 the film companies had conglomerate aspects. RKO was associated with United Fruit, Atlas Corporation, National Can Company; 20th Century-Fox with General Foods, Pan American Airways, New York Trust and National Distillers; Warner Bros. had affiliations with J. P. Morgan & Co. and American Power and Light. It was with the shibboleths of the *Daily Worker* that Sullivan, fan of the HUAC and enemy of all whom it condemned, wrote in the New York *Daily News:* "Reason that Hollywood big shots rushed to New York . . . and barred the ten cited by Congress: Hollywood has been dealt a blow that won't please Wall Street financiers, who have millions invested in picture companies. Wall Street jiggled the strings, that's all."

It was believed by the credulous that dismissal and open blacklisting of the ten would have a shamanic effect. Sacrificed for the commonweal, these few wretches would serve to quiet the furious deities.

They remained implacable. Thomas gloated: "Those Hollywood big shots were pretty high and mighty at first, but they got off their high horse, all right. Maybe after another lesson or two they will be able to run their industry on a safe, sound American basis." The *Chicago Tribune* sneered at "the death-bed repentance of Eric Johnston."

The producers regrouped. They had fired the ten; what in God's name did the Committeemen want? Two days after the Waldorf announcement, members of the Screen Writers' Guild received a telegram asking them to join with Dore Schary and other executives who sought "to acquaint you with the intent of the producers' statement . . . and to disavow any intent of a witch hunt."

At an assembly of the Guild, Dore Schary spoke for his colleagues. The producers, he said, had prepared a three-pronged program. First, as announced, they would fire and blacklist what was now labeled the Hollywood Ten. "We do not ask you to condone this," he assured an audience that included seven of the ten. Second, no one who was believed to be a Communist would be hired. "We do not ask you to condone *this*," Schary repeated. Third was the classic panacea for movie *tsorus*: a massive public-relations campaign to renew Hollywood's image —a campaign that eventually produced the hallowed slogan "Movies Are Better Than Ever." As Schary descended the platform, accompanied by producers Walter Wanger and Edward Mannix, who remained silent throughout, he walked slowly up an aisle, examining the faces of the writers. In the front row, within reach, was Dalton Trumbo. Each producer stopped, bent over, touched a soft hand to Trumbo's unyielding shoulder, and moved on. *Nothing personal, kid,* said the gesture; *business is business.*

What had been rumor was now doctrine; the blacklist had begun.

2

When the tactics of the Ten came to analysis, they were seen—by sympathetic as well as disdainful historians—as morally repugnant and self-defeating. We have already discussed Murray Kempton's altering views. In A *Generation on Trial,* Alistair Cooke called the unfriendly witnesses "squalid and rowdy"; Eric Bentley, comparing Lawson's prose style with that of his inquisitors, says delicately: "Bullshit equals bullshit." Does it? Those witnesses who preceded the Ten would seem worthier of epithets. Contemptuous in the deepest sense, they pandered to the centripetal tendencies in government and helped accelerate the coming hysteria.

Yet the events of 1947 cannot be considered a scale on which the Ten rose as their opposition sank. In crucial aspects the defendants aided in the abasement of due process. After the hearings many of them tried to blame their attorneys for their situation. In fact, Bartley Crum had been falsely assured by certain clients that they were not and never had been Communists. When evidence proved otherwise, Crum said nothing; the betrayal of trust was a *fait accompli*. Later, when Crum asked why he had been lied to, a client replied, "We thought you were a classic bleeding-heart liberal; we thought we could use you to advantage." More than two decades later Trumbo was still slandering his lawyer in published letters, but by that time Crum was dead.

Many of the nineteen mocked the findings of the committee. They derided Louis Russell for producing Communist Party cards when everyone knew that the name had been changed to the Communist Political Association. Gordon Kahn sneered at the hearsay constructs of Ginger Rogers' mom. Lawson swore he would reveal his politics to the country at large—and never did. In partial answer for this reneged promise, Trumbo, in his apologia for silence, wrote: "The accused men made their stand before the Committee to reestablish their right of privacy not only in law but in fact . . . privacy in relation to political opinion means secrecy. What principle, then, is served by defending the right of secrecy in law only to reveal the secret in life?"

But Trumbo and most of his colleagues were about as secret as a skywriter. Lela Rogers may have been a carnivorous parakeet, but, as it turned out, Clifford Odets *had* been a Communist. So had Ring Lardner, Jr., Larry Parks, Albert Maltz, Lawson, Ornitz, Bessie, Cole, Dmytryk, Trumbo. These men and others far less guileful would live to hear themselves described by Congress as "dedicated agents of a foreign conspiracy." Their notion of secrecy was a stage whisper that could be detected three thousand miles away, their very vocabulary *was* a live giveaway, their notion of practical Marxism derived from remote distances. For them experience was no substitute for literature—mainly pamphlets and "front" literature of enormous pretense and ephemeral quality. Agents? Neither they nor the Committee knew what an agent was. They were no longer even catalysts by 1947. They were only precipitates, fallout from an organic chemistry neither they nor their censors could comprehend.

FIVE

Schary felt wretched about the whole historical process. "I was faced with the alternative of supporting the stand taken by my company or of quitting my job," he explained with sorrow. "I don't believe you should quit under fire. Anyway, I like making pictures. I want to stay in the industry. I like it."

Yet there were limits. In 1948 the Golden Slipper Club of Philadelphia voted Schary their Humanitarian Award for producing *Crossfire*, written and directed by blacklistees Scott and Dmytryk. The humanitarian politely declined to pick up the award. In his stead came Eric Johnston, always glad to stump for his employers, bearing his customary freight of platitudes. "Intolerance," he told an appreciative audience, "is a species of boycott, and in any business or job boycott is a cancer in the economic body of the nation. The film business," he added, "knows no such thing as discrimination. In Hollywood it's ability that counts."

Also *chutzpah*, and a high tolerance for self-delusion. The columns continued their chatter; the cameras kept whirring. The sky had not fallen. The town endured. But even the meanest extra, the sleaziest geek, knew the pervasive sense of wrong, the overhang of fingerless guilt and anxiety. Employment of actors and writers was the lowest since the pre-depression slump. Early in 1947 close to fifty features were in production. Early in 1948, half that number were before the camera.

Fear and resentment fed on each other. Sam Wood went around saying Congress ought to make everybody stand up publicly and be counted. "Communists," he argued, "are a danger and a discredit to the community."

His ally Ayn Rand, ever happy to advocate her homely philsophy of profit-as-revelation, issued a little pamphlet entitled *Screen Guide for Americans*. Published by the Motion Picture Alliance, it gained a wide circulation at the studios. *Screen Guide*'s headings, like its philosophy, were a festival of negatives: Don't Smear the Free Enterprise System, Don't Glorify the Collective, Don't Deify the Common Man, Don't Smear Success, Don't Glorify Failure and, most important, Dont Smear Industrialists. "All too often," Rand felt, "industrialists, bankers and businessmen are presented on the screen as villains, crooks, chiselers, or exploiters. It is the *moral* (not just political but *moral*) duty of every decent man in the motion picture industry to throw into the ashcan, where it belongs, every story that smears industrialists as such. . . . It is the Communists' intention to make people think that personal success is somehow achieved at the expense of others and that every successful man has hurt somebody by becoming successful. . . ." The *Guide*'s most frequently quoted advice was: "Don't let yourself be fooled when the Reds tell you that what they want to destroy are men like Hitler and Mussolini. What they want to destroy are men like Shakespeare, Chopin and Edison."

The Screen Writers' Guild magazine offered a counter-pamphlet in opposition to the HUAC. Its feature item was an acute though overly hearty editorial by Lillian Hellman entitled "The Judas Goats."

"Why this particular industry, these particular people?" she wanted to know.

Has it anything to do with Communism? Of course not. There has never been a single line or word of Communism in any American picture at any time. There has never or seldom been ideas of *any* kind. Naturally, men scared to make pictures about the American Negro, men who have only in the last year allowed the word Jew to be spoken in a picture, who took more than ten years to make an anti-Fascist picture, these are frightened men and you pick frightened men to frighten first. Judas goats, they'll lead the others, maybe, to the slaughter for you. The others will be the radio, the press, the publishers, the trade unions, the colleges, the scientists, the churches—all of us. All of us who believe in this lovely land and its freedoms and rights, and who wish to keep it good and make it better.

They frighten mighty easy, and they talk mighty bad. For one week they made us, of course, the laughingstock of the educated and decent world. I suggest the rest of us don't frighten so easy. It's still not un-American to fight the enemies of one's country. Let's fight.

But no one was in the mood for combat, least of all filmmakers. Even the most apolitical among them began to parse the credits of the unfriendly. As it happened, about 30 percent of the Unfriendly Nineteen's films *had* been concerned with social justice—as compared with 10 percent for other filmmakers. Convict labor, dust-bowl farmers, municipal corruption were their natural subjects—along with the bread-and-butter, nuance-free entertainment that constituted the staple American product. John Howard Lawson was capable of *Algiers* ("Come with me to the Casbah"), but he had also written *Blockade*, the first important film about the Spanish Civil War. (In retrospect, even that seemed sanitized. When Walter Wanger gave Lillian Hellman a private exhibition, she told him that it was vastly entertaining but there was one lingering question: Whose side was it on? In an effort to hype the film, Wanger wired Secretary of State Cordell Hull that Franco's agents were in Hollywood, planning to subvert the release of the movie. Franco's government, as it turned out, had never heard of *Blockade*. The Communists had. They tried briefly to use it for their own purposes. But they were far more concerned with a 20th Century-Fox project entitled *The Siege of Alcazar*: the war from the Falangist side. The film, after sufficient hollering from both poles, was never made.)

Producer Jerry Wald remembered that Alvah Bessie had inserted some "Red" material in *Action in the North Atlantic*. Alan Hale and Dane Clark were on deck as an airplane engine sounded off screen. The men looked skyward.

CLARK

It's ours!

HALE

Famous last words.

CLARK

(*pointing*)

It's one of ours, all right!

CUT TO:

CLOSE SHOT. SOVIET PLANE

—its red star painted plainly on the fuselage. The helmeted and goggled pilot dips his wings and salutes the ship below as Clark's voice comes over.

CLARK

(*shouting*)

Soviet plane off the starboard bow!

Lester Cole had been responsible for *Charlie Chan's Greatest Case* and *The Romance of Rosy Ridge*; on the other hand, in a picture about a boys' school he had made the football coach paraphrase La Pasionara, the Spanish Communist: "It is better to die on your feet than live on your knees."

So it had gone with Trumbo, Dmytryk—and the other writers who had dared to exhibit a social conscience. True, they were responsible for pap, but they were also concerned for the Little Man, about whom Jack Warner wished to hear no more.

That little man had been the center of a genre: John Garfield, Alan Ladd, Dane Clark, Richard Conte, Dick Powell played him. He was the guy in *Johnny O'Clock* and *Force of Evil* back from the army, from prison, from the streets, cleaning up his life or his town. Encased in a huge suit and a fedora wide enough to shade a garden, he came on in nervous black and white, the blacks very dark and the whites harsh enough to hurt the backs of the eyes. His backchat echoed Raymond Chandler and James M. Cain, and it smacked of the streets. You could imagine Gary Cooper or John Wayne coming home to a ranch; you could not imagine John Garfield anywhere but in an apartment. The little men were remembered years later by the youth of Europe, blinking back the war, clinging to the nervous images of the B picture. For them, the little man and his bleak-and-white surroundings were an aesthetic principle, the bedrock of the *nouvelle vague*. But in 1948, in America, there was no room for aesthetic sensibility.

At the beginning of the year *The New Yorker* sent Lillian Ross to Hollywood to take the town's blood pressure; she found it 160 over everybody. An executive in charge of script approval told her of Hollywood's new self-censorship. "It's automatic, like shifting gears," he explained. "I now read scripts through the eyes of the DAR, whereas formerly I read them through the eyes of my boss. Why, I suddenly find myself beating my breast and proclaiming that I love my wife and kids, of which I have four, with a fifth on the way. I'm all loused up. I'm scared to death, and nobody can tell me it isn't because I'm afraid of being investigated."

"At some parties," the analyst observed, "the bracketed guests break up into sub-groups, each eyeing the others with rather friendly suspicion and discussing who was or was not a guest at the White House when Roosevelt was President—one of the few criteria people in the film industry have set up for judging whether a person is or is not a Communist—and how to avoid *becoming* a Communist."

Billy Grady, the flamboyant casting director at MGM, refused to believe persistent rumors that the FBI would take over his job. "What does a G-man do?" he asked in a baggy-pants monologue. "A G-man sends guys to Alcatraz! Ha! I'd like to see a G-man find a script about Abraham Lincoln's doctor in which we could work in a part for Lassie." As for the Red menace, Grady figured, "There are fifty thousand people in this industry, and all they want is the right to take up hobbies. Spencer Tracy takes up painting. Clark Gable takes up Idaho. Dalton Trumbo, who got the sack, takes up deep thinking. Take away their hobbies and they're unhappy. For God's sake, Tracy doesn't paint when he's acting. Gable doesn't shoot ducks. Trumbo doesn't think when he's writing for pictures. I say let them keep their goddam hobbies. They're all capitalists anyway."

Amor patriae was the order of the afternoon. The Paramount Choral Society was apostrophized in a program printed by their employers: "Where, but in a true democracy, can a group of employees take over the directors' quarters, using them as their own, to meet and pursue a cultural interest, encouraged by their directors? Is this, then, a cold, impersonal industry? Is this supposedly a country lacking in musical heritage? No! This is America. This is Democracy. . . ."

At MGM, where Louis B. Mayer now personally approved the purchase of *all* scripts, including cartoons, the commissary menu informed guests that meat would not be served on Tuesdays. "President Truman has appealed to Americans to conserve food, an appeal all of us will heed, of course."

"Roosevelt was a good politician," Bogart admitted. "He could handle those babies in Washington, but they're too smart for guys like me. Hell, I'm no politician. That's what I meant when I said our Washington trip was a mistake." William Wyler thought that he could not make *The Best Years of Our Lives* now, and that the United States would produce no more films like *The Grapes of Wrath* or *Crossfire.* "In a few months we won't be able to have a heavy who is an American," he maintained. An untainted writer agreed. "For years I've been writing scripts about a Boy Scout-type cowboy in love with a girl. Their fortune and happiness are threatened by a banker holding a mortgage over their heads, or by a big landowner, or by a crooked sheriff. Now they tell me that bankers are out. Anyone holding a mortgage is out. Crooked public officials are out. All I've got left is a cattle rustler. What the hell am I going to do with a cattle rustler?"

Newly released films seemed dangerously obsolete. *The Treasure of the Sierra Madre* was to have begun and ended with a quote from the book: "Gold, Mister, is worth what it is because of the human labor that goes into the finding and getting of it." Warner Bros. informed the director, John Huston, that the line was to be deleted. "It was all on account of the word 'labor,' " said Huston. "That word looks dangerous in print, I guess. You can sneak it onto the sound track now and then, though."

Some of Billy Grady's capitalists initiated actions for breach of contract and damages. Some were fired because of the standard "morals clause" in their contracts. This finely drawn paragraph had been invented to protect the studios against sexual scandal of the Arbuckle-Chaplin variety. ("The employee agrees . . . that he will not do or commit any act or thing that will tend to degrade him in society or bring him into public hatred, contempt, scorn or ridicule, or that will tend to shock, insult or offend the community . . . or prejudice the producer or the motion picture, theatrical or radio industry in general.") Its vague, all-purpose legalese made it quite serviceable for political indiscretions. But not all contracts contained the clause. Trumbo's, for example, had none. A lot of good it did him; MGM summarily dismissed Trumbo anyway, unconcerned by his suit for reinstatement and damages.

Four others also began actions for breach of contract and damages. Lardner sued for some $5,000 per week until August 1948, Cole $4,000 a week until September 1949. Dmytryk and

Scott sued RKO for back and future losses. They had made their tough little report on home-grown anti-Semitism, *Crossfire*, for $595,000 in twenty-two days. The picture was expected to gross three million dollars. "I sure hated to lose those boys," mourned their producer, N. Peter Rathvon. "Brilliant craftsmen, both of them. It's just that their usefulness to the studio is at an end."

Very early in the year the first offer of rehabilitation was wiggled indiscreetly at Trumbo, a large hook in a short worm. Like most effective Hollywood agents, Philip Berg had mastered the ten-percenter's basic tactic: always put your client on the defensive. He harangued Trumbo for "making long speeches" before the HUAC—although the writer's longest speech was 75 words and Ayn Rand's longest was 1,636 words. Still, Berg wished to be generous and tolerant. When Trumbo confessed his financial plight, Berg was willing to arrange a loan at only slightly usurious rates. Moreover, he suggested an exit from the blacklist. A friend of his, Westbrook Pegler, would fly to the Coast to meet the agent and the Ten. If Trumbo felt diffident about inviting the others, he could meet Pegler alone, to speak freely of the motives that had prompted him to behave as he did before Congressmen. Abject regret could be stated and, after a sufficient period, something could be worked out with the studios. Strapped for cash, Trumbo said nothing; his silence was refusal enough. Later, in a letter terminating his relationship with the Berg-Allenberg Agency, he wrote: "I am fully aware—albeit with sadness—that there are men in this country so wanting in self-esteem that they are perfectly willing, for a matter of money, to deal with anti-Semites. But neither I nor any other of the ten is such a man. Two of our number lost their jobs solely because they made a picture against anti-Semitism, and we take a certain pride in the fact that neither cash nor contract can tempt us into any kind of relationship with an anti-Semite—not even if he be sponsored by Mr. Berg, and referred to affectionately as 'Peg.' "

Rehabilitation was not the only avenue to survival. There was also the black market: scripts written by the blacklistees and signed with pseudonyms. Hal E. Chester, who had produced Alvah Bessie's last film, *Smart Woman*, arranged several assignments—rejiggering a screenplay for one and a half weeks at $500 a week, then an original screenplay for a flat rate of $750 for four weeks, and finally a $400 deal to metamorphose an unworkable idea into a polished screenplay.

Through George Willner, a sympathetic literary agent who was soon to be blacklisted himself, some of the Ten also received assignments—under assumed names and reduced salaries. Once Trumbo had earned $3,000 a week. Now, as he had it, work consisted of writing "three times as fast for about one-fifth of my former price."

The secular blacklisters heard of the pseudonyms and the reduced rates. They did what they could to police the studios. Hedda Hopper told her readers, "Ring Lardner, Jr., one of the unfriendly witnesses in the Un-American Activities probe, got another job. He was hired by Lewis Milestone. Let's take a look at Lardner's new boss. Milestone was born in Chisinau, Russia, and came to this country years ago. He found many friends here. . . . He has a beautiful home in which he holds leftish rallies, is married to an American and has made a fortune here. But still his heart seems to yearn for Russia. Wonder if Joe would take him back?"

Lardner, whose humor refused to flag, wired Milestone: "Please start salary checks immediately or tell your publicity department to stop name-dropping." Milestone responded: "Have checked publicity department and they say no telling what comes out of the Hopper. Admire your work but cannot consider hiring you because of birth in Illinois. Prefer one of the original thirteen states. . . ."

In Washington, portents were legible, but few cared to read them. The 1949 case of the United States v. Judith Coplon, for example, was a textbook case of hysteria costumed as jurisprudence. The accused was a moony, irresponsible Department of Justice employee who had passed classified documents to her Russian paramour. Miss Coplon could easily have been dismissed and exiled. Instead, the government elected to give her a showcase trial. The defense demanded that Coplon's entire FBI file be entered in evidence. Attorney General Tom C. Clark vigorously opposed the move—the files were crammed with chatter and unprovable innuendo as well as solid evidence. Yet the government was afraid to dismiss the case; the Truman administration needed constant proof of its anti-Communist bias.

The files were entered in evidence. A report from a "confidential informant" advised that Fredric March, Canada Lee and Norman Corwin of CBS were "outstanding fellow-travelers." Lee, the outstanding black actor of his era, was to be killed by this disclosure. Helen Hayes was listed as a performer in a 1945 skit for the benefit of the American Society for Russian Relief; Danny Kaye had spoken at a New York rally entitled "Crisis Coming, Atom Bomb—for Peace or War."

Save for these listees, no one was more appalled at the lapse in evidentiary standards than J. Edgar Hoover. In an official FBI memorandum to Bureau field officials, the Director complained that he had "urged the Attorney General to seek a mistrial or a citation for contempt rather than produce these reports with consequent devastating harm to the FBI's responsibility for internal security, as well as the disclosure of as yet uncorroborated information in our files concerning individuals."

The first Alger Hiss trial proceeded furiously. During the proceedings J. Parnell Thomas faced Whittaker Chambers and Hiss and shouted in a tone strongly evocative of the Hollywood hearings: "Certainly one of you will be tried for perjury." (On December 15, 1948, Thomas' prediction was realized. But by then the prophet had vanished like the Cheshire cat, leaving only his gloat behind. A month before, Thomas had been indicted on charges of Congressional payroll padding.)

The Ten savored the irony on their tongues. Although

Trumbo and Lawson were sentenced to $100 fines and a year in prison, both maintained a naïve confidence in the appeals courts. "I don't think I'll go to jail," Trumbo predicted. "The constitutional issues involved in this case are so clear that if I go to jail there just aren't going to be enough jails. Half the country will be building them and the other half will be in them."

Trumbo's prophecy was reinforced by the election results of November. Representatives Vail of Illinois and McDowell of Pennsylvania, two of the members of the Hollywood HUAC subcommittee, were defeated for re-election. Sixteen of the seventeen representatives who voted against the citation for contempt were returned to office. Alvah Bessie, Ring Lardner, Jr., Samuel Ornitz and Adrian Scott gave out the news that they were "writing novels"—hence available for screen work. Dmytryk was in England, working on *Spotlight*, a British movie. Trumbo was readying a play for Broadway; Lester Cole was also writing a play. Herbert Biberman continued to spend his days and nights writing and speaking for the Ten.

Trumbo, whose dynamism was undiminished by misfortune, had enough time between black-marketed scripts to fight a few backstairs duels. In the *Saturday Review* he exchanged hostilities with Arthur Schlesinger, Jr., who had called him a hack and implied that Trumbo's interest in human rights began and ended on the lots of MGM. Trumbo replied that the historian paid "lavender lip service" to the libertarian tradition and worked him over further in a self-congratulatory pamphlet, *The Time of the Toad*, singing of himself and against the encroachments of the Cold War. In it we learned that the real danger to America came from "the non-Communist left," and that the Russian Jews had been misinformed. "In the Soviet Union," Trumbo declared, "3,500,000 Jews live under the protection of laws which ban discrimination of any kind."

In the late forties Trumbo employed his wife's surname as a *nom du contraband*. But here he found himself undone—by

one of the Ten. The restless, unthinking Biberman had circulated a petition to reverse the lower courts' conviction. It was,
in time, published in *People's World*, furnishing future investigators with still more names, among them Cleo Fincher
Trumbo. Her husband shot an angry note to his colleague:
"You may ask why I am upset. For eighteen months I have
been carefully building up the name Fincher in the motion
picture industry as a legitimate writer. Today by telegraph I
have received (1) a cancellation of a screen credit in that name,
and (2) the abrogation of a job for which the contracts had
been made out but not yet signed."

Yet Trumbo continued to work and be compensated—in a
manner of speaking. The King Brothers wanted scripts to come
in at under $6,000 per. Sam Spiegel tended to be late with
payments. In order to meet absurd deadlines, the author would
have to go without sleep. By the end of the year Trumbo had
been cured of his blithe security. Jail seemed fairly certain now;
plenty of time to sleep there, he decided.

Still, Trumbo was blessed. No meals missed, no diminution
of ego or zeal. He had the plague, but he would survive. The
others were not so sure. Actors like Larry Parks, one of the
original Unfriendly Nineteen, and Sterling Hayden, who had
been a very vocal supporter of the Good Committee, and John
Garfield and J. Edward Bromberg, who had been cornerstones
of the Group Theatre, and petition-signers in the thirties—all
began to find themselves without good roles. They had not
been forced to go before J. Parnell Thomas; nonetheless they
were on the studios' new blacklist. They were not alone. Anyone who had been mentioned at the hearings, or who had been
too active in the unions, too noisy at meetings, too "controversial" in the forties, was suddenly regarded as a possible
threat. Had not the American Legion just picketed theaters
where Chaplin's *Monsieur Verdoux* unreeled? Had not the
protests been so severe that the film was withdrawn from circu-

lation? And that was Chaplin, for God's sake. What about Fox, or Warners, or Columbia?

At RKO the term for a politically unfit actor was "too tall"; at least, that was what his agent was told. By the time the performer heard the news it was decoded to mean "Blacklisted baby, go sell shoes. You're through." Columbia hired a public-relations firm to investigate the backgrounds of writers and actors. Benjamin B. Kahane, vice president of the company, began a provisional liaison with the American Legion.

"If we checked on a writer or actor," he assured the curious,

the report we received was not that he was on a blacklist or any kind of list, but a report setting forth facts and information. Such a report, for example, would state that there was no information that was found which linked him with the Communist Party or any "front organization" designated by the U.S. Attorney General as subversive.

In other instances, the report would state that the person was identified as a member of the party or was involved in some way with suspect organizations. They would specify full details on the report. We would then examine the reports.

In most instances we would discuss the report with the person's agent, who would in turn discuss the matter with his client. In the majority of cases, we would receive a letter of affidavit negativing or explaining the alleged connection with the party or party front organizations.

The "negativing," the burden of proof, remained on the accused, who sometimes would not even remember the circumstances in which he had signed his petition or allowed his name to be merchandised by the Spanish Civil War refugees or the anti-lynching organizations. By now the Attorney General had been given fresh and unwanted assistance by California State Senator Jack B. Tenney. Composer of "Mexicali Rose," ex-union executive, presently seeker of Reds in high places, Tenney headed the State Senate Committee of Un-American Activities. In a freehand copy of the federal model, Tenney published his own committee report of subversives and front organizations, bound, of course, in red. Among the suspect groups was the American Civil Liberties Union, which Rankin himself had overlooked.

"The beauty of Tenney's publications," wrote Lee Mortimer in Hearst's *Sunday Mirror*, "is that the citations may be repeated or republished without fear of civil or criminal action, because they are the official reports of a legislative body, issued under the imprint of the State, and thus are privileged."

Bound in two volumes, Tenney's little Un-American Activities Committee report dropped hundreds of names. Some were imperishable subversives of another time. Like the radio comedian's old standbys, Brooklyn, the La Brea tar pits and mothers-in-law, they could be mentioned to an audience with guaranteed response. Charlie Chaplin, Lillian Hellman, Anna Louise Strong and all the other old protesters were old money, granting respectability to Tenney's parvenu investigators. Among the new suspects were Danny Kaye, Gregory Peck, Edward G. Robinson and Artie Shaw. Such non-entertainers as Bartley Crum and Robert Kenny were also listed for their temerity in defending, said the report, "the brutal, inhuman and treacherous doctrines of Marxism-Leninism-Stalinism."

Pushed by their frightened studios, the performers drafted statements.

Gregory Peck: "I have been denying these allegations for several years and will do so once more. I am not now and never have been associated with any Communist organization or supporters of communism."

Artie Shaw: "I don't understand what they are talking about. I don't think they do either. I have never traveled in a Stalinist orbit, unless that orbit includes the United States."

John Huston: "The Tenney report is yet another example of

that Senator's vicious campaign to smear the names of his betters in loyalty and obedience to the principles of our democracy."

Gene Kelly: "I am not a communist, never was a communist and have no sympathy with communist activities. The only line I know how to follow is the American line."

Like *The Red Network*, the Tenney Report depended heavily on researchers who, in turn, depended on discarded letterheads and yellowed copies of the *Daily Worker*. Among the most avid examiners of waste paper was an anti-Semitic hatemailer named Ed Gibbons, who sporadically published *Alert*, a "nationalist journal." *Alert* was listed in the *First National Directory of Rightist Groups, Publications and Some Individuals in the United States*. Rightist was perhaps the kindest term: Carey McWilliams called it a "smear sheet" and revealed that Gibbons had been hired by the Tenney committee at a salary of $220 a week.

The revelations did nothing to reverse the tides. Albert Maltz's new and apolitical novel, *The Journey of Simon McKeever*, was purchased by 20th Century-Fox—which soon afterward announced that it was all a terrible mistake, that the picture was never going to be made. Alvah Bessie, hapless from 1947, was far more typical of the blacklistees without big credits or a heavy studio investment in his reputation. From Bessie's melancholy autobiography, *Inquisition in Eden*, the reader can get some measure of the mental state of a blacklistee circa 1948. The tough veteran of the Spanish Civil War, ex-critic of the *New Masses*, who treasured his ironic resemblance to the elegant British actor Sir Cedric Hardwicke, became just another out-of-work laborer walking the harsh Los Angeles streets. His few movie assignments completed, Bessie found himself, like a salesman demoted from salary to commission, closing in on old friends, drawing overdrafts on emotional debts. His former producer Jack Chertok (*Northern Pursuit*) had removed the picture of Henry Wallace from his wall and was now boosting the Du Ponts. "I don't approve of the position you took in Washington," Chertok grumbled. Bessie pleaded, "It'll be a question of eating pretty soon." The producer was unmoved. "You should have thought of that before you got messed up in all this stuff." Instantly remorseful, he offered to telephone his friend J. Edgar Hoover. "I'll call him up right now and say 'Look Edgar, this is a friend of mine. He may have some screwy ideas, but I *know* he's not a traitor to his country. I'll vouch for him and I'm asking you to go easy on him.'" When Bessie coldly refused, Chertok offered the customary hand-on-the-shoulder farewell: "I'll tell you how much confidence I have in you," he said. "You go to Russia and you come back and tell me it's *good* and I'll believe you."

The hell with the small time, Bessie thought, and called on Charlie Chaplin.

Long before the subversive scare, even before the Wheeler atrocity, Chaplin's extra-sexual capers had annoyed politicians and galled industrialists. Back in 1936 in *Modern Times* the dehumanized Charlie went crazy, stepping from the factory to tighten the foreman's nose, fire hydrants and the buttons on women's dresses, ridiculing the authority that fought against new unions. When objections were voiced in Detroit, Chaplin tried to explain: "I was only poking fun at the general confusion from which we are all suffering." The businessmen knew better: the Tramp was tramping on the Gross National Product.

In the same film he created another gag of enduring editorial power. Chaplin waved a danger signal at a truck driver—and the funny cops came down about his head: the Tramp was inciting crowds with a Red Flag. Thirteen years later the gag had lost its savor. Bessie had become the tramp with the flag, and Chaplin welcomed the exile to his estate. Over a long afternoon the melancholy scenarist spitballed a desperate idea: how about a film of Don Quixote, with Walter Huston as the Don and Chaplin as Sancho? Chaplin listened with consuming interest and gave a brief review: "They'd crucify me." As Bessie climbed back into his old Hudson, the sixty-year-old comedian shook his hand and walked rapidly away. Bessie looked down in his palm and found a tightly folded $100 bill.

Three weeks later the money had gone. Bessie made another house call, this time to Lee J. Cobb, the actor he had praised in another epoch, when Cobb was an ambitious stage actor and Bessie was the ruminative drama critic. Back in 1940 Bessie had called Cobb's performances "pure, stunning, dignified and heartbreaking." And Cobb had written him a fan letter. They had become friends in Hollywood; surely that liaison could be tested for a loan of $500. "There's nothing in the house to eat," pleaded Bessie. Cobb, then under contract for $1,500 a week, regretted that he could not advance any cash—although he was willing to pick up Bessie's grocery bill. Bessie turned vituperative.

"I forgive you," answered Cobb, showing him the door. "I can understand how a man like you, who's been through what you've been through and who's going to prison, can say a thing like that to an old friend." Cobb stood in the entrance of his new home. "I hope you'll come to see me again," he orated. "You're a revolutionary, you know. Go *on* being a revolutionary. Go on being an example to me."

SIX

VLADIMIR: *You want to get rid of him?*
POZZO: *I do. But instead of driving him away as I might have done, I mean instead of simply kicking him out on his arse, in the goodness of my heart I am bringing him to the fair, where I hope to get a good price for him.*

SAMUEL BECKETT,
Waiting for Godot

1

HISTORICAL PREJUDICE and personal vendetta grew inseparable. It was no longer clear in 1949 when Hedda Hopper referred to Metro-Goldwyn-Moscow whether she meant the studio's HUAC-revealed tradition, or simply its new chief of production, Dore Schary. "If I promise to put no more messages in my pictures, will you be my friend?" Schary pleaded. "Yes," agreed Hedda, "but I doubt if you will. You're too full of your own ideas."

Ideas; these were the principal foe. In the new decade the right would exorcise them. Those guardians of America built their high new watchtowers on the solid waste of external cir-

cumstance: the Russians had the bomb and were garroting
Berlin. China had fallen. Klaus Fuchs, the polite intellectual
traitor, had confessed. At home, Alger Hiss was adjudged guilty,
yet Dean Acheson, Secretary of State, let it be known that he
would not turn his back on his old protégé.

Given the red weather of 1950, the Hollywood Ten were
unable to slow their plummet. Their past associations, the
diddling of their lawyers and the conduct of their case had
made them casualties of the New Insensibility. But, as one of
the best of them, Albert Maltz, admitted, two miscalculations
marred any efforts at vindication. One: "Repeated assertions
that I *was* answering the Committee's questions instead of
merely taking the position that the Committee had no right to
ask me the questions and I was refusing to answer them on
Constitutional grounds. Since all of us did something like this,
it resulted in a certain confusion. . . ." Two: "The witnesses
. . . self-designated title 'The Unfriendly Nineteen' did themselves no good. For the phrase took on a sinister connotation.
. . . From the public relations point of view, this has been an
unfortunate title. . . ." It had become a great case but not a
good one. Its arguments yellowed and cracked in the hand; there
were clearer, more present dangers.

During the early Hollywood hearings, junior Senator Joe
McCarthy dropped in to watch the investigatory methods of
the HUAC. When Chairman Thomas asked the freshman if he
cared to make some personal interrogations, McCarthy politely
declined. "I just came over to watch the very excellent job you
gentlemen are doing," he said. "I am here merely to listen, and
not to ask questions."

He listened well. Now, as the Senate rowdy, he permuted
the subversive issue like a jazz trombonist, sliding the Reds-in-
Government issue from 205 to 81 to 116 to 10 to 121 to 106.
Yet, with this federal example, the entertainment blacklist still
remained narrow and ill-defined until June 1950. Then, within
a few weeks, three events expanded the rolls of the proscribed

and gave the decade its style and bias. The Supreme Court, under Chief Justice Vinson, refused to review the cases of the Ten, thereby bringing the case to the headlines for the last time, satisfying the lower courts and the Hollywood studios that justice had been dispensed.

At almost the same instant North Korean troops marched across the 38th Parallel, committing the adminstration to a more formidable position of anti-Communist militancy. From here on, native Communists, fellow-travelers, sympathizers, dupes, petition signers, certain liberals and all aggressive civil-libertarians would seek redress elsewhere; damned if the label "Soft on Communism" would adhere to the Truman administration, with its new loyalty oaths and its fresh police action in Asia.

The final event—the publication of a thin white paperback—seemed so trivial that few newspapers bothered to record it. *Red Channels* had, in June, a cheap and irrelevant air.

2

In the beginning, the author of *Red Channels* was Savonarola in a burlesque house. The house was Phillips H. Lord, a packaging company whose product included such hyperthyroid shows as *Gangbusters* and *This Is Your FBI*. Radio broadcasting in those days was expensive and flamboyant; Vincent Hartnett was small, thin-lipped, resolutely drab. In the broadcasting business, ethics were variable; Hartnett's principles never wavered. He believed with unblemished sincerity that atheistic godless Communism tainted the American air. Rip Van Winkle was not a tale to him. It was a blueprint. The snoring country, uninformed, was shortly to awaken to find the Church desecrated, the land socialized, the national soul enchained.

His colleagues at Phillips H. Lord could never figure the little guy out. They were interested in the fast buck; Hartnett's mind seemed elsewhere. With good reason. The ex-Naval Intelligence officer had stumbled upon the reactionaries' home truth: History can be bribed with patience. Nothing was permanent, Hartnett realized. Even the drift to the left could be halted. And 1950 was the year to apply the brakes. Hartnett's decision was prompted by an incident at Phillips H. Lord the year before. William Sweets, a director whose past was clouded with membership in suspect organizations, had found his career abruptly terminated because of a letter-writing campaign. The writers had bombarded advertising agencies with complaints about the "Communist director" of *Gangbusters* and *Counterspy*.

Initially, the Phillips H. Lord management had dismissed this campaign as lunatic fringework. Clarence Francis, president of General Foods, and Walter Mack, of Pepsi-Cola, were not so sanguine. For three weeks the Lord office negotiated vainly with tense sponsors and their tenser advertising agencies (Biow for Pepsi-Cola, Young and Rubicam for General Foods). The word, at last, came back: *Nothing personal, Bill. But you're through.* Sweets stayed on to finish the broadcasting season, but he was no longer considered competent to cast his own talent. After all, reasoned Phillips H. Lord management, it was known that leftists hang out together—surely *that* was proven at the '47 hearings.

Variety picked up the story under the headline RED SCARE NUMBING VIDEO: "Situation, which has already hit video via the firing of director William Sweets for his alleged political beliefs, has staggered video to such an extent that the problem of clearing talent from fellow-traveler charges has become all-important. According to one network talent chief, clearing property rights on a story or play has been the biggest stickler heretofore in staging dramatic shows. 'Now,' he said, 'we spend our time trying to satisfy our top brass that the actors have never been on the left side of the fence.' "

Attorneys could clear property rights. But who would clear a man? Hartnett, early in 1950, received the call. Now he sat in his office, gathering strength for the crusade that would consume an industry.

3

In the spring of 1950, Ed Sullivan, maliface of the electronic vaudeville *Toast of the Town*, invited the lean, carroty hoofer Paul Draper to appear on his show. This was to be the most disastrous appearance of a dancer since Salome. Draper's Aunt Muriel, it appeared, had long been a favorite hate-object of the old right, whose newspapers referred to her as a "notorious Moscow favorite."

Upon the announcement of Draper's appearance a Greenwich, Connecticut, housewife named Hester McCullough began an independent probe for subversives. "I guess you might say I was always on the lookout for them," she explained with shining eyes. She found two close by: Muriel's nephew and his partner, the harmonica virtuoso Larry Adler. The partners' associations, she announced to a gentleman from the *New York Times*, made them "pro-Communist in sympathy." Each, she felt, "should be treated as a traitor." Certainly neither should be allowed to appear on national television.

The entertainers immediately sued Mrs. McCullough, claiming "allegiance solely to the U.S. under the Constitution." The housewife quieted down and Sullivan fatuously assumed that the welkin had finished ringing. It had scarcely begun. Cholly Knickerbocker (Igor Cassini) plus the two Hearst reliables George Sokolsky and Westbrook Pegler demanded that Sullivan's sponsor, the Ford Motor Company, cancel the booking. The company, assured by Sullivan that the barrage was mere journalistic envy, refused. Paul Draper appeared, did his number and danced off to a theater full of cheers. But the columnists did not stop their editorials, nor did the cranks cease their complaints.

Ford received 1,294 angry letters and telegrams, many of them duplicates. Clusters were sent from the same post office. Eight percent denounced "leftists" and "pinks" who should, in fairness, be returned to Stalin. Thirteen percent found Communism a threat to Western civilization. The rest were simply shocked: how could that nice Mr. Sullivan be so deaf to his country's distress? Mr. Sullivan would not be so handicapped again. Three days later in a letter to the president of Kenyon and Eckhart, Ford's advertising agency, the MC stated his frozen distress over the appearance of "a performer whose political beliefs are a matter of controversy." The obligatory disclaimer trailed like a disconnected electric cord: "You know how bitterly opposed I am to Communism and all it stands for. You also know how strongly I would oppose having the program used as a political forum, directly or indirectly."

The idea of anyone directly employing the Ed Sullivan show as a political forum was amusing even to Pegler. But indirectly —that was a problem of mandarin refinement. What, after all, was the prominent characteristic of the Red conspirator? Disguise. Your average Commie agent, ran the fifties logic, was the custodian of *two* personae: one for the people he betrayed, another for the people he obeyed. With the correct guises a Red could infect an advertising agency, a sponsor, a program—the world. Among such people, what represented reality? What was illusion? That enigma, which had been piquing philosophers for five thousand years, presented very little difficulty for Vincent Hartnett. To the secular blacklister, all who were not wholly innocent were to be summarily damned. Every man's past was amber in which all discretions lay preserved. From 1950 on, if anything called attention to itself—a petition, a mention in the *Worker*, an attendance at a meeting—the guilty could, no, *must* be rooted out and banished. The tainting of American air was not a metaphor to Hartnett; it was revealed truth. In that air television and radio messages mysteriously hovered on their way to the aerials on American roofs and cars. Who could clean that air? Who could provide the filter? Hartnett, of course. But even he could not do it *all* alone. He needed the support of an organization of intelligence, discretion and proven Americanism. American Business Consultants (ABC to its clients) volunteered for service.

ABC had deep spiritual affinities with the Federal Bureau of Investigation. Indeed, it was in the Bureau's corridors that ABC's three founders first discussed big-league subversion. John G. Keenan was an FBI supervisor in 1945, and two of his brightest agents, Kenneth Bierly and Theodore Kirkpatrick, used to kick the Red menace around during lunch. Kirkpatrick remembered the sessions: "We used to talk about how little the public knew of some of the details of the Communist movement. Some of the facts that were just routine to us, facts being brought in by us and others day to day and actually being buried in the files."

Yet J. Edgar Hoover continued to define his organization as an arm, not a brain. The FBI, he insisted, carried out policy; it did not make it. That, recalled Kirkpatrick, was "a very frustrating sort of thing, particularly to any individual who is impatient."

Jobs for Red-hunters were scarce immediately after the war. Keenan quietly entered a law firm; Kirkpatrick became assistant to the protection manager at Bloomingdale's. But he confessed, "I was unhappy there. It seemed to me small, petty. It was concerned with shoplifting when here the Communists were trying to take our country." In 1946 Bierly finally emerged from the Bureau: the trio was ready to begin.

In 1945 Alfred Kohlberg, the crusty millionaire importer and lobbyist for Chiang Kai-shek, decided to publish a two-fisted anti-Communist publication entitled *Plain Talk*. The FBI men signed on as his researchers. But they were restless entrepreneurs, anxious to found their own blacklisting business. In 1946, Bierly, Keenan and Kirkpatrick opened offices in Washington, D.C., billing themselves as John Quincy Adams Associates. JQAA intended to supply information about subversives to clergymen, union leaders and "persons frequently approached by charitable and civic organizations who are anxious not to support a hidden Communist cause." But, despite some frantic lobbying, the emerging blacklisters failed to win a permanent rating as a non-profit organization. They dissolved their corporation and soon resurfaced at 55 West 42nd Street as American Business Consultants. In 1947 they hit the mother lode. From the start ABC enjoyed a bull market in Reds, investigating names for $5 each, sometimes clearing or accusing hundreds—if the client was big enough. They also launched a new publicaton, *Counterattack*, a legal-sized mimeographed periodical exposing Communist influence in American corporations. Subscriptions were hawked by door-to-door salesmen who started at the top of an office building and worked their way down. The publication was mailed to churchmen, educators and government agencies. Copies were sold to the management of Bendix Aviation, Du Pont, General Motors, Metropolitan Life Insurance Co., R. J. Reynolds Tobacco Co., F. W. Woolworth. ABC leaned heavily on its old references. An employer remembered the merchandising technique: "The salesman didn't exactly say Keenan and Kirkpatrick still get a look at the FBI files, but he had a moth-eaten letter which pointed up their former association. His whole approach was the 'fear technique,' implying that the firm might get in a lot of trouble if we didn't have an investigation made of our people or, at the very least, take several subscriptions to *Counterattack*."

The hard sell had a pleasing effect for the men at ABC. Emboldened by the subscription list, they flushed subversives everywhere, under the unspoken motto: *no exposé too large, no spy too small*. Radio chatterbox Mary Margaret McBride was criticized for advertising Polish hams, the Fredric Marches for their membership in a number of organizations the United States Attorney General had condemned. *Counterattack's* incessant mentions of Fredric March and Florence Eldridge proved effective—so effective that the Marches sued ABC for $500,000. They had been one of the highest-paid acting teams in the country, second only to the Lunts. In 1948, after the denunciations in *Counterattack,* they filed a joint return of $2.58. The case was settled out of court and the Marches were generously allowed to file an anti-Communist statement in the newsletter. For six months afterward, claimed March, the calls for his services "could be counted on the fingers of one hand with a finger or two left over."

ABC's accusations took a considerable dip after that, and the firm went back to the safe policy of clandestine public relations. But they continued to underline their origins in promotional literature: "Ex-FBI Agents Expose Communists" had a nice lilt to it, the kind that Winchell could hype: "*Counterattack* (an anti-Communist newsletter) is edited by former G-men who have names and other data at their fingertips."

But by 1950 those fingertips had drummed a lot of desktops, waiting for a live issue. From time to time *Counterattack* had published a "special report," a supplement to its customary four legal-sized pages full of CAPITALIZED NAMES of subversives and brief paragraphs warning of new conspiracies. The special report on Henry Wallace's Progressive Party (labeled "Commugressive" in *Counterattack*) was especially well received. But that had been in 1948. Now in 1950 the subscribers were bored and hungry. The ABC men, with their copious files, were introduced to Vincent Hartnett and *his* copious files. The quartet suddenly conceived a new method of cleansing the broadcasting industry. "We felt it might be good to come out with something documented and do it publicly," Beirly remembered. "Lay it on the line and sell it over the counter to try to clear the air."

In the months following Draper's catastrophic appearance,

Ed Sullivan had grown dependent on the *petit*-Richelieus who advised the columnist on political theory. Sullivan boasted to his readers, "Kirkpatrick has sat in my living room on several occasions and listened attentively to performers eager to secure a certification of loyalty. On some occasions he has given them the green light; on other occasions he has told them 'Veterans' organizations will insist on further proof.' " Sullivan had thus proved his loyalty. On Wednesday, June 21, 1950, he was granted the privilege of prediction. "A bombshell," he wrote, "will be dropped into the offices of radio-TV networks, advertising agencies and sponsors this week with the publication of *Red Channels*."

The bombshell was the most effective blacklist in the history of show business. A trifle over 200 pages, paperbound, it was Dilling for the fifties. No authors were credited, although Kirkpatrick referred to himself as the publisher and Hartnett privately called the book "my *Red Channels*." Like all its cruder predecessors, the volume was decorated in red. Below the title a microphone canted to the left. Behind it, a gross crimson hand prepared to seize control. Inside, Hartnett's brisk intro brought the reader up to date. "With radios in most American homes and with approximately 5 million TV sets in use, the Cominform and the Communist Party USA now rely more on radio and TV than on the press and motion pictures as 'belts' to transmit pro-Sovietism to the American public."

An unidentified "former head of a Soviet espionage ring" gave a dire prediction—in the terse copy of a laxative commercial: "What American businessmen and the American public do not seem to realize is that these people are playing for keeps, with no holds barred. They don't lose time just making resolutions or having meetings. They're *activists!* Until we Americans learn to take prompt, effective actions, too, they'll win every round!"

To debase the Red currency, Hartnett appropriated the vocabulary of the left. There *was* a blacklist in broadcasting, he allowed. But it was owned and operated by Red fascists. "Those who know radio and TV," he wrote darkly, "can recite dozens of examples of anti-Communists who, for mysterious reasons, are *persona non grata* on numerous programs, and who are slandered unmercifully in certain 'progressive' circles. That this system should be so prevalent is a matter for utmost consideration by those who employ radio and TV talent."

Finally, *Red Channels* clarified the business of suspicion and presumptive innocence with a quote from *Broadcasting Magazine:* "Where there's red smoke there's usually Communist fire."

All of this was grillework before the main design. Part Two contained the germ of the book: an Alphabetical Index of Names. Some listees were connected with more than forty suspect organizations, some with only one. Many of the groups had been defunct since the late thirties, some had existed only during the war; one, Artists Front to Win the War, had had a halflife of one meeting.

It was unsurprising to find Adler and Draper there, with references to "Depositions filed in the McCullough case, 9/49." Nor could there be much astonishment at the appearance of these familiar stalwarts without whom no blacklist could claim thoroughness: Lillian Hellman, Dorothy Parker, Irwin Shaw. But there were many unfamiliars in the catalogue of dupes and fellow-travelers: Irene Wicker, a children's entertainer, billed as the Singing Lady; Judy Holliday, the new comedienne and star of *Born Yesterday;* Jean Muir, featured player of the thirties films. Still others were only vaguely familiar to the public, who confused them with baseball players or politicians in neighboring states: Leon Janney, Ralph Bell, Joe Julian. William Sweets, the banished Gangbuster, was there, though he had been out of the business for a year and sat, exiled, in an antique shop in Vermont. Luther Adler, already so heavy and avuncular that everyone had forgotten that he was the original Golden Boy, was listed by an organization he had joined when he was slim; his freshest association was in 1939, at the sunset of the Group Theatre. Millard Lampell, novelist and TV writer, found himself twice cited for having been pro-Wallace. Gypsy Rose Lee, the witty ecdysiast, had been attacked by the *Daily Worker* as far back as 1937, when strip-teasers were called "shameful creations of capitalism." Nevertheless, she had been prematurely anti-fascist, and the *Worker* had reported her (incorrectly) as the sender of a telegram to Dr. Edward Barsky, head of the Joint Anti-Fascist Refugee Committee (cited by Attorney General Tom Clark as a Communist front).

For some, their presence in the little white-and-red book meant annoyance but not annihilation. Lillian Hellman refused to look down to denounce; Arthur Miller had been accustomed, lately, to critiques. It was only three years ago that Jack Warner had been so noisily disgusted by the quintessence of Ibsenism in *All My Sons*. In 1948, when the Waldorf Peace Conference was organized to welcome Dimitri Shostakovich, Miller had been warned by press agents that, theater party-wise, it would be a mistake to attend. But, he recalled, "I just felt that, having been invited, if I turned it down I would be turning myself down, so I went." He encountered "nuns on their knees around the Waldorf-Astoria, praying for the souls of those within, and enormous, loud and violent picket lines." The mission of the conference was never clarified; as Miller remarked later, "The amazing kind of spaghetti that was being cooked there—you couldn't follow one thread more than two inches." Miller did not allow for the investigatory skills of ABC, which would never lose track of the spaghetti.

Louis Untermeyer ceased to appear as a guest on panel shows; he did not stop anthologizing. Nor did Aaron Copland and Leonard Bernstein find themselves long diverted from high, arcing careers. But the tension varied inversely to fame or genius. As the list bounced down from composers to producers to directors and performers, the book exerted a pressure equal to that of the Mindanao Deep. Finally, at the regularly salaried level, there was no hope at all. A producer, crocked beyond discretion, confided to Lampell: "Pal, you're dead. I submitted your name for a show and they told me that I couldn't touch you with a barge pole. . . . Don't quote me . . . I'll deny I said it."

Soon after *Red Channels* appeared, NBC announced the television version of *The Aldrich Family*, a long-running radio comedy. Mother Aldrich, said the press release, would be played by Jean Muir. The name of the actress was perhaps more familiar to blacklisters than to casting directors. Muir, an attractive, rather eloquent actress of the second rank, was suspected of subversion back in her starlet days. In 1940 a Communist renegade with the Dickensian appellation of John Leech had testified in private session with Martin Dies. Leech had personally observed Jean Muir at a left-wing party; he provided similar evidence against James Cagney, Humphrey Bogart, Fredric March, Franchot Tone, Luise Rainer and Francis Lederer. Singly, these stars appeared before the Congressman; singly, he granted them absolution. Give Dies a single insect and he could spin a web. But Leech's stuff on Muir was insufficient even for the Texas Congressman. The blacklisters would have to wait a decade before they could try twice for the same crime. In *Red Channels* the actress found an italicized paragraph near her name: "Cited by a former California Communist as having attended Communist study groups. . . ."

By their intended use of Jean Muir, NBC and General Foods, sponsor of *The Aldrich Family*, upset Kirkpatrick. It was one thing to have *Red Channels* attacked by the watery liberalism of the *New York Post* and the *Herald Tribune*. But this! Yet, for ABC to lodge a protest to network or sponsor smacked of bad form; it would give persecution an unsavory reputation. Kirkpatrick therefore telephoned the redoubtable Hester Mc-Cullough. She had just seen the Adler-Draper case end in a hung jury. Crusaders are never quite happy with neutral conclusions; if blood is not drawn, how can honor be satisfied?

Besides, Mrs. McCullough had been stimulated by her brush with celebrity. When she and her husband went to Hollywood to gather evidence for her lawyer, Hedda Hopper had taken the McCulloughs to lunch at Romanoff's. "A lot of people came up to meet us," she told friends, "movie stars, I mean important people like that, and all of them knew my name. In every place except Greenwich I'm appreciated for what I am."

Now Mrs. McCullough listened to Kirkpatrick's atrocity story and made her decision. "I knew," she was to recall with evangelical zeal, "this was a fight that had to be won." She began by dialing the National Broadcasting Company—and was pleasantly astonished to learn that she was not the only patriot to protest the new Mother Aldrich. She also learned that Young and Rubicam, agency for General Foods, was vulnerable, as all service industries are vulnerable, because they depend on the wills of the abstract public and the concrete client. She called a Y&R executive in her neighborhood.

"But, Mrs. McCullough, she's just an actress," pleaded the voice. "What harm can she possibly do?"

"Until all the loyal Americans have been put to work," came the answer, "I don't think people like that should be on radio and television."

Mrs. McCullough found the next exchange memorable: "He said something about a relative of his having died a few hours ago, and he wanted to go, but I insisted on his listening to me and told him that in times like these personal matters don't count.

"I think he finally understood what I was talking about, but it took a little time."

The Plimsoll line of protests edged to the danger point: twenty. Numbers were traditionally extrapolated by the network; fifteen complimentary postcards were taken to mean approval by millions of viewers. A score of plaintiffs was interpreted as a catastrophe that dwarfed the Sullivan fiasco. Draper, after all, was a one-shot. Muir was supposed to be on *every goddam week.* After a brief postponement of the show, General Foods delivered its hard line:

"In taking this action," the company said in an official release,

> General Foods wishes it understood that it is in no way passing judgment on the merits of the protests it has received.
>
> The basic policy which General Foods has established and uniformly observes in matters of this kind is as follows:
>
> One of the fundamental objectives of General Foods' advertising is to create a favorable and receptive attitude toward its products among the largest number of consumers.
>
> The use of controversial personalities or the dicussion of controversial subjects in our advertising may provoke unfavorable criticism and even antagonism among sizable groups of consumers. Such reaction injures both acceptance of our products and our public relations.
>
> General Foods advertising, therefore, avoids the use of material and personalities which in its judgment are controversial.
>
> In accordance with the policy expressed above, General Foods has instructed its advertising agency, Young and Rubicam Inc., to arrange with Stellar Enterprises [producer of the program] for the replacement of Miss Muir as a member of *The Aldrich Family* cast.

Muir helplessly protested that if she were truly guilty of pro-Communist charges she could be summarily fired. Instead, she had been compensated in full for her eighteen-week contract. Her protests grew dim and, finally, inaudible.

A choir of sympathetic liberals promptly denounced *Red Channels,* American Business Consultants, General Foods and Young and Rubicam. The prominent civil-rights lawyer Arthur Garfield Hays angrily invited the listees and their attorneys to gather at his office. Hartnett, receiving word of this new Red maneuver, tried to enlist the announcer Kenneth Roberts, then working on a Philip Morris program. Roberts' profitable days were nearing a close, hinted Hartnett . . . unless, somehow, he gained a clearance. And how would that be obtained? the announcer inquired. Suppose, said the blacklister, Roberts was to furnish him with the minutes of the Hays conference? Roberts hotly refused—but Hartnett need not have worried. Hays' notion of a proper counterattack was a series of ineffectual libel suits. Besides, much of the information in *Red Channels* was true enough. At the meeting, few listees offered to repudiate their associations. Disavow the Committee for Arts, Sciences and the Professions, the Wallace rallies, the petitions? How could they? They had organized them. For them to deny the past was to live like Dracula, without a shadow. Hays listened to the speeches and the venting of egos. There was to be no action, he sensed, none triggered by *this* gathering. As the harangues proceeded, Hester Sondergaard sneaked a look at Bella Abzug, the bright, aggressive, chunky lawyer then seeking her first cause. The actress passed a note to a pouter pigeon of an actress named Madeline Lee (Mrs. Jack Gilford), who later recalled the moment as an epiphany. "Hester and her sister Gale were two beautiful and delicate redheads—all dignity and all talent. You must remember that Gale had already won an Academy Award and was an ornament to any meeting. Both sisters were the absolute opposite of the un-Christian New York bolsheviks invented by the blacklisters. When Hester passed me the note, I thought, here it comes: some tedious point of order in an already tedious day, or else a righteous speech that I had to give because I had the loudest voice. I unfolded the note. It said, 'Tell Bella to cross her legs.' It was *that* kind of meeting."

It was *that* kind of season, full of restraint on the part of the damaged, of contempt and raucousness from their enemies. Only occasionally did the press acknowledge the existence, much less the virulence, of a blacklist. In the *Herald Tribune*,

John Crosby had some intriguing questions to put: "How much money are the editors making by exploiting the hatred of Communism shared by all of us? Where does the money come from? What sort of record did the editors have in the FBI and why aren't they still in it?"

Max Lerner called the blacklisters "the locust-plague of the democratic harvest. . . . What they say in effect to Jean Muir and to the many others, often nameless, who are their victims, is 'I veto you.' Which means, 'I annihilate you.' Sometimes I wonder whether the animals in the jungle, falling on their prey, also think of themselves as patriots."

American Business Consultants, artificers to the stars, had no time to answer the razzberries from the liberal press, which already felt it must announce its own anti-Communism before it dared lecture extremists. Critics of ABC would be put down by the proper authorities, at the appropriate occasion. In the meantime, there were Sokolsky and Pegler. "Guilt by association is an old and respected principle of jurisprudence," wrote Peg in his best backroom tone. "If you hang out in a low resort and are picked up as a low character, that is your fault. A reporter of experience will recall loaded patrol wagons unloading after Saturday night raids."

When the dust settled, Sokolsky discussed Muir's brief sympathies for the Spanish Loyalist cause in 1938. "Let's look at the facts," Sokolsky said, and gave a three-paragraph summary of the events from April 14, 1931, when King Alfonso left his Spain, and March 28, 1939, when Generalissimo Franco gained control of the country. "I am not trying to show off my knowledge," the columnist assured the reader. "I looked this up in *An Encyclopedia of World History*. . . . But I cannot see in all this why an American who was not a Communist or a fascist could get all steamed up about it."

The column was encapsulation of the blacklisters' new style. It was the know-nothing who was knowledgeable—*he* could look up what he wanted in an encyclopedia. The intelligent were the ones who were corrupted by knowledge. Involvement was out; people interested in politics outside their own sphere were, at best, activists. Activism, in this revised system, was dangerous in the same way that water was intoxicating, because you got drunk on it whether you mixed it with gin, bourbon or wine.

Yet the Muir victory left ABC strangely unappeased. When General Foods continued to receive a bad press for its abrupt capitulation, Kirkpatrick discovered some more suspect organizations to which the name Jean Muir could be attached. Excitedly he telephoned an executive at General Foods. "I can offer additional data," he panted. "Mr. Kirkpatrick, you've already done too *much* for us," came the reply. "Goodbye." Click.

In Illinois, Edwin Clamage, chairman of the American Legion's Anti-Subversive Commission, lectured the state Legion convention. As evidence of the Red network, he introduced the name of Gypsy Rose Lee, soon to appear on the American Broadcasting Company's radio show *What Makes You Tick?* What made Gypsy tick, boomed Clamage, was fellow-traveling.

The reverberations were immediate. Wire services picked highlights from the Clamage speech, and several hours later Robert Kintner, president of the American Broadcasting Company, telegraphed the Illinois Legion: "If you have evidence [of Lee's alleged pro-Communism], please wire me." Otherwise, Kintner said, the stripper would go on as scheduled. Clamage suddenly remembered the old army game. Hell, *he* had no special insights, he said. He was only reading from the little book. "The entire matter could be easily clarified and the answer should come not from me," Clamage grumbled, "but from the publishers of *Red Channels*."

Kirkpatrick icily declined to open any more files. "We are not adding any further documentation to the information already published." *What Makes You Tick?* went on with Gypsy Rose Lee. There were no further protests.

Nor did the front page soothe the blacklisters. Henry Wallace had just resigned from his Progressive Party, belatedly and sadly cognizant that it had become another front of raucous insignificance. Lee Pressman, former counsel of the CIO, long since discredited, confessed in Washington that he had indeed been a Communist member. At Congressman Nixon's urging, he named his associates.

In August 1950 the Ten received their sentences in Washington; Biberman and Dmytryk held up their hands to their colleagues with six fingers extended; they alone had received a judicial break: six months in jail instead of twelve.

Out in Hollywood the left was now mere detritus from the Popular front. George Beck, a scenarist whose CP membership had long since lapsed, was approached by his old comrade Mortimer Offner. In this crisis, would Beck consider rejoining? "I said no thanks," Beck recalled. "He didn't press me, particularly. He did, however, rather sadly comment, 'Gee, it's tough. Everybody is leaving. And nothing will drag them back in.'" The Party had reached its ebb—at the time when the blacklist needed it most.

Given these conditions, American Business Consultants had to reconstruct the lineaments of the enemy. Of *course* he seemed anemic and shadowy, ABC said; that was the way of the Red: to lie, to pretend weakness and even death, like the puff adder cornered by the American eagle. ABC adopted a more urgent tone: its subscribers were conscripted in the new fight; switchboards at networks rang with Pavlovian timing whenever a listee was scheduled to broadcast. Norman Rosten found his scripts unwanted; the producers told him they needed a "new approach." Rosten, who had once co-written a drama with Arthur Miller, brooded about his loss of powers, unwilling to accuse. "It could be coincidence," he said, shaking his head. "But it's awful damn strange." Actress Carol Atwater suddenly found that she wasn't right for the part—any part—on television. The wistful tragicomedian Jack Gilford was just as amusing as before. Zero Mostel, the waterbed that walked like a man, was just as exuberant and entertaining as he had been. But producers suddenly stopped laughing at both performers. Robert Lewis Shayon ceased producing. Ireene Wicker, the Singing Lady, lost her sponsor, the Kellogg Company. "It was," said a General Foods spokesman stiffly, "merely a matter of business." The Singing Lady, who had only one affiliation in *Red Channels,* was bewildered. The paragraph beside her name claimed that she had sponsored the Committee for the Reelection of Benjamin Davis, the black Communist. Wicker journeyed to 55 West 42nd Street in an effort to gain clearance. She had never heard of Benjamin Davis, she told Kirkpatrick. He answered, Clamage-style, by blaming it all on the *Daily Worker,* where he had seen her name. Perhaps Miss Wicker was innocent, he continued, but how was he to be sure? What had she done to express her *opposition* to Communism? Well, his guest replied, she had conducted an "I'm glad I am an American because" contest for children. She had recorded a series based on American history. She had allowed her only son, later shot down in Europe, to enlist in the Royal Canadian Air Force in 1940 during the Stalin-Hitler Pact. What more could she say? Kirkpatrick remained unconvinced. Only when Wicker's attorney finally obtained the nominating petitions for Ben Davis, examined all thirty thousand names and failed to find Wicker among them did Kirkpatrick relent. Ireene Wicker's anti-Communist statement was printed in *Counterattack.* But she was not re-hired, after twenty-five years on radio. She had created controversy. And controversy now equaled sin.

Tom Glazer, the folk singer, also sought absolution. In 1948, when every fellow-traveler was stumping for Henry Wallace, he had campaigned through New York for the Democratic state committee; he had made several contributions to the International Rescue Committee, which aided Iron Curtain refugees. That was all very well, countered Kirkpatrick; still it was not enough. "Can you tell me about any *arguments* you've had with Communists?" he demanded. Glazer could not think of any. Nevertheless, he too was allowed to enter a patriotic statement in *Counterattack*; he, like Wicker, found no new broadcasting assignments.

Friends of ABC were delighted to assist in the ballooning of the enemy. Rabbi Benjamin Schultz of Yonkers, New York, was the obverse of those Christians who used to be enticed into office in the old leftist Teachers' Union because, as one of them admitted, "they needed goyim badly." In the fifties the black-listers were predominantly Catholic and leery that they might be grouped with those other notorious anti-Communists, the Nazis. Therefore they welcomed the Jews in the traditional role of semi-precious converts to the Cause. Schultz, whom the great rabbi Stephen Wise had called "unworthy to be a member, not to say a rabbi of a Jewish congregation," was pathologically aware of the predominance of Semitic names in show busi-ness—hence in show-business blacklists. With the China lobby-ist Alfred Kohlberg he formed the rabid American-Jewish League Against Communism. The League's membership sel-dom exceeded four hundred; out of a total budget of $29,000, $10,000 went to Schultz as salary. But Schultz was a master of the numbers racket. When he worked in aid of ABC, complain-ing to networks or sponsors, he liked to consider himself the representative of "two million citizens of this state."

After 1948 he found himself without a pulpit; after *Red Channels* he didn't need one. The telephone would do. When, for instance, he heard the talking blues number "Old Man Atom," Schultz became distraught. The lyrics (written five years before) were a loud shade of red:

> . . . "If you're scared of an A Bomb
> Here's what you gotta do:
> You gotta gather all the people in the world with you
> Because if you don't get together and do it, well-uh

The first thing you know we're gonna blow the world
plumb to-uh . . . thesis: Peace in the world
Or the world in pieces."

The message, the rabbi told his followers, was only a smudged carbon of the Stockholm Peace Petition, then being circulated by the Communists. The AJLAC made no public statement and issued no press release. Instead, quietly, Schultz employed the letter-and-telephone gambit with astonishing results. Within a month the major record companies, RCA Victor and Columbia, withdrew their best-selling records of "Old Man Atom" from circulation.

Not everyone could be a member of Schultz's platoon, yet every good American could join the crusade. Karl Baarslag, full-time official of the American Legion's Americanism Commission, praised *Counterattack* in his own lower-case blacklist *summary of trends and developments exposing the Communist conspiracy*. And he gave a blueprint for American action: In writing or phoning radio sponsors and others (here he understandably shifted to caps) MAKE NO CHARGES OR CLAIMS.

"Merely state that you buy their products or services and enjoy their radio or TV shows but that you disapprove or object to so-and-so and desire that they be removed. Nothing else . . . don't let the sponsors pass the buck back to you by demanding 'proof' of communist fronting by some character about whom you have complained. You don't have to prove anything. . . . You simply do not like so-and-so on their programs. . . ."

By September, like iron filings repolarized, businessmen began collecting at the right terminal. *Tide*, the trade magazine, interviewed major sponsors and printed their findings: "88 percent said that they believe advertisers and agencies should concern themselves with artists' or writers' ideologies. Only 10 percent disagreed; only 2 percent had no opinion. Further, almost eight out of ten (77 percent) held that advertisers and agencies should concern themselves with artists' or writers' *past* ideologies as well. . . ."

In October, Kirkpatrick addressed the Radio Executives' Club on the subject of blacklisting: "I don't say you shouldn't hire the performers listed in *Red Channels*. I *do* say that those who continue to support Communist Party causes since June 23, 1950, must take the consequences. Anyone who has continued to support a Communist cause since June 23 is just as much . . . an enemy of our country as if he were in Korea passing ammunition to the Communists." (June 23 was an odd date—one day after the publication of *Red Channels*; two days before the Korean War began. It was unclear to the executives which day was paramount to Kirkpatrick, but in all other respects the audience got the message.)

The same month, Vincent Hartnett briefly left his home and office at 22nd Street to appear at the All-Peoria Conference to Combat Communism. The gathering was one of a series of "anti-subversive seminars" sponsored by the super-alert Illinois American Legion.

"You in the audience," said Hartnett, "hold the purse strings for most entertainers. Big corporations and radio stations will listen to you. Wire, phone or write your requests." With frigid delivery, Hartnett went on to reiterate his charges against activist entertainers and attacked the new Attorney General, J. Howard McGrath, for his defense of performers like Jean Muir. (McGrath, as it turned out, had not mentioned Muir or any other entertainer; he had, however, maligned "vigilante groups who intimidate radio personalities.") The road company of Arthur Miller's *Death of a Salesman* was soon to appear in Peoria. It was "a Communist-dominated play," said Hartnett, uniting in his text such Party-fronters as Miller, producer Kermit Bloomgarden, Lee J. Cobb, the original star, and his replacement, Albert Dekker. "You have your choice of supporting or denying support to any entertainer, playwright or artist. Why should you support such a performance?" Hartnett asked, especially

since a great part of the income from the Peoria appearance
would go directly to the Communist Party or its affiliates.

Protests from Miller, Bloomgarden, Dekker and the Authors'
League were immediately dispatched to the *Peoria Journal-Star*.
But no far-off howls could distract the Peoria Junior Chamber
of Commerce or the men of the American Legion's Peoria Post
No. 2. They insisted that the city manager of the Publix-Great
States Theatres cancel the performances. When he refused, the
Legionnaires announced a giant boycott; the play went on as
scheduled to a small audience. It was an emboldening experi-
ence to the Legion, sort of a *Red Channels* in the round.

Finally, in December, the main resistance crumbled, save for
a few solid left-wingers whose names would be duly filed and
hounded. Station WPIX in New York canceled a series of programs for a Charlie Chaplin festival. The program manager,
Warren Wade, had received about twenty protests when the
series was announced. The most effective was from the Hudson
County, New Jersey, post of the Catholic War Veterans.

That the films were ancient was irrelevant to the CWV.
Said their official spokesman, "It makes no difference if the pictures were made five, ten, twenty or more years ago. Entertainment for art's sake just does not exist when you talk about Communism. People who talk that way have no basis for fact."

By the end of the year CBS made its own genuflection to the
new history where time and quality had no meaning. Joseph H.
Ream, executive vice president of the Columbia Broadcasting
System, had received a surfeit of telephone calls, wires and
letters. In a general memo he told the network's employees:

We are faced with a new crisis in our national life. The
President of the United States has declared a national
emergency.

If we are to fulfill our obligations and responsibilities as
radio and television broadcasters in this new crisis, we must
do at least two things: first, we must make sure that our

broadcasting operations in the public interest are not interrupted by sabotage or violence; second we must make sure that the full confidence of our listeners is unimpaired.

Translation: Every one of CBS's 2,500 employees was to sign and return a loyalty oath testifying to unbelief in the Communist Party, U.S.A.

A minor office employee refused to sign and was hastily dismissed. Other officials were allowed to resign silently. A folk singer turned producer, Tony Kraber, listed in *Red Channels*, made no attempt to hide his past. When Ream asked him to resign, he told Kraber, "The network is bigger than any of us." But, Kraber complained, he had signed the loyalty oath. "Oh, that," replied Ream. "That doesn't mean a thing."

It did, though. The calculated frenzy of the blacklisters had brought unexpected dividends. By the New Year, American Business Consultants, with new clients and an assured future, had only one lingering regret about *Red Channels*. Keenan expressed it: "We made a mistake in charging only a dollar. . . . We didn't think there'd be such a hefty demand for it. We should have charged two bucks a copy. Now we're smarter than we were then."

SEVEN

VLADIMIR: *I'm afraid he's dying.*
ESTRAGON: *It'd be amusing.*
VLADIMIR: *What'd be amusing?*
ESTRAGON: *To try him with the other names, one right after the other. It'd pass the time. And we'd be bound to hit on the right one sooner or later.*
                    SAMUEL BECKETT,
                    Waiting for Godot

"Geez, Mr. Hayden, only the other night me an' the missus was saying: 'Now, that Hayden's a real nice manly actor—' Always admired you, Sterl; never did think I'd ever be serving *you* with no subpoena . . . Here, I'll slip it to you quiet like; then I guess if I was you I'd sure go call my lawyer." . . .

"All right, we'll have to move fast. I'll contact Wheeler, their Hollywood investigator. Meet me tonight—my office —eight o'clock sharp . . . And by the way—better bring your wife—and also you might wear that rosette that goes with the Silver Star."

"Yes, Martin." (Oh, thank God for [my lawyer] Martin

Gang—thank God I went to the F.B.I.—Martin knows what to do.) . . .

"But my God, Martin, he's in every single shot from now till the end of the picture. If we stop shooting now, we're dead. Jesus, imagine the losses. You've got to get the Committee to hold off. Otherwise it'll be a disaster. And this had to be my first production." . . .

"Sterlin'—one word of advice. Go straight, tell the truth. Ask yourself: 'What will my children think?' Always make them proud of you."

"Doc, I can't go through with it. Since the subpoena two weeks back I've tried and tried to convince myself. They knew I was a Party member—they don't want information, they want to put on a show, and I'm the star. They've already agreed to go over the questions with me in advance. It's a rigged show: radio and TV and the papers. . . . Co-operate and I'm a stool pigeon. Shut my mouth and I'm a pariah."

"I suggest, Mr. Hayden, that you try and relax—just lie down . . . Now then, may I remind you there's really not much difference, so far as you yourself are concerned, between talking to the F.B.I. in private and taking the stand in Washington." . . .

Now counsel sounds his pitch pipe and I begin to sing. Once I begin, what follows seems almost anticlimactic.

Strange. In almost all countries a man who collaborates with those who would punish freedoms arouses the hatred of his countrymen. And yet today, in the United States of America, the way to loyalty is this—down the muddy informer's trail. Very strange indeed.

S. Hayden, *Wanderer*

Thus Sterling Hayden, starring in the Washington remake of *The Informer*. In the spring of 1951 the House Un-American

Activities Committee manifestly disagreed with one paragraph in *Red Channels*. Television was all very well in its place, they said, but Hollywood was still where the action was, where big names could be snared, where the ancient embarrassments of parties for the Party, speeches, advertisements, petitions could be strip-mined and merchandised. Hollywood—there was your REAL *Red Channels*. *Counterattack* and its allies had no quarrel with this renewed crusade against the movies. They lived on names; the more the Committee flushed out, the more private investigations, clearances, probes, fees. The greater the anxieties, the more subscribers. There was ever bigger money in Reds in 1951.

Edward G. Robinson, the sawed-off hero of gangster films and screen biographies, had suddenly grown cold at the major studios. So early in 1951 he was forced to make an incalculably long and wearisome journey. The man in whose home the Hollywood Nineteen had first concentrated back in the fall of 1947 went voluntarily to the HUAC to testify, under oath, that he was not and never had been a Communist or knowingly a fellow-traveler, that, at worst, he had simply been a liberal Democrat. Representative Donald Jackson of California, who had replaced Senator Richard Nixon, was unhappy with press reports that the actor had been given "an implied clearance." Nothing of the kind, *he* implied. The new and massive investigation of the film industry would make 1947 look like a college musical. *No one* was to be excused this time.

It began in March with the appearance of Larry Parks, chain-smoking while he waited to play out his base tragedy. In Parks' Communist years the Committee would have disdained him; he was then only a bit actor. But when the open-faced kid mimed Al Jolson's numbers in *The Jolson Story*, Parks enjoyed a swift, miraculous rise to the big time. Parks himself could not believe his change of fortune. Indeed, he confessed to the Committee that in college he had majored in chemistry and minored in physics. "I sometimes wonder," he mused sadly, "how I got into my present line of work." Present was the correct term; there was to be no future.

In the morning the witness confessed his peccadillos but could not be specific as to dates and associates. Compared with the '47 hearing, this tribunal was already ahead on points. The Committee, bright with anticipation, pressed Parks for more revelations. Parks, agonized, begged off: "I ask you again, counsel, to reconsider forcing me to name names. . . . I don't think that this is really American justice, to force me to do this. . . . Don't present me with the choice of either being in contempt of this Committee and going to jail or forcing me to really crawl through the mud to be an informer. . . ."

Even Representative Francis Walter had asked Frank S. Tavenner, counsel, what possible use names would be when the Committee already knew them. But there was no such word as lenity in Tavenner's Malemute code. The witness would sing the low notes, not merely the accessible middle range. "Who were the members of the cell to which you were assigned?" Tavenner insisted. Parks pleaded, "This is what I have been talking about. . . . I am no longer fighting for myself, because I tell you frankly that I am probably the most completely ruined man that you have ever seen. I am fighting for a principle. . . . I don't think that this is fair play. . . . These are not people that are a danger to this country."

Counsel was amazed by this unexpected digging in of the heels. Counsel would decide what constituted ruin. Counsel would define fair play. Counsel would be the judge of danger and safety. Parks, looking down from unaccustomed heights, grew dizzied and nauseated. As abruptly as it all began, the resistance was finished.

Counsel: If you will just answer the question, please. . . . Who were the members of the Communist Party cell to which you belonged?

Parks: Well, Morris Carnovsky, Joe Bromberg, Sam Rossen, Anne Revere, Lee Cobb, Gale Sondergaard. . . .

The chairman, John S. Wood of Georgia, seemed discomfited by this pocket theater of cruelty. Walter assured the witness, "You could get some comfort out of the fact that the people whose names have been mentioned have been subpoenaed, so that if they ever do appear here it won't be as a result of anything that you have testified to."

This was always to be the case; the witnesses were never to provide any revelations. There were no longer any secrets from the House Un-American Activities Committeemen. In their tireless obsession they were reminiscent not of inquisitors but role-players repeating the dry scape of Beckett.

The example of Parks was too near and harrowing for the next guest, Mr. Sterling Hayden. The outsized actor rearranged his life for the Committee's pleasure, posing before the television cameras, patiently answering all questions in meticulous detail. "Few stoolies have played this hall who were better prepared than I," Hayden remembered, seeing it forever in the historical present. "I have nine pages of neat notes typed out on filing cards. And on the tenth page is an index of dates, names, places, and an itemized list of donations to seditious causes dedicated to the liquidation of segregation and racial prejudice and other minor hatreds."

Hayden had served in the Office of Strategic Services in liaison with Tito's Partisan forces. He came back "all steamed up," he testified, ready for ideological training. When Bea Winters, a secretary at his booking agency, told him to "stop talking and join," he wavered, then signed on. He attended some twenty weekly meetings of his cell. Most of its members were anonymous working stiffs, technicians, grips, stagehands. But he *could* identify Karen Morley, the actress. When Hayden dropped out, she tried to persuade him to rejoin. By then, he assured the Congressmen, he had rediscovered his red-white-and-blue-blooded heritage. The Committee thrilled at this disclosure.

Emptied, Hayden rose slowly from the stand and went out

into the long marbled hallways with attorney Martin Gang's voice raucous in his ear: "Hear 'em? Hear 'em? Mark my words, boy, you are going to emerge from this thing bigger than ever before. I wouldn't be at all surprised if you became a kind of a hero overnight. Wait till they hear about your testimony out on the Coast tonight. . . . Why, you're going to end up smelling like a rose."

He smelled through pictures like *Kansas Pacific, Hellgate, Cry Baby* and *Arrow in the Dust,* increasingly glazed and consistently empty, like Kafka's hunger artist who could never eat simply because he could never find anything he liked. A decade later Hayden finally cast up his repentance in the peculiar and moving autobiography *Wanderer.* And he was free.

With Larry Parks as the reluctantly cooperative witness and Sterling Hayden as the fully cooperative witness, the Committee needed only a whole *un*cooperative witness to make its set complete. Howard Da Silva, powerfully built manual laborer turned actor turned *Red Channel* listee, obliged them by invoking the Fifth Amendment in a rich bass. At the close of Da Silva's testimony, Representative Charles Potter of Michigan, annoyed with the witness' recalcitrance, voiced the Committee's dominant fantasy: "If the Soviet Union should attack the United States, will you support and would you bear arms for the United States?"

Da Silva's answer, that the prime issue of the day was peace not war, was adjudged immaterial and incompetent. The gruff performer left the Committee and, in the professional sense, fell off the edge of the earth. Da Silva, veteran of forty films, abruptly found himself in the province of the surrealists. He was unemployable not only in the future but in the past. Just before his Committee appearance Da Silva had appeared before the cameras as Captain of the U.S. Cavalry in the RKO film *Slaughter Trail.* Producer Irving Allen announced that celluloid containing images of the actor would be excised and the role re-enacted by Brian Donlevy at a cost of $100,000.

As other uncooperative witnesses passed in review, they joined Da Silva in the new limbo. There, people appeared like ghosts in the fantasy movies of the forties. They could be seen, yet not touched. They were dead—and yet they moved. Gale Sondergaard, who had won an Academy Award as a supporting actress in *Anthony Adverse*, seemed to have offended the Committee principally because she was married to Herbert Biberman of the Hollywood Ten. She invoked the Fifth, refused to name names and lost her own identity. When the perennial mother-type Anne Revere used the Fifth, Walter Winchell delightedly announced that she would go the way of Da Silva. George Stevens, producer and director of the recently completed A *Place in the Sun*, denied the report. Anne Revere, he said, in what passed for defiance in those days, will not, repeat not, be cut out of this picture. But she was never to regain her status or income.

The King Brothers, surreptitious buyers of Dalton Trumbo's black-market scenarios, gave voluble approval of the Committee. Maury, the loudest of the Kings, told the world, "We here will give a job to these fellows if they'll go ahead and tell who these rats are. It'll help to clean out these rats. We don't want the fellow who *can* talk to be scared to talk."

Edward Dmytryk needed no such invitation. In jail he had told Ring Lardner, "You writers can write under other names. What the hell can a director do?" To Biberman he had confessed, "Herbert, I'm the same guy I always was. But I'm going to work. In the studios." To Albert Maltz he had insisted that he was still opposed to the Committee, that he was heart and soul against the Motion Picture Alliance, that he was still Eddie—but that it was necessary for progressives to go underground for a while.

After four and a half months in jail (about a third of the time he had spent in the Party), after swearing to Maltz, "I'm never going to go to prison again," Dmytryk let it be known that he wanted to meet "the toughest anti-Communist in town." The most reputable of the toughs was Roy Brewer, leader of the International Alliance of Theatrical Stage Employees (IATSE), chairman of the AFL film council, chairman of the executive committee of the Motion Picture Alliance for the Preservation of American Ideals. Adamantine as he was, Brewer, like his compatriot John Wayne, sometimes seemed a little too liberal for the resurgent right. After Parks' testimony, Wayne had rallied round: "I think it's fine," he said, "that he had the courage to answer the questions and declare himself. . . . The American public is pretty quick to forgive a person who is willing to admit a mistake." Following a public chewing out by Hedda Hopper, the Duke allowed as how his early benignity was a "snap comment." The long interval of silence between Partyhood and confessional was "not to Larry Parks' credit . . . we do not want to associate with traitors." Hearst labor columnist Victor Riesel, binary enemy of racketeers and radicals, groups he tended to confuse, agreed. "The hell with Parks," he snapped. "And *all* the late confessors." Yet Brewer held to his stubborn belief that even the worst criminals could be rehabilitated—at what he called "a tough and drastic" price. Dmytryk's price was the total repudiation of his past, the naming of names, the posture of anti-Communist militance and the revision of history, tailored to suit his rehabilitators. Now, before the HUAC, Dmytryk numbed the legislators as he cleansed himself. At one point the director sadly remembered Lawson's insistence upon democratic solidarity: "I can truthfully say I had much more opportunity to observe the workings of the Communist Party while I was a member of the Hollywood Ten than I did while I was a member of the Communist Party." Then, in an unguarded moment, he gave away the show:

"What would you call the final test of credibility of a witness purporting to be a former Communist?" demanded counsel. "Would you say the test of credibility would have to be primarily the willingness to name names, places, and circumstances surrounding such membership?"

Dmytryk: "I personally believe so. That is why I am doing it."

Like earlier witnesses, Dmytryk was certain that the Party never realized a tenth of its ambitions. Members controlled the Screen Writers' Guild for a brief, delirious moment, and ignited the studio strike of 1945, he claimed. But no Red ever got on the board of the Screen Directors' Guild (he was the one who tried). The Party's sole consolation became that of the studios: loot and celebrities. "I think over a period of years," said the witness, "particularly when the love feast was on between Russia and America during the war, and for some years afterward, a great deal of money was taken from Hollywood." Among the big names who took it: John Howard Lawson, described by Dmytryk as the "high lama of the party," Frank Tuttle, who had directed seven Bing Crosby hits, and Jules (*The Naked City*) Dassin.

After naming twenty others as Communists, Dmytryk was considered fit to direct actors in the King Brothers' new film, *Mutiny*, a nice safe picture about the War of 1812. Albert Maltz, both saddened and enraged by the comrade with whom he had once been spiritually and physically chained, attacked Dmytryk as a man of "flexible conscience . . . quickly and cheaply refurnished" who "lied and befouled others with his lies." Maltz recalled the empathetic conversations with his former friend and evoked a Christmas scene when Dmytryk, post release, watched Herbert Biberman play with his infant son. "Who but the blind, the stupid and the prejudiced will believe anything Dmytryk says?" Maltz consoled himself.

This was merely the gate of betrayal. The nation's new climate created a series of breakups that seemed infinite and excruciating. Like Maltz, the wounded seldom looked beyond their own hurt. This visceral response was understandable, perhaps inevitable. But it was also another instance of the left ripping and flogging itself, repeating the lesson it could never learn. Its troops had once stood firm on some forgotten barricade; it was assumed that the fervor would last unto death. But in the fifties loyalty became a debased word; life was too long, and severance pay too high for comradeship. Only the very strong, or the very principled—or those who had no other choice—would find the blacklist an annealing experience. The others, the disenchanted and the opportunists, chose three courses: hysterical anti-Communism, clownishness or a self-abnegation unequaled outside the Moscow Trials.

Scenarists Richard Collins and Paul Jarrico, for example, were comrades and collaborators on Hollywood musicals. Collins—who, like Hayden, had revealed his past to the FBI—grew fearful of his future. He lived, he said, in "a nightmare that in the event of a war I would be considered a friend of the Soviet Union when actually I was an enemy." Two weeks before Collins testified, Jarrico had asked him not to be a stool pigeon. Collins told his ex-partner that he would not name names on one condition—that Jarrico assure him that he would not help the Soviet Union in case of a war with the United States. Jarrico hedged; Collins sang. Among the names in his lyrics were Jarrico and a scenarist named Martin Berkeley. The writer promptly telegraphed the HUAC that he was not now, nor had he ever been, a member of the Party. But when Berkeley was called to the stand, he labeled himself "a damn fool" and manically babbled the names of a hundred subversives. Another witness wrote an apologia to Herbert Biberman which was almost unbearable in its candor: "I have come to recognize that I was not formed in the heroic mold. Unfortunately, my father and mother bred a moral weakling. I'm truly sorry, but because I am what I am I'm going to work and get paid for my cowardice." And there was more debasement to come. The genial, low-pressure director Carl Foreman, named by Collins, answered the Committee with considerable forbearance, patiently refusing to act the part of character assassin. Even when the name of the dreaded Dmytryk was introduced, Foreman declined to jump through the hoop. "I don't think it is very important as to what I think," he testified. "I think it is important to Mr. Dmytryk what he thinks."

But Foreman clambered under the awning of the Fifth Amendment, and when he returned to work he found his partner and old army buddy, Stanley Kramer, a most unpleasant adversary. Soon the partners on *Champion, Home of the Brave, The Men, Cyrano de Bergerac, Young Man with a Horn* were not speaking at all, and there were rumors of legal action to be taken by Kramer. Foreman and his lawyer, Sidney Cohn, appeared one day in Kramer's office. Kramer, ultra-correct in hair, suit and manner, refused to meet Foreman's eyes or to talk to him. "Tell your client," he informed Cohn, "I want to buy him out. Otherwise I will destroy this company." Cohn, in a dry-iced voice, scolded Kramer: "Little boy, you better get someone I can talk to. Someone grown-up. Because we're not about to sit by and watch you wreck us."

Foreman found an unexpected ally in Gary Cooper, star of the new Kramer-Foreman production *High Noon*, member of the Motion Picture Alliance, a loyal and honorable man—and a surprising one to those who thought honor was the exclusive property of the old left. Cooper affectionately addressed Foreman as "Uncle Carl" and openly offered to buy stock in the scenarist's new film-making company. But even Coop was not immune to pressure. His pals in the Alliance lectured him on the subject of subversion and diplomacy until, on a fishing trip in Montana, Gary Cooper found it necessary to give the newspapers a message in highly decipherable code. "I have received notice of considerable reaction" (*sic*), he said, "and now I feel it best for all concerned that I should not purchase this stock." Frank Tuttle's turn came. The director shamefacedly gave a *précis* of his Party career from the mid-1930s to 1947. "There is a traditional dislike among Americans for informers," he said to his shoes, "but there is need for informers now." He had remained a Red for so long, he said, because the Party is kind of "mental incest. You see and talk only to those who are close to the Communist way of thinking. . . . It took me a long time to think for myself."

"You have rendered a great service to us of this Committee," Representative Walter told him. But Tuttle had not rendered himself any service. His producers refused to distribute any more of his pictures; money for two new films was withdrawn and he had been asked for permission to remove his name from a new movie. Walter was aghast at this fresh example of Hollywood duplicity. "If employers withhold employment they will discourage people who wish to make their contribution to this Committee," he griped to Hollywood management.

The HUAC pushed on, acquiring new power and showing, daily, less inclination to compassion. Attorney Martin Popper told the Committee that his client J. Edward Bromberg was a victim of rheumatic heart disease and introduced a doctor's statement certifying that the actor had recently experienced "a frank attack of congestive failure." Walter was not mollified. "I know," he told Popper, "having practiced law for a great many years, that you can get doctors to make statements as to almost anything."

In very quick order, Bromberg was brought before the Committee to list his credits (*Hollywood Cavalcade, Mark of Zorro,* some of the Charlie Chan pictures), to invoke the privileges of the First and Fifth Amendments, and to admit that he had told the press that "the record of this Committee has been such that its effect has been to deprive people of their livelihood . . . it is in the nature of a witch-hunt calculated to scare a lot of people beyond those who are involved in the hearings."

Bromberg was in very obvious distress during the questioning, so obvious that Representative Wood asked if he desired to have "a little recess." "Mr. Chairman," admonished Martin Popper, "that should have been thought of before the subpoena was issued." "On that point," returned Wood, "the witness's appearance here was deferred until we found that he was engaged in his usual avocation" (*sic*). Bromberg refused a recess, finished his clenched testimony and walked cautiously from the room. He had less than seven months to live.

Abraham Lincoln Polonsky, the reedy intellectual screen-writer turned director, soon to be blacklisted out of the business, made a business trip to Pacific Palisades during the new hysteria. Like a man long accustomed to battle, he refused to stop planning merely because of the Committee. What the hell, either the bullets had your number on them or they didn't. For years he had wanted to adapt *Mario the Magician*; for the first time Thomas Mann seemed eager to discuss it.

But as it turned out, what Mann really wanted to talk about was politics. The old *émigré* asked Polonsky what his plans were: the director said that he planned to "get a little money together, go over to Europe and make the picture." "I would advise you to stay there," said Mann. "Fascism is coming to America." Polonsky, the radical, replied that he didn't believe that fascism was imminent at all. "Perhaps *reaction* is coming to America," he admitted, "but that's not quite the same thing." "Well," the old man insisted, "I have had the European experience. I am leaving. As much as I love this place, I have to leave it. This is not the country that I became a citizen of."

Mann's drama was not lessened by the farcical characters who enacted it. Marc Lawrence, a narrow, pockmarked performer who specialized in the role of low henchman, continued his career in civilian life by giving the Committee a ten-page gossip column. Lionel Stander, he said, dangled an irresistible invitation to join the Party: "Get to know this stuff and you will make out more with the dames." Lawrence dropped a handful of names in the collection plate, called his former associations "a great and unholy mistake" and labeled himself "a curious kind of 'shmoe'"—a theme that would be repeated, with variations, by scores of repentant witnesses. If there was any doubt now about the hand-in-glove affair of studios and Committeemen, Representative Jackson blew his cover by congratulating Lawrence for his splendid memory. "You should have less difficulty in learning scripts than some of the people who appeared here," he said, beaming.

Among those who would have dramatic difficulty in learning scripts was the toucan-like Jeff Corey, who, after being named by Marc Lawrence, admitted that he knew the actor. "He played an informer with great verisimilitude, in a picture called *Asphalt Jungle.*" John Garfield, a bigger star with a longer history, fared almost as badly. He had known all the old leftists from the days of the Group Theatre, a fact that had not escaped *Red Channels.* To provide proof of his cleanliness, Garfield, like Louis B. Mayer before him, offered his bad notices. The *Daily Worker,* for example, had called him "a little punch-drunk" for playing in a religious play like *Skipper Next to God.* Representative Harold Velde, ex-FBI, was less interested in the text than in the source. How was it, he wanted to know, that the witness looked at a Communist newspaper? "They review all plays," answered Garfield. "There is nothing sinister in my question," Velde persisted. "Do you remember where you obtained the copy?"

When Garfield insisted that no one had ever recruited him for the Party, Jackson offered a crumb of autobiography: "It might interest you to know that attempts were made to recruit *me* . . . and I was making $32.50 a week." "They certainly stayed away from me, sir," Garfield protested. "Perhaps I looked like better material," mused the Congressman.

In the end, Garfield dutifully praised the Committee and knocked the Reds, who, he felt, should be outlawed. "Otherwise," he asked plaintively, "how do you protect people like me?"

But the Committee had no intention of protecting anyone like Garfield. Even after the star had been praised for his cooperation, Representative Potter shook his head. "It seems incredible that you could be identified with movements which, looking back now, the Communists have used, without suspecting it."

Will Geer, character actor, whose wife was the granddaughter of the farm-labor organizer "Mother" Bloor, was through in Hollywood after his appearance and invocation of the Fifth Amendment. More offensive to the Committee than Constitutional privilege was Geer's placid humor. He was another of the witnesses to hear the hypothetical question: "In the event of an armed conflict in which the U.S. would find itself opposed to Soviet Russia, would you be willing to fight on the side of the United States?" Geer, then forty-nine, replied that he would grow vegetables, as he had done during World War II, and play hospitals. "It would be a wonderful idea," he added, "if they put every man my age in the front lines and in Washington, fellows on the other side." The Committeemen, who thought gags improper unless they were recited by elected officials, told him he was leaving under a cloud. Geer exited, commiserating with Wood and his staff: "We all of us have to appear in a turkey once in a while."

Writers found very little difference between 1947 and 1951 except that the HUAC had researchers and a less livid approach. Like downed kites, each writer twitched flatly under the Committee's wind of outrage. The lack of revolutionary fervor, the utter absence of agitprop in pictures, depressed the Congressmen. Waldo Salt had concocted *Wild Man of Borneo* and *Rachel and the Stranger*. Paul Jarrico, it is true, had written the dreaded *Song of Russia*. But he had enjoyed greater success with the Technicolor musical *As Thousands Cheer*. Daniel and Lilith James had written the stage musical *Bloomer Girl*. Sam Moore had written the radio hit *The Great Gildersleeve*. Fredrick Rinaldo specialized in Abbott-and-Costello pictures. Yes, Michael Wilson *had* written *A Place in the Sun*, adapted from a novel by the Communist Theodore Dreiser. But during the years of his subversion he had been responsible for Hopalong Cassidy pictures.

Any probe of past associations provoked a common response: I decline to answer on the grounds of self-incrimination. Many witnesses, however, voluntarily told the Committee that they were not *now* Communists. Why stop there? asked the studio executives and the agents. Why refuse to divulge the past? One need not follow Parks through the mud or Marc Lawrence into the canary cage. One could simply admit his prior Communism, name the terminal date and go home. Or could one?

An important witness attempted that course, and his progress was microscopically examined by those who expected to succeed him on the tumbrel. Sidney Buchman was no ordinary writer; he was the highest-ranking executive the Committee would find in its seine. A cultivated, prolific scenarist with some mysterious ability to hold Columbia Pictures' Neanderthal chief, Harry Cohn, in check, Buchman had been responsible for some twenty films, including the classic comedies *Theodora Goes Wild*, *Holiday* and *Here Comes Mr. Jordan*. The executive readily admitted his old membership in the Communist Party from 1938 to about 1945. He spoke freely about the dislocations of the First World War, his own rather unfocused idealism and his inability to accept and follow the tergiversations of the Party line. Fine, said the questioners, settling down to the entree. Now, in whose houses did the members meet? Who were the members of his group? Buchman took a long breath, wondered aloud if his answer would conclude a career which had taken twenty years to build, and then regretfully declined for three reasons. "First," he explained, "because these persons never planned, committed or suggested an illegal act. Secondly, the names of such a person or persons already have been made public by you and I therefore do not see how it will aid you if I repeat it. Thirdly, it is repugnant to an American to inform upon his fellow citizens."

At the close of Buchman's testimony, his attorney noted that the witness had been on so long only two members of the

Committee remained in the room. This did not constitute a legal quorum—a scruple that proved highly expedient.

Buchman was again subpoenaed; this time he delayed because of ill health. The Committee refused to believe him—you can get a doctor to testify to anything, after all. They fined him and began contempt proceedings.

These were merely *pro forma* punishments; the Committee was satisfied to learn that Buchman was washed up at Columbia. Harry Cohn, appalled, he said, at the Committee's revelations, had not even bothered to say goodbye to his most trusted assistant. Despite the pretense of deep shock, however, Cohn had been fully aware of Buchman's radical tendencies—all studio heads had full dossiers on their employees. Not too many years before, William Wyler had asked Paramount to hire Lillian Hellman to adapt *Sister Carrie*. Paramount executive Barney Balaban had reluctantly showed Wyler some choice items from the Hellman portfolio, some true, some false, all placed there by the supposedly secretive FBI. Columbia enjoyed much the same privileges. Cohn had once told Hellman, "I don't care who you meet with. But go out of Hollywood for lunch. I mean, who's going to follow you? What I don't see, I don't know." But in 1951 King Cohn could no longer afford to wear blinders. He, too, hated to lose his boy. It was just that Buchman's usefulness to the studio was at an end.

A third type of witness appeared during these hearings. Having achieved recognition for non-political performances, these artists did not wish to appear shmoes. Nor did they wish to lockstep with the professional Red-baiters. They wanted, simply, to be let alone to resume their careers. Budd Schulberg, whose book *The Disenchanted* was shortly to be published, exhumed his old disappointments for public delectation. The old Lardner critic was a lot wiser now. He recalled his break with the Party. *What Makes Sammy Run?* had at first obtained a rave from the *Worker*. The critic hailed it as "*the* Hollywood novel." But the chieftains saw degeneracy in the book. The critic recanted in classic Muscovite style: "It is precisely the superficial subjective attitude shown in my review which reflects the dangers of an 'anti-Hollywood' approach. The first error I made," he admitted, "was in calling the book *the* Hollywood novel."

Schulberg did not tell the Committee that before his appearance he had telephoned his friends with a reassurance: on the stand Schulberg would not name any of *their* friends "unless absolutely necessary." His word was gold. The names Schulberg introduced were worn smooth from previous mentions.

The next witness was José Ferrer, nominated for an Academy Award for *Cyrano de Bergerac*. Ferrer came on like a penitent fox that had just renounced its appetite for fowl. The rolling bass had a querulous lilt as he insisted that the Ferrer name was misused on Communist fronts, that he was only a poor Puerto Rican who had made good. Yes, he had known a notorious friend of Russia; he had played Iago to Paul Robeson's Othello. But, mercifully, Ferrer had not seen the actor for six years. Ferrer had already been sentenced by hanging judge Ward Bond of the Motion Picture Alliance; on its front page *Variety* reported that in Bond's view, "if Ferrer was willing to swear that he was not a Communist, then he was perjuring himself." Ferrer, not a Communist, never a Communist, judiciously retracted any thought crimes he might have harbored concerning the abolition of the HUAC. Inquired Representative Kearney: "When did you change your mind on that score?" Replied Ferrer, "Well, today, among other things."

With all except the angriest of the Fifth Amendment takers, the Committee tried to stay with the witness to the point of fatigue. Repeatedly the Representatives issued their disclaimer: they wished to blacklist no one, for blacklisting was un-American. Besides, there *was* no blacklist. However, when an alert investigator found that *These Many Years* was sold to Warner Bros. for $20,000 under a pseudonym, Representative Kearney asked agent George Willner: "Is Lester Cole now selling under the name of J. Redmond Prior?" He was indeed, as Kearney already knew and Willner refused to say.

In the end, though this Committee was better prepared than its predecessor, it too was born of those Dickensian children about whom Scrooge was warned: Want and Ignorance. Faint echoes of John Rankin could still be heard through the dreadful homilies of Georgian John Wood: "There can be no odium attached to any person who may have made a mistake and have seen that they have made a mistake and seek to rectify it, because if there was we would give lie to the advent of Jesus Christ in this world, who came here for the purpose of making possible forgiveness upon repentance."

Again the Committee had sent innumerable buckets down the well only to raise them clanking and empty. There was no subversion in films; there never had been. The rabid, babbling Martin Berkeley admitted that most of the comrades' time was spent trying to refurbish the screen's mean and farcical treatment of the Jew and Negro. None of the Communists had written a scene more offensive than that of a Russian girl teaching an American how to drive a tractor—and even that had been excised by 20th Century-Fox. As to the always compelling matter of money, contributions to the Party had indeed been made. George Beck remembered the agent Willner bidding him up at a fund-raising affair: "Beck offers fifty. Is anybody going to match it . . . now Beck offers a hundred . . . one hundred and fifty." But the cooperative ex-Red Leopold Atlas reported that dues were always in arrears. Dmytryk's business manager allotted him $25 a week allowance and forbade sizable contributions to the Party. To the HUAC the most impressive Communist front was the Hollywood Democratic Committee. But its funds were squandered on Democrats running for election. By Murray Kempton's estimate, the Party would have been fortunate to net as much as half a million dollars out of its Hollywood fronts in fifteen years.

This was not what the HUAC wished to give out. Instead, it

told the country that the propaganda machine had been un-covered and destroyed, that the financial conveyor belt from Hollywood to Stalingrad had been halted. Names were thrown to the papers and reprinted in the Committee's annual report, and the public was asked to subscribe to Beaumarchais' jubilant theme: "Vilify, vilify! Some of it will always stick." Subversion was now a glamour stock; few legislators up for re-election could afford to pass up the investment. No one bothered to examine the Congressmen's most significant disclosure: the Party's lethal enemy was not the Committee but the Party. All but the saddest hacks and the most imbecilic reformers had long since found the dogma indigestible. With unconscious irony the Committee had noted that Richard Collins, the loudest in-former, had been among the last to jettison his membership.

The wounded, now unemployable, sought shelter from the blacklist in the wrong places. Their labor unions were all march-ing to an indifferent drummer. The Artists Managers Guild, the Hollywood AFL Film Council, Independent Office Workers, Screen Actors' Guild, Screen Directors' Guild, Screen Pro-ducers' Guild, Screen Writers' Guild, Society of Motion Picture Art Directors—all wrote a collective letter to Chairman Wood: "We beg to call to your attention the following: This country is engaged in a war with communism. Eighty-seven thousand American casualties [in Korea] leave little room for witnesses to stand on the first and fifth amendments; and for those who do we have no sympathy."

At MGM a studio investigator under the command of Dore Schary tapped the memories of players. He cornered comedian Ed Wynn's delinquent son Keenan, confronted him with items recalling his and Henry Morgan's satire of J. Parnell Thomas and membership in such shocking pink groups as the Holly-wood Anti-Nazi League. The studio has been good to you, the investigator assured Wynn. It wanted to continue to be pater-nal, but, well, there was the business of names. Who had attended meetings with him?

Wynn filled his face with blanks. He would like to help, he commented, but he had never been very good at names. Besides, he was just a studio brat in those days, a green comic taking on the world. What did *he* know? The investigator was not buying excuses that day. "Wait a minute." The actor brightened. "There *was* one guy . . . I remember now. Dore Schary went with me."

"O.K." The clearance specialist shrugged. "If you can't think of any names, you can't think of any names."

EIGHT

America has its army ants, called legionaries, which differ from true army ants in that they do not move in a mass but run rapidly in single file. They also stay in their bivouacs much longer. They live by hunting other insects, storing their meat and carrying it with them when they move—usually at night under a cover of leaves. Most legionaries are almost blind.

PETER FARB,
The Insects

A PLAGUE IS GENERAL; its carriers specific. New epidemics and faded memories have obscured the importance of Lawrence Johnson to the blacklist. A white-haired, avuncular grocer in Syracuse, New York, he became at once the most unlikely and effective spreader of moral disease. Professionally, Johnson was merely the owner of five supermarkets in obscure, upstate neighborhoods. Privately, he was a dangerous patriot who believed implicitly in the past.

In this, he was not very different from his entrepreneurial betters: Henry Ford, who had his reconstructions at Dearborn;

144

John D. Rockefeller, whose Williamsburg restoration evoked a fossil time before fossil fuels; Walt Disney, with his famous plastic replicas of the vanished natural life. Johnson's evocation was an elaborate ante-bellum store. Some items, he boasted, went clear back to 1815. He collected ancient campaign buttons, antique toys and piggy banks with an enthusiasm he was shortly to transfer to the collecting of subversives. Where Johnson walked, contradictions flowered. His emporia, for example, constantly featured sales; yet none of the stores was listed in the Syracuse phone book. During the war their owner had been called too often by housewives wheedling for sugar. He had insulated himself then, and saw no reason for becoming public property simply because rationing was off. Yet he was frequently possessed by the itch to communicate. When the National Association of Food Chains made an educational film about the history of food products, Johnson volunteered for the part of an old storekeeper. He played the white-haired, benign old gaffer with authentic warmth. It was his closest association with show business, and it might have remained his sole one.

But early in 1951 Johnson's daughter Eleanor, encouraged by the HUAC hearings, began an exclusive police action against performers whose convictions she found odious. Her husband, John Buchanan, had recently been recalled from the Marine Reserves and shipped to Korea. By late spring Mrs. Buchanan had arranged a meeting between her father and members of American Legion Post No. 41 in Syracuse. Suffused with the thrill of utility, she wrote to the Legionnaires: "Dad and I were pleased that you agree manufacturers can be persuaded to remove Communist sympathizers from their advertising programs on radio and television. As you gentlemen pointed out . . . the task is too great for me alone."

The Molly Pitcher of the blacklist, Mrs. Buchanan would not drop back from battle. She mailed letters to Syracuse housewives enclosing material from *Red Channels, Counterattack* and the indispensable *Daily Worker*. By midsummer she had worked out a picturesque speech and patter. The local Kiwanis ate it up.

"My husband," she told them, "a veteran of World War II, never received a penny for being a member of the Inactive Reserves. When he was recalled to service it meant leaving the small town on the Hudson where we'd been so happy, the company in which he'd been found to be a valuable asset, my small but interesting teaching position at Vassar College. . . . Faced with the prospect of being apart from one another, I asked him one day why on earth he'd ever signed up in the Reserves. He answered quietly and simply in one word, 'Patriotism.'"

The word gained new shadings when the Reservist reached Korea. "I have not been sick," he wrote his wife, "which is a blessing, in this land of loose bowels and bodies. The flies go from the dead Gook twenty feet away, to the fish heads he left behind, to my C rations, so I'm glad my stomach is strong."

After excerpting Jack's letter, Eleanor Buchanan brought her speech to a rousing close: "Well, my stomach isn't that strong. It sickens me to know of those banquets engineered by Red sympathizers on radio and television to raise funds for their henchmen, and those do-nothing patriotic citizens who discuss the wrongs of the world over a dinner table while my quiet, unassuming Jack ate his lunch, surrounded by dead Chinese." Encouraged by her smash performance before the clubmen, Mrs. Buchanan went on to the Rotarians, the American Legion and the Syracuse Advertising Club. Her furious complaints, crammed with documents, were sent to NBC, CBS, Kraft Foods, Philco, Borden. She also issued a white list of actors whose patriotism was unsullied and who, by the revised fairness doctrine, should be given preference in casting offices. Like phagocytes, she reasoned, they could be employed to drive the red cells out of the body patriotic.

Here Eleanor Buchanan suggested the wilder shores of hate,

shire of the embittered playwright and pamphleteer Myron C. Fagan. Even before *Red Channels*, Fagan had published *Red Treason in Hollywood*, followed by the incarnadine *Documentation of the Red Stars in Hollywood*. This pulpy document, held together with howls, imprecations and two staples, provided the blacklister with hundreds of names, from Larry Adler to Sam Zimbalist. It had but one hero, Fagan, whose Song of Myself ended: "Two Thousand Years ago a Man named Jesus died on a Cross for Peace on Earth and the Salvation of Man's immortal soul. . . . It is possible that this year *I* shall die*— on a different kind of a cross—for the safety of America and, God grant, the Peace of the Universe. If so it will be a good Death in the sight of God!" While he was alive, Fagan wished to boost as well as knock. A list of touchables was proffered. "Ever mindful of the actor's sensitivity as regards 'billing,'" he wrote, "we list the Loyal Names alphabetically rather than in order of appearance." There followed a unique roster. Like Eleanor Buchanan's, it favored the familiar intolerants: John Wayne, Ward Bond, Adolphe Menjou, Robert Taylor. Both lists carried separate places for ventriloquist Edgar Bergen and for his wooden dummy, Charlie McCarthy.

In a year when Fagan's *nudnik* soliloquies could be purchased by studios and networks, the accession of the Syracuse grocer must be considered as natural as death. Over sixty, settling into his sunset years, Lawrence Johnson accepted a commission as field marshal in his daughter's war. With Eleanor's help he reinforced the liaison with local Post No. 41 of the American Legion. The veterans soon circulated their own version of *Counterattack: Spotlight*, which issued its own blacklists. For additional support, Johnson organized the Veterans Action Committee of Syracuse Supermarkets, a group whose relation to Johnson was that of Charlie McCarthy to Edgar Bergen. When Johnson stubbed his toe on a subversive, the Legionnaires

---

* Fagan was still thriving in 1973.

howled. Networks and sponsors received angry warnings from the Action Committee, signed by Francis W. Neuser, Commander. Neuser never employed his full title: Fruit and Vegetable Buyer for Johnson's supermarkets. Members of Post No. 41 would no longer have to wait until Memorial Day to take their courage out of mothballs. In an atmosphere reminiscent of a bunker somewhere north of Seoul, the troops received incessant counsel from Johnson's crony John K. Dungey, chairman of the Post's Anti-Subversive Committee. Under his supervision, Post No. 41 issued its own version of a body count, entitled "Monthly Box Score." An early one enumerated their victories and high ground still untaken:

The Weavers .... Finito

Jack Gilford .... He and Fledermaus struck out.

Philip Loeb (Jake on Goldbergs) .... Done for good we hope.

Artie Shaw (A *Red Channels* Listee) ...... Radio Station WOLF still using his records—how come?

Jose Ferrer ...... Maybe we should not see his new motion picture, and how come the big *Life* Mag. spread?

Judy Holiday [*sic*] ....Ditto above regarding her new picture.

George S. Kaufman .... What about him and Sam Levenson on LUCKY STRIKES' TV show "THIS IS SHOW BUSINESS"?

Gilford was a perturbing triumph to Johnson. Early in 1951 Arthur Godfrey had carelessly permitted the comedian to appear on his TV show. Godfrey's sponsor, Liggett and Myers, was so discomfited by Johnson's armies that the network's chief executive, J. L. Van Volkenburg, fired off a series of excuses to Syracuse. "Mr. Gilford's appearance on the show took place during the absence on vacation of the regular director-producer," wrote the president in a tone that evoked Mr. Dithers apologizing for the misbehavior of Dagwood Bumstead. "He was engaged

GANG BUSTERS : *Members of the House Un-American Activities Committee at a New Jersey rendezvous. From left to right: Rep. Richard Vail (R., Ill.); Chairman J. Parnell Thomas (R., N.J.); Rep. John McDowell (R., Pa.); Robert Stripling, Chief Counsel; Rep. Richard Nixon (R., Calif.).*

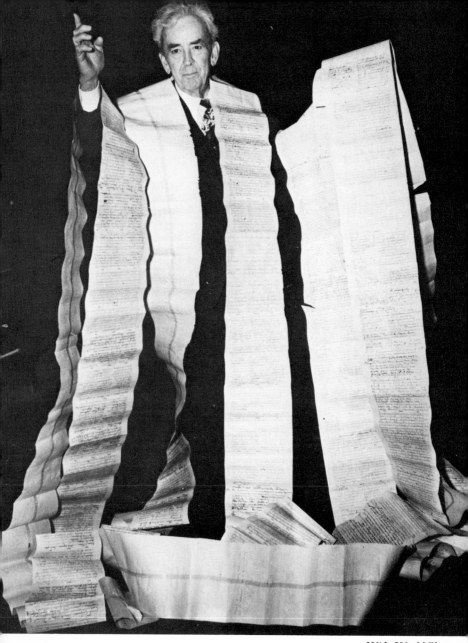

AND NOW, A WORD FROM OUR SPONSORS: *Rep. John Rankin (D., Miss.) proudly displays a scroll of signatures from citizens who backed the 1947 HUAC investigation of American motion pictures.*

THE GANG THAT WAS BUSTED: *Some of the Hollywood nineteen pose after leaving the committee room. From left to right: (front row) Lewis Milestone, Dalton Trumbo, John Howard Lawson, and legal counsel Bartley Crum; (center row) Gordon Kahn, Irving Pichel, Edward Dymytryk, and Robert Rossen; (top row) Waldo Salt, Richard Collins, Howard Koch, Albert Maltz, Herbert Biberman, Lester Cole, Ring Lardner, Jr., and another attorney, Martin Popper.*

CONTEMPT OF CONGRESS: *For their refusal to cooperate with the HUAC, ten Hollywood film-makers were sent to the federal penitentiary. Here, Albert Maltz and Ring Lardner, Jr., are cuffed together on their way to jail. Lester Cole and Herbert Biberman are inexplicably free-handed.*

ABOVE: *Director Elia Kazan*
BELOW: *Director Edward Dymytryk, one of the original Hollywood Ten*

FOUR WHO TALKED. AND TALKED: *Three foundering careers were saved by cooperative testimony before the HUAC. Among the old leftists who gave evidence against their former comrades:*

Harris & Ewing

ABOVE: *Clifford Odets, former ornament of the left theater*   BELOW: *Actor Larry Parks, who confessed his ex-Communism under pressure, made only one more film.*

Wide World Photos

FOUR WHO DIED: *The plague terminated lives as well as careers. Among those whose deaths can be clearly attributed to the blacklist were:*

John Zimmerman

ABOVE: *John Garfield, whose last hours were spent vainly trying to "clear" himself* LEFT: *Mady Christians, the "Mama" of* I Remember Mama.

Wide World Photos

Life (Sharland)

ABOVE: *Philip Loeb, hounded even when unemployed* RIGHT: *Canada Lee, seen addressing a rally to save the FEPC, the sort of activity that placed him on FBI files.*

International News Photos

THE BLACKLISTERS: *Two of the top investigators and compilers of the proscribed entertainers: Vincent Hartnett (*ABOVE*), described by Michael Harrington as "the perfect spoiled-priest type."* BELOW: *Theodore Kirkpatrick, editor of the blacklisting periodical* Counterattack, *could have been J. Edgar Hoover's model for the handsome, hard-hitting ex–FBI man turned show business Red-fighter.*

Roy Stevens

through a reputable talent agency for a *one-time* appearance on the basis of his previous performances on television . . . as well as for his performances in the comic role in *Die Fledermaus* for the Metropolitan. He was on tour with this opera throughout the nation from April through July of this year."

Wielding a copy of this white flag, Johnson entered the offices of the Metropolitan Opera Company, George F. Babbitt swinging his niblick in the Temple of Culture. The grocer had been preceded by mail from all the best people, Legionnaires who formally demanded the separation of Jack Gilford from a living. Here, the confident Johnson suffered the common delusion of the parvenu right—that old money suffers from the same fears as new money. In fact, though the opera patrons were to the right of Louis XIV, they were used to mahogany heritage, not plywood patriotism. They considered themselves morally as well as culturally oversubscribed. For them, subversion was a matter for policemen and people in trade. They were, in short, sponsors of Richard Wagner, not Arthur Godfrey. The Met management, in its turn, was far more concerned with *Aïda* than *The Boys from Syracuse*. Johnson was courteously steered out to Broadway, muttering about the Red menace and hinting darkly that the Bat could yet be brought down in the provinces.

When *Fledermaus* played Syracuse, Post No. 41 was out with signs and chants. The crowds were ugly, the attendance disappointing. A representative from the Met management was hastily summoned to receive (and reject) the new definitions of degenerate art. *Fledermaus* had perhaps struck out, but blacklist headquarters considered the triumph pyrrhic. Gilford, after all, could still earn money; to Johnson this indicated a breach of the democratic process. He would soon see to repairs.

As for the Weavers, the Un-American Activities Committee of Post No. 41 had been organized because of them. Dungey had heard a recording of "Good Night, Irene," realized that this was the selfsame quartet slandered in *Counterattack* and featuring Pete Seeger, a *Red Channels* listee. The Weavers had been scheduled to appear on Dave Garroway's low-key Sunday-night show from Chicago. Three days before the telecast the network let it be known that complaints had been received from "the usual groups." The Weavers were canceled. Several weeks later *Counterattack* congratulated the Ohio State Fair upon banning Seeger and his friends, though their names were still included in the fair's program. "There wasn't time to conduct an investigation," the fair board announced. "And rather than support any act about which there was the slightest doubt it was decided that it would be better to eliminate it."

Blacklisted performers began to get compensatory kicks out of the Restoration-comedy appellations of their villains: Fagan, Leech, Dungey, Hartnett. In much the same fashion, the Hollywood Ten had enjoyed the knowledge that J. Parnell Thomas was baptized John Feeney. But the forced mirth smacked of the gallows. The real laughter sounded from the other side of the blacklist. Francis McNamara, the new editor of *Counterattack*, liked to sit in on the grilling of showfolk seeking clearance. "You should see the big act some of them put on in this very office," he chuckled. "It's a panic to hear them!"

By the middle of 1951 neither side was laughing. Even in churches the Devil had been replaced by the Bomb. Einstein had gone on television to warn that "general annihilation beckons." Fear had become a way of life. History had wholly reversed its tides. Members of the left swirled around, giddy and directionless. Every day seemed to edge them closer to the falls. The very headlines seemed to fight them: the Rosenbergs were sentenced to death; Korea was going badly; Joe McCarthy's influence was reaching its apogee. The censorious tone of Eleanor Buchanan reached the Senate floor, when the Senator instructed wounded veterans to tell Secretary of State Dean Acheson that "you and your crimson crowd betrayed us . . . if you want to at long last perform one service for the American people you should not only resign from the State Department but you should remove yourself from this country and go to the nation for which you have been struggling and fighting so long."

Way back in the entertainment section more immediate misfortunes were recorded. For refusing to divulge certain contributions to the Civil Rights Congress, Dashiell Hammett was given a prison sentence. He was also banished from the memory of the radio audience. His side-of-the-mouthpieces *Sam Spade** and *The Thin Man* were barred from broadcasts, as if they, too, had been trustees of the CRC bail-bond fund.

As resentment became policy, every liberal gesture had an elongated shadow. A librarian in Bartlesville, Oklahoma, was dismissed because she subscribed to the *Nation,* the *New Republic* and the *Negro Digest.* Dorothy Bailey, after fourteen years with the U.S. Employment Service, was discharged because someone called her a Communist. She denied the charge, but could not find the someone. These cases, which had once seemed as remote as the Yalu, abruptly entered the insular domain of show business when the American Civil Liberties Union decided to cite them in its radio program, *Friday Is a Big Day.* The occasion was the commemoration of the 105th Anniversary of the Bill of Rights. The show was careful to present a steep anti-Red bias ("In almost half of the world, the sound of knocking comes much too often, usually at around three o'clock in the morning . . ."). Nevertheless, more than four hundred complaints were received by the National Broadcasting Company, most of them furious at the script's "pro-Communist line." Hardly any of them came from the customary addresses.

The secular blacklisters, suddenly powerful, were at once delighted and appalled. Public response was their *sine qua non.*

---

* The principle of guilt by association was never more efficiently encapsulated than in the case of Howard Duff. Because of his interest in the Hollywood Ten, Duff found himself listed in *Red Channels* as: "Actor—Screen, Radio. Has title role in radio's 'Adventures of Sam Spade' created by Dashiell Hammett."

Yet they alone wanted to trigger the response. The mob acting independently is, after all, as profitless to the demagogue as to the judge. The people must be taught upon which lawns to trample, over which trees to sling the rope and whose bodies shall dangle there. This new hysteria began to weaken the rightists. It had been different when they were all hungry, scrounging in unfamiliar provinces. Now, the American Business Consultants found that they could not stay together through thick.

Of the troika at *Counterattack*, Kenneth Bierly, by his own description, was the leftist. "Keenan," he maintained, "was more the businessman and was certainly the most right-wing of us, and Kirkpatrick was kind of in the middle, whichever way the wind was blowing."

The chill wind from the right kept knocking Bierly down; after a series of acrimonious skirmishes, he left his colleagues to set up as Kenby Associates. His new function, he told the curious, was "partly to get people out of the trouble that *Red Channels* got them into." The publication, he belatedly perceived, "has been used in many frightening ways that I am against. I don't think I've changed my position. . . . It's just that now I feel it's being used to keep innocent people out of jobs, and it shouldn't be. I'm against that."

Moral indignation was not only tardy for Bierly, it was remunerative. Among his first clients was Columbia Pictures, which hired him "to clear up the confusion about Judy Holliday." The actress had starred in *Born Yesterday*. Both she and its author, Garson Kanin, were cited by *Red Channels*. The ponderous rumbling of the Catholic War Veterans and the American Legion troubled the earth beneath the feet of King Cohn. Bierly was a pro; the tremors soon disappeared. The threatened picket lines never formed—the CWV contented themselves with mimeographed handouts—and the columns soon found other victims. The ex-FBI, ex-ABC man confessed shyly, "You might put it that I had something to do with getting the facts, the true facts, to the right people."

But Bierly could not be everywhere. Private HUACs, dwarf McCarthys and typewritten blacklists flourished beyond the established fiefs. Despite his excellent counsel, Ed Sullivan again incurred displeasure when Lena Horne was booked to appear on his Sunday-night show. The day before Horne's appearance, Jack O'Brian, broadcasting columnist for the *Journal-American*, wrote: "It was no secret along radio and TV row today that the sponsor and the advertising agency were considerably perturbed about what was believed would be certain public resentment [over the singer's appearance] and anxious to correct the latest display of Sullivan's booking genius. That it might take on the proportions of the Paul Draper controversy . . . was deemed almost a certainty. . . . Amazing, isn't it, that so many of these pink teas seem to 'just happen' to the Columbia Broadcasting System?" The network vainly attempted to substitute another singer, Carol Bruce. It found that the American Guild of Variety Artists was serious about removing all its members from *Toast of the Town* if Lena Horne did not appear. Later, Hubbell Robinson, Jr., righteously defended his employee: "Ed Sullivan's record over the years as a vigorous fighter of Communism, subversives, and all un-American activities is too well known to require further elaboration by CBS."

Neither Sullivan nor Robinson announced that Lena Horne had been cleared not only by them but by the publishers of *Counterattack*. Her manager, Ralph Harris, later admitted in the *Amsterdam News* that Miss Horne met with Ted Kirkpatrick and "settled the matter." The Harlem paper happily reported that Miss Horne had not promised to change "her opposition to Jim Crow and oppression. No other commitments have been exacted from the star, . . . despite the fact that the ex-FBI man usually requires a signed statement, recanting past associations and promising to espouse only anti-Communist statements."

With Caligari gaining full control of the asylum, systems and instincts went into reverse. The accused was guilty until innocence had been clearly established. The accuser was the judge, the past was the present, decency was evil.

The American Civil Liberties Union dispatched novelist Merle Miller to investigate the phenomenon of blacklisting. A CBS executive, granted a cloak of anonymity, told him that the network now preferred mediocrity to excellence. "The trouble with people who've never joined anything and therefore are 'safe' for us to use," he lamented, "is that they usually aren't very good writers or actors or producers or, hell, human beings."

Bobby Sanford, a talent agent, waved a list in front of the ACLU correspondent. "There are seventeen names . . . some of the biggest in the business. I don't even bother suggesting them any more. The other day I got a call from this producer, and he says he wants somebody for the lead in one of his shows. He asks me, 'Who've you got like John Garfield?' I say, 'What do you mean, who've I got like Garfield? I've got the boy himself. Why don't you use him?' And this producer says, 'We just can't do it. I'm sorry, but we just can't, and you know why we can't.' "

In autumn of 1951 the blacklist grew darker still. In the Legionnaires' box score, the first of the targets could be transferred from missing in action to destroyed.

Mady Christians, the Mama of *I Remember Mama*, lecturer in drama at Columbia University, veteran of more than sixty European and American motion pictures, had been obsessed with the plight of the displaced person. She had interested herself in the Spanish Civil War refugees and ousted German writers; she had been a guest of honor at the United Nations and member of the American Committee for the Protection of the Foreign Born. These and other offenses were noted in *Red Channels*; save for the Committee for the Foreign

Born, all the organizations listed had ceased to exist between 1940 and 1946. Christians was visited by men who called themselves investigators; her friends were unsure whether the men were from the FBI or the Senate Subcommittee on Internal Security. The telephone rang less often. The jobs vanished. Grown suddenly ill and tired, she began to suffer what some dismissed as psychosomatic illness: high blood pressure. Her health briefly improved when the Maugham TV Theatre offered her a role in *The Mother*, sponsored by Tintair. A week before rehearsals were to begin, she was informed by the producer that it was all a mistake; she could have full salary but not the role. Shortly afterward the actress suffered a massive attack of hypertension and was removed to Flower Hospital. When she was allowed to go home, she wrote an old friend, "I cannot bear yet to think of the things which led to my breakdown. One day I shall put them down as a record of something unbelievable." The secular blacklisters had made her the classic figure of their century, the exile. Several days later, on October 28, she collapsed at the home of a friend in Connecticut. Cause of death, wrote the attending physician, was cerebral hemorrhage.

Playwright Elmer Rice, an old friend of the actress, had another medical opinion. "She stood for what is best in American theater and life," he wrote in a seething eulogy. "As a reward she was slandered, falsely accused, hounded by investigators, deprived of employment, faced with destitution. There is no use appealing to the consciences of the McCarthyites; obviously they have none. But perhaps the martyrdom of Mady Christians will set freedom-loving citizens thinking about what is happening to art and to democracy in America."

Perhaps. But not yet. Rice, appalled at the metastasizing of the blacklist, waited a month and then resigned from the Playwrights TV Theatre, a group of dramatists whose works were performed on ABC-TV's Celanese Theatre. After John Garfield had been barred from the Celanese revival of Rice's *Counsellor-*

at-Law, Rice lit into Ellington & Co., the advertising agency for the Celanese Company: "I have repeatedly denounced the men who sit in the Kremlin for judging artists by political standards," he told them. "I do not intend to acquiesce when the same procedure is followed by political commissars who sit in the offices of advertising agencies or business corporations."

Jesse Ellington, the executive responsible for clearances, insisted that Celanese Theatre would nevertheless proceed with *Counsellor-at-Law*, starring the sanitized Alfred Drake, who had explained his past to the satisfaction of Kirkpatrick. Ellington pleaded: "We've tried to lean over backward to live up to the best traditions of the theatre and to avoid any of that political thing in casting. But when you get somebody who may cause a lot of bad publicity for your program, you have to be a little careful—it's an ordinary political safeguard."

If euphemisms are the anesthesia of language, surely no more deadening terms existed than "controversial" and "that political thing." Under them the little world of entertainment writhed. No one seemed to hear the afflicted, now reduced to voiceless silhouettes. Owners of conscience, like Elmer Rice, seemed to speak in an incomprehensible tongue, Mandarin falling on Cantonese.

In December, in the *New York World-Telegram*, columnist Frederick Woltman, a sort of anemic Pegler, took note of another fatality. J. Edward Bromberg, weary, ill, unable to work in America, had gone to London to appear in Dalton Trumbo's play *The Biggest Thief in Town*. One matinee day the star had failed to appear. In Bromberg's little apartment the body lay sprawled; a police physician attributed the death to "coronary occlusion."

Under the heading RED BLEEDING HEARTS TRYING TO MAKE MARTYR OF ACTOR J. EDWARD BROMBERG, Woltman paid his last respects: "The actor . . . was actually a victim of 'the un-Americans,' the Communists say. . . . *Red Channels* lists more than 15 CP Front connections of the late Mr. Bromberg.

With American soldiers dying in the Far East and the nation's economy and welfare threatened by world-wide Soviet aggression, the Communist in America, surrounded by his chosen enemies, is subjected to a certain stress and strain nowadays. It could scarcely be otherwise. To the end, the ailing Mr. Bromberg chose not to take sides against the Communist enemy. A victim of whom?"

One of Woltman's bleeding hearts was Clifford Odets, who, like Rice, disputed the coroner's verdict. "The English have strange phrases for such matters," Odets sorrowed. "I, for one, would like to suggest in a paraphrase of their terminology, a possible verdict of 'death by political misadventure.' "

Odets was a genius of the human condition writ small and performed loud. He had an instinct for what men told their wives in their bedrooms at night, what explosions occurred at dinner tables and in back rooms. He speculated on his old friend's last days, told of the three Bromberg children, remembered "this warm . . . considerate and masculine man of steady ethic and Left-liberal orientation.

"Men are growing somehow smaller," Odets concluded, "and life becomes a wearisome and sickening bore when such *unnatural* deaths become a commonplace of the day now that citizens of our world are hounded out of home, honor, livelihood and painfully accreted career by the tricks and twists of shameless shabby politicians banded into yapping packs."

It would be charitable to fade out here on Odets, to remember him, finally, at the memorial. For this speech is the finish of the old Odets, the playwright of commitment and rhapsodic despair. Within six months he too will shrink out of weariness, terror and incapacity. Even now his powers are fading and his work is not so actively sought. His fire has become neon; his divorce has been costly. He is selling off his Paul Klees, wondering about the success of *Clash by Night,* the film of his old play, adapted by someone else. (Perhaps the seeds of self-betrayal have always been there. The old Communists are fond of recalling Odets' crankiness when his first wife, Luise Rainer, gave her staff a night off and served the guests herself. "In Hollywood, one has servants," Odets told her. "Otherwise why come here?" And in *The Big Knife* he had a Devil's advocate—i.e., producer Stanley Hoff's representative—make a plea for compromise: "Your wild, native idealism is a fatal flaw in the context of your life [in Hollywood]. Half-idealism is the peritonitis of the soul—America is full of it! Give up and really march to Hoff's bugle call.") In the end, Odets will be in the blacklister's color guard, marching in lockstep with the worst of them.

At the time Odets saluted Bromberg, both names were circulated in still another catalogue of the leprous. The *American Legion Magazine* was no shoddy product hastily capitalizing on old obsessions and fresh power. Its advertisements were the same as those of the *Saturday Evening Post:* Armstrong tires, Gordon's gin, Ford automobiles. The coated pages displayed a format of substance and style. The publication was well edited, and if it was without criteria, except those of bad taste, the same could be said of many publications of larger and more influential circulation. The *Legion Magazine* enjoyed an impact far outside its audience. Hollywood studio men, for example, turned its pages with wet thumbs, praying that their names would not be in it. For, early on, the Legion had been persuaded that the governmental investigations of entertainers were flops. It was time, the veterans figured, to call in the National Guard. In October, American Legion conventionaires instructed the magazine editors to "publish all information on Communist associations of all people still employed in the entertainment industry."

In its December issue the magazine was ready with its Hollywood exposé, a feisty article entitled "Did the Movies Really Clean House?" by J. B. Matthews. Once the author had been an inexhaustible fellow-traveler, piping his followers through the glades. None of them was aware that the journey led to the slaughterhouse. None but Matthews; he lived to expose any organization, any member. He had formerly felt that he and the thirties were twins. What nonsense, he came to realize. It was, the fifties he was born for. Here, in a generous climate, he could be a reverse prophet, seeing everything backward in perfect focus, talking and writing of radicalism gone cold. He would heat and season it for those who cared to listen, and to pay. "I don't consider myself a crusader," he liked to say. "I am engaged in a very interesting field of investigation. To me the letterhead of a Communist front is a nugget. And I make a good living at it."

Nuggets and dust gleamed in the *American Legion Magazine*. Sixty-six suspects were named by Matthews, entombed in his coarse prose. "It is silly," he wrote, "to suppose that guys like Albert Maltz or dolls like Anne Revere were ever meant to do the dirty manual work of throwing up barricades in the streets." No, he contended, the Party probably never had more than three hundred official members in Hollywood. The Red aim was the fellow-traveler, the chump who would kick in his enormous salary check, subvert the labor unions, doctor the scripts and lend his prestigious name to fronts and petitions.

Even now, Matthews figured, Commies were working on American sound stages and cavorting in American swimming pools. Seventeen of Matthews' sixty-six may have appeared innocent to the reader, but they had signed an *amici curiae* brief defending the Hollywood Ten. Others had appeared before the HUAC; still others had suspect "affiliations." Toward the end of his article Matthews decided to appear even-handed. "It is only fair," he wrote, "to call attention to the fact that Warner Brothers also produced the recent and deservedly anti-Communist film, *I Was a Communist for the FBI*."

Matthews' article provoked new tremors in Hollywood and New York. The film companies requested meetings with the new president of the American Legion, Donald Wilson; American Business Consultants was hired by CBS, which feared a Matthewsian article on the broadcasting business. They need not have worried. Matthews was soon to forsake show biz for the high criticism; he would become executive director of Senator McCarthy's investigating committee.

Into this cheap chaos came the Hollywood Ten, their sentences complete, their lives irreparable. Dmytryk had recanted. Ornitz was dying. Maltz fled to Mexico, where the newspaper *Excelsior* immediately characterized him as the leader of an incendiary group of revolutionaries. In fact, all that the displaced writer had tried to organize were his own thoughts. Trumbo, Lardner, Cole and Scott attempted to live by other names, since their own were unemployable. The black market would always have a use for distress sales; writers were employed at the usual 80-percent discount. Bessie was especially luckless. He had never been fully established as a scenarist and his contraband work had almost no value. He was not a big enough nonentity.

Lawson's jail sentence allowed him, at last, to finish his history of American freedom. The Party had insisted on innumerable revisions. With tedious fidelity, Lawson had listened and rewritten. Its fatigued, airless arguments won a publisher but few readers. The thirties radicals had made the past their most lethal foe; now *they* were the past. In Union Square, where he appeared for a leftist rally, Lawson seemed to fade not merely as a writer but as a symbol. On the temporary dais an old radical whispered to the young man at the microphone. Mr. Lawson, he insisted, should be introduced to the audience. Witnesses remembered the announcement with a shudder. "And now," said the speaker, "I want to introduce a great fighter for peace, a man you all know. . . . What did you say his name was?"

Biberman resolved to make no compromises. The studios did not want him? Very well, he did not want the studios. His next work, he told friends, was to be a trenchant cinematic statement about injustice, American-style. Biberman had been away from that style too long, shut off first by the amnion of press-agentry, then by coterie politics and finally by jail. It was in there, on his last day of imprisonment, that Biberman received word of what had happened to the country outside. A drug pusher, looking for someone lower down the human scale, pointed at last to the outlawed director. "He'll be back," the junkie shouted. "He pushes worse'n I do!"

Outside, the sun shone on the righteous. While Biberman received his lecture, the Veterans Action Committee received its new stationery. It showed drawings of a crisp white grocery, shelves stocked with American produce, floors paced by clean and beaming employees. "Let's Keep 'Stalin's Little Creatures' from Crawling All Over These Products" read its secondary message. The primary one decorated the checkout counter. Below the jingling cash register was the irrefutable legend: FREEDOM RINGS HERE.

NINE

"*Red Channels* was a piker," conceded the advertisement. Vincent Hartnett, running hard, was promoting his expertise in the *Brooklyn Tablet*, a lay Catholic publication promulgating the Devil theory of history. Secularists, Roosevelt and the Jews were three of its frequent quarries. All three were mere guises of the Evil One.

The *Tablet*'s primed audience was given the barker's full spiel: "Now hear the full, documented exposé of Communists and Communist fronters in TV, Radio, the Stage, and your daily newspaper! A must for every Holy Name Society, Knights of Columbus Council, Catholic War Veterans Post." Hartnett was, in the view of Hartnett, "the nation's top authority on Communism and Communications. . . . Wire, phone or write, now," he urged, "to insure early booking." In the New York area the lecturer's fee was about $50 per talk, roughly a penny per subversive. Out of town the rates were higher.

In the same issue Hartnett demonstrated a will to live by his own categorical imperative. In a letter to the editor he complained of lascivious calendars displayed at a local pharmacy. They featured "scantily clad women" at the tobacco-and-candy counter, where any child could gaze upon them. Scandalized, Hartnett had taken his custom elsewhere.

Shortly afterward another lay Catholic publication, *The Sign,* imitated the *Tablet* mentality. "What About *Counterattack?*" inquired its vigorous article. The text, by Arnold Foreman, praised the earnest blacklisters of ABC and cited Hartnett for his "firsthand knowledge of certain Communist activities in program production." It should also have praised him for mimickry and adaptation. The blacklistees were not the only ones who could employ pseudonyms. There was no Arnold Foreman. There was only Vincent Hartnett, journalist.

The principle of economic sanction was applied with more profound effect by Lawrence Johnson. Under his aegis, Post No. 41 and the Veterans Action Committee had a roster of new recruits: Army, Navy, Marine and WAAC veterans, all anxious to keep Communist frontiers the hell out of show business. Mailing lists grew so long that the secular blacklisters sent out form letters. "To everybody in Retail Foods," they read, "To Retailers, Wholesalers and Consumers," "To All Super Market, Chain and Independent Operators; To Buyers, Merchandisers and Everyone concerned with the retail industry."

For Hartnett, blacklisting was quite literally money in the bank. He was a mercenary in the Cold War; at an established fee he would examine the political background of any person: $5 for a first report; $2 for additional checking. A thorough checkup, a full compilation of letterheads, petitions and advertisements in Red periodicals would run the client about $20. His new looseleaf blacklist, File #13, was $5 a copy, and for $500 "qualified persons" (i.e., persons with $500) could rummage through his files.

To the Syracuse organizations the remuneration was spiritual. By 1952 they were eminences, however gray, who had mastered the arts of coercion. Their crank letters, sent at will and in concert, displayed an arrogance unequaled outside an editorial cartoon. Upon the appearance of Jack Gilford on the Jerry Lester show, the Action Committee asked its readers to write the president of the American Chicle Company. "Ask him if the boys who are dying and being captured and maimed in Korea would chew his gum if they knew how he encouraged a Communist Fronter like Gilford to try to regain lost prestige . . . ask the General Manager of the S.O.S. Company if these boys who are fighting to maintain the Freedom of our country . . . care to have their loved ones at home continue to use S.O.S. Scouring Pads?"

The Block Drug Company, manufacturers of Ammident Tooth Paste, sponsored *Danger,* a TV adventure series. The Action Committee very shrewdly reasoned that the show was controlled by those who fought a final, hopeless action against blacklisting. "Since April 15th of this year," said the *Bulletin,* "the Block Company have used many Communist Front sympathizers. . . . Among these are—Walter Bernstein, Martin Ritt, Salem Ludwig, Will Lee. . . . Do the makers of Chlorodent, Colgate or Ipana tolerate the use of Communist Fronters in their advertising? NO!"

Johnson himself appealed to fellow supermarketers for succor. "The Block Drug Company," he wrote, "has salaried and given credit to such Communist Fronters on their show 'Danger' as Walter Bernstein, Martin Ritt, Salem Ludwig, Joshua Shelley, Lee Grant. Is it necessary to use these Communist Fronters to sell toothpaste or any other cosmetic or beauty aids? Does the Colgate-Palmolive-Peet Company use Communist Fronters to sell Colgate toothpaste? Do Lever Brothers find it necessary to employ people who give aid and comfort to a foreign power in order to promote their toothpaste, Chlorodent? What do you advise?"

By general consensus it was decided to adopt the democratic mode. Accordingly, Leonard Block of the Block Drug Company was informed of Johnson's offer: in his markets, tubes of Ammident and Chlorodent would be placed next to each other. Above the Chlorodent a sign would dangle: "Lever Bros. try not to use any of Stalin's little creatures in their advertising." The sign over Ammident could explain why the Block Drug

Company preferred Communist Fronters to loyal American performers. The loyalty of CBS, too, could be measured in this consumer poll. Customers would be asked, "Do you want any part of your purchase price of any products advertised on the Columbia Broadcasting System to be used to hire Communist Fronters?" Two boxes could be allocated for voting Yes or No; it was, Johnson concluded, the American way.

Industry, always an enthusiast for flag-raving, rapidly acquiesced. Stuart Peabody, vice president of the Borden Company, journeyed to Syracuse, listened to the blacklisters, then soothed them with a trophy they never tired of exhibiting. "Dear Larry," Peabody wrote, "I want to tell you again how grateful I am for the time and help you gave me on Tuesday. It is not exaggeration to say that my eyes have been opened as a result of your cooperation.

"The same goes for Francis Neuser and his group. He mentioned the fact that they are unpopular, but I know he isn't right. No one could meet them without being impressed by the honesty and zeal with which they are pursuing this fine cause, and with their obvious determination to be completely fair."

Paul M. Hahn, president of the American Tobacco Company, was delighted to report that he had shaken the subversives from his company's show, *The Big Story*. Procter & Gamble's Howard J. Morgens wrote Johnson that a stay in Syracuse was "pleasant and instructive. . . . We honestly feel that we also have been taking effective action in this field," he maintained, but added an emergency clause: "In any case, as a result of our contacts with you and your associates, our operating methods are being reexamined and will be tightened wherever possible. If you have any further suggestions to make about our radio and TV talent, I'd consider it a personal favor to hear from you directly."

The private sector was enthusiastically joined by the government. It was natural that the HUAC vibrate sympathetically at the gongs of Johnson, Hartnett, American Business Consultants and their colleagues. But the U.S. Chamber of Commerce endorsement proved a bright surprise for the secular blacklisters. Its annual report on subversion, *Communism, Where Do We Stand Today?* acknowledged the salutary effects of *Red Channels:* "Much furor and considerable unfair reporting has occurred over this publication. The attack . . . in certain circles, made much of the alleged unsubstantiated mass of rumor and gossip, which it was alleged to contain. [That] was plain bad reporting. Listings of 'front' connections were factual, with the source indicated." This, after Kirkpatrick acknowledged that no sources were checked and that no listee was consulted prior to publication. The Chamber, like the HUAC in *its* annual report, counseled businessmen against giving direct or indirect financial support to Communism by employing artists who contribute to Red causes. This boycott, the Chamber emphasized, did *not* chasten persons for their political beliefs. It was merely "denying indirect financial aid to a movement which is essentially treason."

Counterattack, expanding in influence and billings, felt the need for additional expertise. It summoned one of its star salesmen: a government witness, a consultant to the Senate, the New York Board of Education and Police Department, and, incidentally, a professional perjurer. As a street arab in the Bronx he had earned the sobriquet Kid Nickels. As an adult, the porcine Harvey Matusow had never grown too fat to stoop for the small change. He described his commission at ABC as "the happiest in my blacklisting career. *Counterattack,*" he trilled, "afforded me the opportunity to get into the glamorous limelight of show business. I felt the full meaning of the words, 'the pen is mightier than the sword.' "

The voice was equally formidable. When Jack Gilford was booked on the Colgate Comedy Hour, Matusow learned that the Yankees' star catcher, Yogi Berra, was also scheduled to appear. Matusow called the Yankee office, identifying himself as a loyal Yankee fan and red, white and blue-blooded American. "I've supported the Yankees for years," he complained. "And I think it would be a very wrong thing for Berra to be on a show which added prestige to a known Communist-Fronter like Gilford."

His call exacted a pledge from Jack Farrell, assistant director of public relations for the club. Something, Farrell promised, would be done about it. Matusow recognized the reply as the standard reply to crank callers. He telephoned Farrell sixteen more times, employing a variety of voices. Matusow boasted to the gang at ABC, "It was a voice technique I had developed through my hobby of working with puppets."

The final puppet bought Farrell's weary surrender: "Look, Mister, you really don't have to get so excited. I don't think Yogi Berra knows the difference between communism and communion."

With that one-liner, Farrell broke away and summoned executives of WNBT. The station, he told them, was too small for both Berra *and* Gilford; it was one or the other. The WNBT man hastily assured Farrell that Gilford would be booted; he was only a comedian, after all, and a controversial one. Baseball players were beyond cavil; as the Yankees liked to say after a ball-field collision, "X-rays of Berra's head showed nothing." "With that assurance," the PR man decided, "we will permit Yogi to take part in the program. But we have a firm policy that no Yankee player can take part in any public appearance, radio, TV or whatever it is, with persons who have been identified by authorized agencies as members of Communist-Front organizations. That's our policy and we're going to stick to it."

For years Matusow had shivered outside the blacklisting estate, offering his matches in the snow. Once inside, warm and dry, he resolved never to venture farther than the gate; he adopted a more-rabid-than-thou attitude which was to carry him all the way to the epicenter of the McCarthy movement. At ABC his violent will-to-smear made him privy to records and statistics. He learned that corporations paid a minimum fee of $5,000 for the company's twin services: "security information" on its employees, and "special informatives" (or, as they were known outside ABC, labor spies). General Electric, Republic Aircraft and several New York department stores commissioned ABC; in addition, subscriptions to *Counterattack* brought in another $100,000. In ABC's enlarged suite, two rooms were allocated for files on Communism and its dupes. Names and organizations were cross-indexed by a code that Kirkpatrick and Keenan had learned at the FBI.

Matusow flourished on conspiracy; where he could not invent it, he found it. One of Kid Nickels' earliest political acts was the shying of a rock through a window of a Young Communist League headquarters. Later, holding a Party card, he sold 320 subscriptions to the *Sunday Worker* and won a trip to Puerto Rico, all expenses paid. But Harvey was never as happy as at the sound of shattered glass. Restored to the right, he learned that tyranny is always better organized than freedom, that the wonderful microcosm of conspiracy was bungled by the Reds. It was the blacklisters who really knew how to organize.

There was no aspect of blacklisting that Matusow's new friends failed to touch, sometimes merely for luck. No longer individual entrepreneurs, they had all come together to pool their talents and their files. Vincent Hartnett (who now billed himself as "Talent Consultant") and Lawrence Johnson had taken to each other; they were "Larry" and "Vince" now, and when Vince wrote to Larry of the American Legionnaires, he called them "your boys." The movement enlisted many soldiers. Jack Wren, a BBD&O account executive, was called "a security officer" who obeyed the strictures of *Counterattack* and *Red Channels*. George Sokolsky, Victor Riesel and Eugene Lyons represented the literati of the blacklisters, interested upon occasion in the rehabilitation of the remorseful. In Hollywood the gruff old Wagon Master, actor Ward Bond, with the union official Roy Brewer, helped to aid the patriotic and cripple the subversive. The American Legion's Americanism Commission provided support; so did Congressional investigators. Lawrence Johnson came to Manhattan more frequently these days, holding court in the Hampshire House, happy to find a bright young man like Harvey so interested in his country's welfare. On lower levels, an actor named Frank Pulaski monitored his television set in the evenings, searching for listable performers. Pulaski, who frequently described himself as a victim of Red censure, was an early example of the blacklist backfire. While working as an announcer in 1948 he complained to his station manager that a newscast reported the existence of a Henry Wallace rally in Brooklyn. "I rasied hell over that," he said. "Not much later, they let me go. The manager said, among other things, that I just couldn't get along with people. But I know what the real reason was." Inexplicably, Pulaski was hired at the radio division of the U.N., where he found that an actor re-creating the speeches of the Soviet delegate "put too much feeling into it. He tried to make it sound convincing," complained the critic. "I'd have read the stuff in a dull monotone." Pulaski was soon let go by the United Nations. When he turned up as guest MC for the Cholly Knickerbocker show, the embittered announcer tried to use career rightists Ralph de Toledano and reformed chief of the U.S. Communist Party, Benjamin Gitlow. Both guests were refused by an official of the American Broadcasting Company; they were, the network decided without irony, too "controversial."

During Matusow's tenure *Counterattack* broadened its definition of entertainment to include the higher forms of creativity. Since they knew nothing about aesthetics, the blacklisters relied upon the sisters Dorothy and Lorna Drew, whose central concern, they told Matusow, was to "rid the fine arts of Communists." To this end, they furnished *Counterattack*, and eventually Congressman George Dondero of Michigan, with information that the Congressman used in eight speeches "exposing Communist painters and sculptors."

Choirboy among Torquemadas, Kid Nickels was an auditor rather than participant at most blacklisting sessions. When his advice was solicited, he threw his rocks very cautiously. At a George Sokolsky seminar, Victor Riesel submitted a rhetorical question: How could the guardians of show business work with the enemies of light? The interrogator insisted that clearances for José Ferrer were meaningless. The actor's testimony was manifestly a studio arrangement to prevent picketing of *Moulin Rouge*; it was *au fond*, said Riesel, a Communist plot to offset the blacklist.

Sokolsky's defense of Ferrer proved unexpectedly vehement. José, he insisted, was providing valuable information on Communism in the American theater. Sokolsky hinted darkly that he could not break the story, even before such trusted associates, but without Ferrer the job of theatrical blacklisting would be much more difficult. The quarreling seniors turned to the frosh for support. Matusow did not hesitate. "I agreed with Riesel," he recalled in the mode of the celluloid counter-spy. "I had been a Communist and could not afford to show leniency toward suspects or I myself would have been open to suspicion."

Johnson sought to show Harvey the further uses of power. One afternoon a cowering ad man offered up a new name that the grocer did not carry: Rosemary Clooney. "We've got nothing on her," Johnson grumbled. The executive tremulously agreed that she had signed nothing, appeared on no committees or letterheads. But, he added, producing a Winchell column, she had been dating José Ferrer. Johnson briskly apologized for doubting the efficacy of the agency's security system. "I guess you can't always catch them," he said. "But you're trying."

After several conferences, the grocer decided that Matusow deserved a piece of the reaction. At Hampshire House, over a quiet dinner, he and Harvey attacked the Schlitz Playhouse of Stars before the distressed ad man Frank Barton of Lennen and

Mitchell, agency for the sponsor. Communist-fronters, Johnson said, were constantly employed on the show. The film must be scrapped. "I don't care if you lose ten thousand dollars by not showing it," he insisted, "you shouldn't have hired those people in the first place."

Matusow was allowed to offer a solution: the producer, not the film, would be destroyed. The new producer would sign a new contract. It would stipulate that if controversial people were used, he would absorb the $10,000 loss. "But," Barton wondered, delivering one of the blacklist's great straight lines, "where can we obtain the information needed to compile our clearance list?" Johnson seemed to find it a fine question, an intelligent question. He nodded to his aide. "What about Harvey?" he asked. And so Kid Nickels found his way to Madison Avenue and 47th Street.

It was not unexpected, this total capitulation of free enterprise. The advertising industry, in the lost dictum of Calvin Coolidge, ministers to the spiritual side of business. If the fifties had been an ideal world, if generosity and charity were the desiderata of the age, clients would have instructed their agents to concoct virtuous campaigns devoted to the protection of the weak and the sheltering of the poor and disabled. But in the real world, business was sick with fear, anxious only to be a corporate version of e. e. cummings' salesman: an it that stinks please. To the interviewer from the ACLU or the *New York Times*, businessmen were willing to criticize Lawrence Johnson and his fellow blacklisters—always with the proviso that they could speak anonymously. When the executives appeared under their own names, they were extremists only of probity and caution. Controversy would be avoided. Security checks would be provided. No show, no commercial would be spoiled by a letter or telegram from Them. Riding this unenviable moral shuttle in 1952, the clients and ad men developed a diplomatic skill reminiscent of Talleyrand. During the revolution of 1830 a street battle raged below the minister's window. "I see that we are winning," he remarked to his aides. "Who are *we*, Monseigneur?" "Hush," said Talleyrand, "I'll tell you tomorrow."

2

Many old radicals could not wait until the morrow. They were uncertain as to who was winning. But it was very clear that *they* were losing. Early in 1952 two principal ornaments of left theater surrendered to the Committee, creating shock waves that still reverberate. Both were virile figures of barely contained violence. Both had carried the spark and ardor of the Group Theatre onto the contemporary stage. To watch them crumble, to witness what amounted to an enthusiastic retreat, was to attend the funeral of an entire movement.

By 1952 Elia "Gadget" Kazan had established himself in the American theater the way a fist establishes itself in a face. The director of Tennessee Williams, Thornton Wilder, Kurt Weill, Arthur Miller, S. N. Behrman, Kazan was as much collaborator as stager. His work was like a life force; he made his actors and writers burn themselves into prominence. Followers of his new reputation had almost forgotten Kazan the actor, the little jolt of electricity in the film *City for Conquest*. There, in one of his final roles, he played a bantam crook knocked off when he turns his back on an armed goon. As the bullets pierce him, Gadge turned to the camera to utter his curtain speech: "Ah, gee, I never figured on that at all."

After ten years his life suddenly mimicked that gangster film. Kazan had always given his back to the HUAC, to Jack Warner and the Motion Picture Alliance. He had constantly dismissed the menace of the philistine. But now it had the drop on him— and he would not allow *City for Conquest* to be replayed in life. At the beginning of the year Kazan and Lillian Hellman sat over drinks at the Plaza. The playwright was depressed and angry at the work of the Committee; the director was dodgy, rambling, incoherent. Unable to get through, Hellman excused herself and dialed her producer, Kermit Bloomgarden. "Gadge isn't making any sense," she told him. "He's not drunk, he's just odd. What's wrong?" "I thought you knew," Bloomgarden told her. "He's going down to Washington to name names." At the taxi stand outside the hotel, Kazan offered a rationale he never disavowed: "All right, I earned over $400,000 last year from theater. But Skouras says I'll never make another movie. You've spent your money, haven't you? It's easy for you. But I've got a stake. . . ."

"I could never understand his terrible, twisted logic," Lillian Hellman was to recall with a special shudder, "his feeling that he had to compromise because he was rich."

Kazan's solipsistic progress took him to Washington in January of 1952, where, in secret testimony, he gave Francis Walter and his Committeemen the posture they desired. In April, for the benefit of the public, Kazan testified in executive session and the transcript was released to the world. J. Edward Bromberg (deceased) was one of the names Kazan disclosed, also Morris Carnovsky, Tony Kraber, Art Smith—Jonahs thrown overboard so that the confessor could float. Although Kazan's memory for names was unfailing, he had trouble with organizations. "My connections . . . were so slight and transitory," he explained, "that I am forced to rely on a listing of these prepared for me after research by my employer, Twentieth Century-Fox." Fox, of course, had relied upon the work of blacklisters, who supplied them with such transitory groups as the American Friends of the Chinese People and the Committee for a Boycott Against Japanese Aggression.

During his testimony Elia Kazan became reminiscent of those peculiar people visited by Lemuel Gulliver on his voyage to Laputa. Rather than converse, the Laputans carried enormous bundles, filled with simulacra of all the things they could think of; when they wished to speak they merely pointed at the object. The witness made no attempt to exchange historical notions with his inquisitors. There was no conversation at all. Toward the end of his testimony Kazan indicated the little models of his work, from *The Strings, My Lord, Are False* ("Not political. It shows human courage and endurance in many kinds of people, including, prominently, a priest") through *A Streetcar Named Desire* ("Not political. But deeply human") to *Flight into Egypt* ("Story of refugees stranded in Cairo and trying to get into the United States"). "Secrecy serves the Communists," Kazan pontificated. "It is my obligation as a citizen to tell everything I know." But to whom? Congress? The American people? The answer lay in the director's bottom line: "I have placed a copy of this affidavit with Mr. Spyros P. Skouras, president of Twentieth Century-Fox."

Once Kazan began, he could not shut up. In an ad in *The New York Times* he ran on: "Liberals must speak out. . . . The motion pictures I have made and the plays I have chosen to direct represent my convictions. I expect to continue to make the same kinds of pictures and to direct the same kinds of plays." Those expectations were, as we will see, both disappointed in the large sense and fulfilled in the small. For the present, the declaration served to gut the old left still further.

A month later Odets himself sat at the confessional, graying, tired, past caring, apparently. He too had been a Communist. J. Edward Bromberg, he said, had recruited him into the Party. Later he told friends that he was "doing less harm by naming Joe than by giving the Committee someone alive." The Party had used Odets shamelessly and the playwright was suing for alienation of affections. He fed the Committee the dead and the living; it consumed them whole, a boa ingesting rabbits. Like the performers and producers before him, the artist was pitiably grateful for bad reviews. "Too often for the health of *Awake and Sing,*" the *New Masses* had said, "a situation is created out of nothing just to get across a wisecrack or a laugh. . . ." *Waiting for Lefty* was only "rather infrequently done by colleges." Before his apostasy James T. Farrell had written, "I don't understand how [Odets] could have written a play so consistently, so ferociously bad [as *Paradise Lost*]. It is mistitled. It should be known as *Lay Down and Die.*"

Finally, Odets gave his tragic summary of the literary situation: "One must pick one's way very carefully through the mazes of liberalism or leftism today or one must remain silent. Of the two, I must tell you frankly I would try to pick the first way, because the little that I have to say, the little that I have to contribute to the betterment or welfare of the American people could not permit me to remain silent."

Like Kazan, Martin Berkeley, Richard Collins, Sterling Hayden and Larry Parks, Odets himself had "named" no one. New investigators with greater facilities had compiled immense dossiers on all the witnesses and their associates. The HUAC needed no fresh identities; to finger a dead man, or a person already named five times, was perfectly acceptable. The significance lay in the rite, not in the sacrifice. Nonetheless, the act gave the speakers a sense of incalculable revulsion. One spring night, as the hours staled toward morning, Tony Kraber answered his doorbell. The visitor spoke in an inhuman whisper, as if he had been on microphone too long. "I named you," he said. And, like a Clifford Odets character, Clifford Odets plunged into the dark.

Scarcely a month later Odets stood at the graveside of another friend abbreviated by the blacklist. At the funeral services Rabbi Louis Newman described the arc of the deceased. "He came like a meteor. And like a meteor he departed." Ten thousand people filed past the oaken bier. Odets, waiting his turn, looked down at the body and turned away to bury his face in his hands. Out in the street two men began slugging each other; one of them had called the dead man a Communist. Even here John Garfield could not rest. The star was dead in Hollywood long before this: *Red Channels* had finished him in 1950. Early in 1951 an ANTA revival of *Peer Gynt* had paid the star $75 a week. After that, nothing significant came his way until a brief Broadway revival of *Golden Boy*. The production was more sentimental than remunerative. Garfield was paid $80 a week for the role that Luther Adler had won the first time around. By then, he—and some fellow performers—were completely bleached by their times. When a Save-the-Rosenbergs petition was sent to him, Garfield wailed, "Can't these people leave me alone!" Later, during a performance of *Golden Boy*, Lee J. Cobb scribbled his name on a routine Actors' Equity petition, went out and performed horribly in Act One. He furiously erased the signature during intermission.

John Garfield's final film, *He Ran All the Way*, was released posthumously. In it he played a criminal in flight, one street ahead of the cops, never certain of the people around him, waiting for the imminent betrayal. The vulgar irony lay upon Garfield's reputation like a cheap shroud. In the days before his death the actor had been ransacking his checkbooks and diaries, searching the memories of friends and professional associates. The HUAC had summoned him again—this time, it was hinted, with some crushing evidence of checks signed to the Party. Garfield kept beating back notions of betrayal by his politicized wife, Robbie. "She never really had time for such things as Party activity," he assured a friend hotly, as if to convince himself as well. "She had three kids and a house to handle, not to mention me." Yet, in 1951 who could be sure of anyone or anything?

Garfield sought his old friend from DeWitt Clinton High School, Arnold Forster. Unlike Garfield, Forster had prospered in the early fifties; he was now counsel for the B'nai B'rith Anti-Defamation League and, incidentally, something of a clearance expert; it was that old business of Jewish names on the blacklists. Forster, in an unofficial capacity, took it upon himself to act as liaison between the secular blacklisters and the afflicted performers and sponsors. Leonard Block of the Block Drug Company had come to him first; Forster had smoothed things over with Lawrence Johnson, soothing egos, standing up for his "client," hinting at an anti-Semitism that was promptly denied by the blacklisters, who mistrusted everyone regardless of creed or national origin. Albert Dekker had come to see Forster with less happy results. "He thrashed around the office, a bull of a man, growing more furious all the time," recalled Forster. "Finally, he just said, 'Fuck 'em! I *won't* compromise, I won't give in, I'll wait them out. I'll lecture, I'll go on one-man tours, but I *won't* crawl to those bastards. Never!' And he *did* go on those tours, and he *did* survive. Larry Adler also came to me. I suggested some statements he might make and he turned on me, called me a fink and worse, strode out of the office and went to Europe. And he was never—well, hardly ever—heard from again. Julie Garfield was far more tractable. Far more understanding. And far more terrified."

The two men collaborated on an article designed to apologize for Garfield's past concern for the poor and the disenfranchised. It was entitled "I Was a Sucker for a Left Hook"; Forster had arranged for *Look* Magazine to print it in a fall issue. Forty-eight hours before his death Garfield was still working through the night with his counsel, doubling back on some stale, half-forgotten tracks from the thirties. He left at 4:20 A.M.; seven hours later he was back. "We went over the record pretty minutely," the clearance expert was to recall, "and I was satisfied that Garfield had never been a member of the CP. He was guilty of two things—of loving people and of being naïve. For his naïveté, he paid with his reputation."

And with his life. John Garfield, born Jules Garfinkel, the first of the Jewish street kids turned movie star, the driven, swaggering womanizer, the open-handed signer of petitions and guest books, had been warned by his doctors to slow down. His heart was badly strained, and his marriage unstable. But the Garfield ego and reputation were even more damaged. He died several blocks from his apartment, in the bedroom of an actress who described herself as a family friend. So the tarnished celebrity was to end as a dirty joke, one of those sharpshooters who died in the saddle. And the words he had composed, the detailed exegeses he had planned to give the Committee, the sixteen-page magazine article all became part of the estate. *Look* Magazine would not publish "I Was a Sucker for a Left Hook," but copies of the article were leaked to some important opinion makers.

The columnists were not unmoved by tragedy. Now that John Garfield had died, wandering in New York, far from her town, Hedda Hopper pronounced a benevolent farewell. "John Garfield's friends and fans are happy," she told her readers. "Before he died he made a full confession."

Ed Sullivan, former pal of Garfield, had once allowed him a guest column to celebrate Hollywood in 1939. Thirteen years later Sullivan had other thoughts:

> The grim and curious coincidence of the deaths of John Garfield and Canada Lee within a few days spotlights the fact that both appeared in *Body and Soul,* made by United Artists in 1947.
>
> *Body and Soul,* as a case history, is of tremendous importance to Americans fighting Communism because it illustrates the manner in which Commies and pinks, in the field of communications and ideas, gave employment to each other.
>
> The picture was directed by Robert Rossen, written by Abe Polonsky, included in its cast Garfield, Canada Lee and Anne Revere. All of them later were probed by the House Committee on Un-American Activities. *Body and Soul* is the pattern that the Commies and their sympathizers in TV networks, agencies and theatrical unions would like to fasten on the newest medium. From the director on down, the Commies insert their members, freeze out those who are on the American side of the fence.

In his haste to join the blacklisters, the harassed, myopic Sullivan even Red-baited like a novice. He omitted Art Smith, who played Garfield's father and who was barred from work following Kazan's testimony, and James Wong Howe, apolitical cinematographer of *Body and Soul*, deemed suspicious because of his willingness to work with Commies. As for Canada Lee, *his* agonies could be traced not to the Committee, but to the Judith Coplon trial—when his name was flushed from FBI files of hearsay evidence. Overlooked by almost every theatrical or film historian, unmentioned by such retentive and bitter victims as Alvah Bessie and Dalton Trumbo, Lee is the Othello of the blacklist, at once its most afflicted and ignored victim.

"All my life," he once said, "I've been on the verge of being something. I'm almost becoming a concert violinist and I run away to the races. I'm almost a good jockey and I go over-weight. I'm almost a champion prize fighter and my eyes go bad." This sense of incompleteness began and ended in Harlem, where he and Adam Clayton Powell had been boys together. Leonard Lionel Cornelius Canegata had been too long a monicker for ring announcers, and before one preliminary he became Canada Lee. There was a sense of the driven aristocrat about him, as if to relax was to sink below one's natural level. When he turned actor, almost because there seemed nothing else to do, he was variously judged a natural, a consummate professional and incredibly lucky. He became famous almost immediately, as Bigger Thomas in *Native Son* on Broadway. Soon after, he reinforced his reputation in an independent production of *Othello*, and as Banquo in an all-black version of *Macbeth*. In Boston he donned white makeup and became the first Negro to play the heavy in *The Duchess of Malfi*; now, said the critics, there was nothing this actor could not do. They had reckoned without the blacklisters. Shortly after his appearance in *Body and Soul* Canada Lee found his contracts canceled, his roles small and dispiriting. It was not black that was hurting him, the producers explained, it was red. In 1949, reduced to penury, he called a press conference to protest his anti-Communism. "I refer to the drivel that has come from the so-called secret files of the FBI about one Canada Lee," he said. "I am not a Communist. This is a simple fact. . . . I believe this constant screech of 'Communism' is only a smoke screen designed to hide very unpleasant facts. . . . I freely admit that my work, my art, my livelihood is very much affected by the irresponsible, nebulous, false insinuations directed at my name. However, I shall continue to speak my mind. I shall continue to help my people gain their rightful place in this America. . . . My duty, my heart is with those in America who do not experience the full realization of the democracy we all talk about and with them I shall always be found, no matter by what names I am unjustly labeled. I take my hat off to no man in my love for my country. I will let my acts speak for me!"

He carried each act on his deteriorating body. By the summer of 1952 he had been banned from forty shows. The American Tobacco Company was the first to bar him; others followed, and soon he was entirely shut out from radio and television. "How long," he pleaded to the editors of *Variety*, "how long can a man take this kind of unfair treatment?"

He could take it for only a few more months. At last, destitute, he delivered an attack upon Paul Robeson. The film industry thereupon relented and granted him one final role, as the Reverend Stephen Kumalo in *Cry, the Beloved Country*, filmed on location near Johannesburg, South Africa.

It was his most controlled and moving performance. The round face carried another face within it; the Umfundisi's emotions forced themselves to lie down in darkness; the voice had the undertone of a cello. Shortly after the film was completed, Lee underwent a sympathectomy to relieve high blood pressure. He returned to New York, oppressed by the *apartheid* world of South Africa and afflicted by failing health, unable to work in his own country. Four TV sponsors offered roles, then withdrew. They would agree to cast him, they said, only if someone else used him first. In the end, the actor went to his friend Walter White, executive secretary of the NAACP. "I can't take it any more," Lee said. "I'm going to get a shoeshine box and sit outside the Astor Theatre. My picture is playing to capacity audiences and, my God, I can't get one day's work." Walter White, placatory, even-tempered, controlled, told him not to make waves. The trouble would disappear, White predicted; the last thing Lee needed now was an infusion of melodrama. The actor obeyed; his curtain speech was delivered offstage, at a meeting in Westchester. He was protesting the death of two Negroes shot down by an ex-policeman who resented their presence in a public tavern. "I try not to be emotional," he said, summoning the Moor's lament, "Haply, for I am black and have not those soft parts of conversation." Lee told his tense, grieving audience, "I am a black man and black men have been killed and I must be emotional. . . . When I think that America, this great and tremendous country, has been built on the backs and sweat of my people, when I think that in every war my people have died for this country; and when I know that my people cannot walk the streets here in safety, I feel bad." A few weeks later, in the spring of '52, he died penniless and alone. Typically, the obituaries made no reference to the blacklist. Several weeks later the claimants for the body began their squabble. The *Daily Worker* called him their own ("They could not make Canada Lee a Cold War stoolpigeon"). Leonard Lyons disagreed. "The *Worker* is trying to claim Canada Lee," he wrote. "The fact is that Lee worked with anti-Communist groups for the past three years. . . . After he made *Cry, the Beloved Country* he told me: 'I'd rather be the lowest sharecropper in Mississippi or Georgia, than live in South Africa. America is the best place for the Negro, for no place else is there any real hope for decent living.' "

As for the indecent dying, nothing could be done. Few doctors sought to battle the plague, and those who did found unexpected enemies. In mid-1952 the American Civil Liberties Union published the Merle Miller report, *The Judges and the Judged.* Playwright Robert E. Sherwood wrote a glowing foreword, praising the accuracy and objectivity of the book, observing that "It is quite clear that whereas the editors and publishers of *Red Channels* and *Counterattack* do not consciously strive for the same objectives as the agents of Communism, their methods and techniques are very similar and so are their standards of morality. . . ."

Miller's report displayed several unfortunate faults. It was tentative; there was a blacklist, it concluded, but its operational techniques were unknown and its lineaments barely shown. (Straining for fair-mindedness, Miller also investigated rumors of a blacklist against anti-Communists, and found only unsupported rumor.) There was no index, so that researchers were on their own, searching pages for a story that would disappear in one chapter, only to surface three chapters later. And, unhappily, the book was wholly supported by unattributed quotes. "Everyone was frightened," Miller recalled two decades later. "It seems odd to think about such dense civilian fear in America, but there it was. Actors were afraid to give me their names, producers, agency people—everyone refused to talk, or would not speak for attribution. Only the blacklisters were brave."

Miller was the first accredited investigator of the blacklist. Perhaps because of his politesse and his manifest desire for scrupulousness, the blacklisters talked to him at length. In *The Judges and the Judged* the record of fear psychosis, of the Muir case, of the beginnings of *Counterattack* in the halls of the FBI—all were presented without prejudice or outrage. Here was CBS honoring the moral objections of its star commentator, John K. M. McCaffery, to the house loyalty oath. "It is impossible," he said, "for a Catholic to be a Communist." Here was CBS President Ream liberally accepting the objection. For John to fill out the statement, he agreed, would be "a sterile insistence upon form rather than substance." The network made no mention of other religions; each case "would be decided on its own merit."

Here was the American Legion advising its members to "organize a letter-writing group of six to ten relatives and friends." "Phone, telegraph or write television sponsors employing entertainers with front records." Interested persons could uncover the names from the American Legion, *Counterattack* and other dependable sources.

Here were the Muir affair, the troubles of John Garfield (described anonymously) and of the kind of ad men who told Cohn-and-Schine jokes—and who kept a copy of *Red Channels* in the bottom drawer of their desks. It would seem difficult to find an objector to *The Judges and the Judged*—save, of course, for the blacklisters. But Miller was not to find his enemies on the right. He was to find them at his side.

Mervyn Pitzele, labor negotiator, and fellow board member of the ACLU, examined Miller's thesis with great disdain. In the pages of the *New Leader* he sought to embarrass the author and discredit the report. "It is only because Miller's book is a report commissioned for and issued by the ACLU that it is worth taking seriously," he wrote. "Otherwise it could be dismissed as just about what could be expected from a man grown firmer in a view he expressed in 1947: 'The real threat to veterans, to the United States, to the world, is not from the left but from the right.' Such a man could be expected to find a mountain of evidence on one side but not a single instance proving that Communists blacklist their enemies . . . in its attack on *Red Channels* the ACLU departs from its principles and this leads to everything that the ACLU has itself condemned: anonymous charges, half-truths, distortions and lies."

The *New York Journal-American* delightedly reprinted Pitzele's rebuttal. Howard Rushmore, the ex–*Daily Worker* critic, now Hearst's authority on Red Thought, devoted a column to the civil strife at the ACLU and quoted Pitzele further: "As for

Miller's 'anti-communism,' he is one of those fellows who believes that the guilt of Alger Hiss is still unproven, that it's only McCarthyism America should be worried about and that the way to fight for 'liberalism' is to say anything which may be persuasive, whether it is true or not."

Miller protested by offering further evidence of the profitable blacklisting done by such professional anti-Communists as Vincent Hartnett and American Business Consultants. It was judged inadmissible. The slipshod investigator, Rushmore reported, had never interviewed the great anti-Communist radio writer Paul R. Milton, although Milton had prepared sheaves of material. We shall shortly see that collector at work; the fact that his "evidence" was not examined by the ACLU was deemed further proof of collusion between Miller and the Reds.

Soon afterward *Commentary*, then in its most confused phase of civism, published an article, "How End the Panic in Radio-TV?" The writer was Louis Berg, editor of the flourishing Sunday supplement *This Week*. *Commentary* billed him as "one of the fairest and most knowledgeable writers in the entertainment field, with two decades of professional experience . . . and an even longer record of concern with civil liberties and political justice." Then, with a wrenching disclaimer that introduced an air of sanctity, should there be any social historians giving grades, the editors added: "The opinions expressed here . . . should not be taken as official views either of this magazine or of its sponsors." This transparent equivocation only served to underline the fear felt even by subsidized magazines. With only a little imaginative faculty the editors of *Commentary* might have guessed the perturbations in the entertainment business. Evidently they preferred not to think about it. As for Berg, he could not imagine what the fuss was about.

"The question raised in *Red Channels*," he wrote, "is not of membership in the Communist party which, Mr. Miller observes unnecessarily, none can prove except maybe the FBI.

The question is one of *collaboration* with the Communists, which *can* be established by the *public activities* of the suspected persons. There is no exact dividing line between the foolish innocents and the guilty, but neither is there one between sanity and insanity. Nevertheless, society may sometimes find it necessary to draw the line." Berg's sophistries formed an anthology of beliefs held by those who felt McCarthy's methods were repugnant but his aims worthwhile. They were the same people who thought the blacklist unfair in the same manner that IQ tests were unfair—they barred some perfectly nice people, but, after all, examiners needed *some* touchstone, didn't they?

"It is intolerable," Berg went on, "that the rascals who shared the guilt at Buchenwald should be permitted to make too handsome a living in the public eye. A free society may have to tolerate its enemies, but it is not called upon to reward them. And is the present less vivid in the mind's eye than the past, and have we not the slave camps of Russia and the war in Korea to jog our sensibilities? More is involved here than the simple right of a man to hold a job and 'an unpopular opinion' at the same time."

Berg proposed a board of inquiry, a more elite blacklist which would "serve the function of getting the truly innocent and innocuous off the hook." This dybbuk, which might slay the lower-class dybbuk, "would have to weigh, by *present* speeches and actions, the sincerity of those who were more deeply implicated in collaboration with the Communists, but who have since disavowed their ways."

Tromping among the ruins of the ACLU's shy, tentative effort, Berg concluded, "Let us, whatever our disagreements on civil liberties, at least put a halt to the shameful procedure that meets the demagogic half-truth with the liberal half-lie. What ever happened to the old liberal conviction that, in the fight for justice, the best weapon is the truth?"

What happened to it was capitulation—by the intelligent,

the gifted and the frightened who could no longer distinguish between a Nazi executioner, a Communist agitator, a signer of petitions and a liberal without a compass.

In 1952 the HUAC was given new aid by the Senate Internal Securities Subcommittee under its chairman, Pat McCarran of Nevada. The xenophobic McCarran made few excursions into the minor field of show business; he preferred proving that the State Department sold out Chiang Kai-shek. But for these few star months his group was willing to examine some buskers. Judy Holliday testified behind closed doors that she was "irresponsible and slightly—more than slightly—stupid." The *Red Channels* listee employed her best Billie Dawn manner before the Senators, admitting that her income had altered a bit since the attacks of the blacklisters. But, she added, "I am not simply turning tail because of that." Her support for Henry Wallace, her registration in the American Labor Party, her signature on suspect petitions—they all grew, she maintained, out of naïveté and impulse. Yes, she *had* sent greetings to the Moscow Art Theatre. "It was a wonderful way to show that artists could still respect each other no matter what their political backgrounds were. . . ."

Her questioner demanded: "Are you in the *habit* of sending telegrams to theatrical groups wishing them well?"

"Only when I feel like it . . . for instance when the Old Vic came here I did feel it."

"Old who?"

Another revelation threw the Senators. "When were you told that the organizations to which you lent your name were Communists?"

Holliday: "I have been told every day for the past year practically . . . by Columbia Pictures, by lawyers, by people that I have hired to investigate me. I wanted to know what I had done."

"You *hired* people to investigate you?"

"I certainly did, because I had gotten into a lot of trouble."

Senator Arthur Watkins was especially pleased with the actress' style and timing. He applauded her answer "I don't say 'yes' to anything now except cancer, polio, and cerebral palsy and things like that."

"You watch it now, do you not?" asked Watkins.

"Ho, *do* I watch it now!" Holliday replied.

Others loudly watched it upon command. Sam Levenson, the bland, ingratiating raconteur, appeared at his own request to scotch rumors about his disloyalty. The smile vanished as he insisted, "I would like to say simply . . . that my father and mother came from [Russia]. . . . I was also born on the other side. I am an extremely grateful American citizen. . . . I believe that I cannot survive as a performer under Communism or fascism. . . ." As additional proof of Americanism, Levenson offered a deposition. "To whom it may concern," it stated, "I can attest to the fact that no evidence of Communist Party membership nor activities in Communist Party fronts have been undertaken by Mr. Levenson during my personal participation in these affairs." It was signed *Harvey Matusow*.

The barrel-bellied troubadour and actor Burl Ives also appeared before the Subcommittee. He assumed the role of chuckleheaded field hand, admitting that he had guitar-strummed at many Communist-sponsored gatherings. "I believe that most . . . sounded like very positive and good things to do. They were known as good causes, so I sang." He had little more to confess; neither did Philip Loeb, dismissed from *The Goldbergs*, now unemployable, informing the Senators of what they already knew and approved—that *Red Channels* had terminated his life's work, both as performer and as union officer.

The apparent eagerness of Holliday and some other witnesses gave Chairman McCarran an opportunity to express his philosophy. "Communism fastens itself like a leech on the careers of prominent entertainers," he stated, remarking on "the striking number of Communist-controlled organizations and Communist-sponsored activities in which some of the witnesses have involved themselves. We do not want to accuse anyone of guilt by association, but it is a dangerous type of thinking that leads people into such involvements."

In the view of the secular blacklisters, McCarran's tone carried a dangerously liberal quality. Victor Riesel expressed their displeasure in an open letter to Holliday, carried by the Hearst papers: "This is to let Hollywood's Oscar-winning blonde, Judy Holliday, know that we weren't born yesterday. . . . Had she gone to Screen Actors Guild sessions in Hollywood she would have learned from Ronnie Reagan and the other officers just what Communist infiltration meant. Like Edward G. Robinson and many others, she says, in effect, she was played for a sucker. . . ." Riesel grumbled, "Now she's free to resume her career. There will not be any demonstration against her. She has denounced the Stalinist world.

"But what will Judy Holliday and Eddie Robinson and all the rest exploited by the comrades do for the world which was besmirched by those to whom they lent their names like casual endorsements of toothpaste?

"They owe the world of decency a debt. Silence and withdrawal from the crusades will not repay that debt. Let them speak out. Now!"

Riesel continued to listen for a stridence to match his own. He seldom found it. Those who worked the same side of the street found greater spiritual rewards in the quiet selling of lists. On the left, the dupes wished only to hide under the bed until the monster went away. Occasionally a hard leftist would break ranks and condemn those conspirators with whom he had once rallied. But there was no choral quality to these confessionals. The loudest of them never gave convincing evidence that they believed in anything more important than personal rehabilitation.

Only in Hollywood could Riesel find a comforting decibel

strength. Working under the band musician's motto, "Loud Is Good," the studios had, at last, released those great anti-Communist movies for which Representative Nixon had thirsted. They were gruff, trivial exercises like *The Iron Curtain, The Red Danube, I Was a Communist for the FBI*, rewrites of the old formulae of Good Peasant Versus Fascist Underground, or Loner Against the Mob. The villain had simply changed accent and style.

Only one anti-Red film exhibited any distinction: *My Son John*, directed and co-written by Leo McCarey, one of the friendly witnesses of 1947. His contribution to the blacklist was personal and original. In an hour and a half it provided the viewers with a view of the primordial thought of the show-business Red-baiter.

My Son John opens with a view of Anytown, U.S.A., a symbolic arena of frame houses and wide, elm-lined streets. This is the forest primeval, the 1952 battlefield for man's political soul. Outside, all is well. Two infantry corporals toss around a football in a scene reminiscent of the flashbacks in *Death of a Salesman*. These healthy, blond American boys are but two fifths of the Jefferson family. Dad, played by Dean Jagger, is a schoolteacher, a Catholic and an American Legionnaire of dogmatic response. Helen Hayes, absent from the screen for seventeen years, was induced to play Mom, a hysteroid who, the script plainly indicates, is enduring a very difficult menopause. Both parents are rubbed raw by their third son, John, a government functionary who has failed to see his brothers off to Korea. After their departure he appears: vain, priggish, haughty and dark-haired, a typical American subversive. How has this family produced him? Through no fault of their own, McCarey indicates. For they have sent him to college. There, amidst God knows what kind of elements, he has learned to mock and despise his origins.

McCarey wished to give his hero faults in order to make him

appear human. In the process Dad became a huge, ludicrous toad. Lurching, drunken, violent, he berates John for his mockery of American tradition. Since Dad cannot argue logically, he expresses his views in the famous World War I song:

> If you don't like your Uncle Sammy,
> Then go back to your home o'er the sea,
> To the land from where you came,
> Whatever be its name,
> But don't be ungrateful to me!
> If you don't like the stars in Old Glory
> If you don't like the Red, White and Blue,
> Then don't act like the cur in the story,
> Don't bite the hand that's feeding you!

To Dad, Communists are "scummies," and intellectuals are a gathering threat. When John's friend, a professor, turns up, he is literally a longhair. When teacher and pupil embrace each other, Dad spits. John, it is revealed, has had an affair with a girl suspected of Communistic leanings; worse, he has a key to her apartment. Yet Robert Walker's ornamented performance hints ominously at homosexuality; corruption, says the film, is one big bag. Mom ascends shrill peaks of neuroticism; Dad, frustrated, gets drunk and belts John with a Bible. Dad's only consolation is Mom's comment, "You've got more wisdom than all of us because you listen with your heart."

Two subordinate characters are of paramount interest in the film: the priest (Frank McHugh) and an FBI investigator (Van Heflin). In McCarey's popular Catholic films *Going My Way* and *The Bells of St. Mary's*, priests are knowledgeable, winning sorts, men equally at home on the ball field or in the pulpit, capable of dealing with every sort of human trauma, including murder. But in *My Son John* the clerical role has been abdicated. Here, the priest is a pink-cheeked, winsome good guy, totally out of his shallowness in political affairs. It is the FBI man who assumes the role of adviser and confessor, praising the cleansing power of confession to John, giving Mom a sense of the world as it is and providing her with a rationale for working with the Bureau against her wayward boy.

McCarey's denouement resorts to the hallowed cornball practice of hare and hounds: pursued by scummies, John is shot at the base of the Lincoln Monument. The reason for his execution is soon made manifest. He has taped a speech, later broadcast to a college commencement. "I was flattered," the voice explains to potential Johns, "when I was immediately recognized as an intellect. I was invited into homes where only superior minds communed. It excited my freshman fancy to hear daring thoughts that I wouldn't have dreamed of when I lived at home—a bold defiance of the only authorities I knew, my church and my mother and father. I know that many of you have experienced that stimulation—but stimulation leads to narcotics. . . ."

There it was, crackpot primer for Americans, inspired by the investigation of 1947, polished by the blacklist mentality and produced for the American public without embarrassment or explanation. Stimulants led to narcotics, colloquy to atheism, intellectual curiosity to Communism. There were cures for narcotics, and there were cures for the other lethal habits, chiefly, if not solely, the Federal Bureau of Investigation and the Church. Catholic critics in *Commonweal* and *America* were somewhat disturbed by the tenor of this epic revelation, but it remained for Nathan Glick, in the self-contradictory *Commentary*, to underline the film's criticism of "the vicious habit of intellectual curiosity" and for Robert Warshow in the *American Mercury* to notice that John was the movie's most interesting, best-fulfilled character. "The hidden logic of *My Son John* seems to be," wrote Warshow, "since we cannot understand Communism, it is likely that what we cannot undestand must *be* Communism. The strongest and clearest image that one takes away from the film is that of the father, and his message is that we must fear and hate the best potentialities of the human mind."

Moreover, Leo McCarey was mistaken not only in his emphasis but in his history. John represents the quirky, fastidious traitor—Alger Hiss, perhaps, as seen by Ayn Rand. In fact, the American Communist tradition always hawked a full-throated masculinity. What Michael Gold and the *Daily Worker* critics promoted was the sweaty man of the left who could write epic poetry on his lunch break at the jute mill. Byron in bib overalls is what they wanted; to them, Proust was "the master-masturbator of the bourgeois literature." John would have revolted them. His wrists were too narrow, his voice too meaching. Yet *My Son John* never really lies. It reveals absolutely, if unintentionally, the deep traditional appeal of the left. For John manifestly did not have to go to college to be converted. He was altered long before, by his father's booming factitious ideology, by his mother's neurotic fear of the new, by his brothers' grinning, incurious acceptance of obscene circumstance. *My Son John* may not have been the aesthetic American film of 1952. But it was surely, in its own strange way, the truest.

TEN

FOR THE CALIBRATIONS of political tenor, '52–'53, no better instrument exists than the evidence of a Washington hearing organized by Senator Joseph McCarthy. The Senator, looming like some great unsexed Cyclops, looked down in every sense on that most unlikely Homer, the small, belligerent James Wechsler, editor of the *New York Post*. Wechsler had been a Communist in his youth, and that error, trumpeted by Lawrence Johnson and amplified by Hearst columnists, had been sufficient to bar him from the TV round table, *Starring the Editors*. Wechsler had left the Party in 1932. He had thereafter criticized the vagaries of the Party line, defended Congressional committees even when he disliked their know-nothing members, and generally promoted in his newspaper a warm tureen of gossip and benign liberalism.

All but the most hostile legislators were content to let Wechsler and his paper alone. It spoke, essentially, to the New York City Jewish community, a group which the right had traditionally written off as unconvertible. Senator McCarthy, almost alone, saw Wechsler as a useful quarry. He had the editor subpoenaed, and began his investigation by informing Wechsler that the *Post* was, "in my opinion, next to and almost paralleling the *Daily Worker*. We are curious to know, therefore, why your books were purchased [by the U.S. Information Service]. We want to know how many Communists, if any, you still have working for you."

This sort of lurching diatribe was McCarthy's standard format for interrogation, permuted by HUAC Committeemen and the secular blacklisters. Wechsler offered the accepted defense: a recent attack by the National CP Committee. The recent Eisenhower victory was, said the chieftains, "a result of the Reuthers, Dubinskys, Wechslers *et al.* who paralyzed independent action by projecting the myth that Adlai Stevenson was an obstacle to the advance of reaction."

Wechsler glared at the Senator. "I am rather fond of this tribute," he said, "and it may perhaps have some bearing on your comment that I have not been active in fighting Communism."

McCarthy struck without coiling: "Did you have anything to do with the passage of that resolution? Did you take any part in promoting the *passage* of that resolution?"

Wechsler stammered a tardy, ineffective denial. "With that single stroke," he recalled, "McCarthy virtually ruled out the whole structure of evidence which I had wide-eyedly assumed would resolve the issue once and for all. Here indeed was a daring new concept in which the existence of evidence of innocence becomes the damning proof of guilt."

Thus all the minutiae, the bad reviews in the *Worker*, the slurs of Reds and fellow-travelers were invalidated. The blacklisted, and those who hovered on some gray list, able to work on some sound stages but not on others, awaited the final exclusion. The last line of self-defense had been severed. The winter of liberties had frozen the earth solid.

Wechsler soon decided that "silence was suicidal" in dealing with the investigators. After a pained delay he provided names of thirties Communists. "I submit [the names]," he stated, "because I do not propose to let you distort or obscure the clear-cut issue of freedom of the press involved in this proceeding."

"I did not see," he later wrote, "how I could persuade my perplexed countrymen that unwillingness to entrust such a list to McCarthy was different from the now stereotyped refusal of Communists to answer questions before Congressional committees."

Here in thirty-five words or less was the moral and psychological dilemma of the period, the true subtext of all judicial debate. The Fifth-Amendment Communist was a tautology to the public and the press. Indeed, Committeemen *liked* witnesses to invoke the Fifth; it produced a guilty verdict without the nuisance of a trial. For his part, McCarthy used the Fifth Amendment in the manner of a judo fighter, making the witness who wielded it fall of his own weight. The Senator's favorite maneuver was to inquire whether the victim had ever engaged in Red espionage. Offered a straight denial, McCarthy would reply, "You have just waived the Fifth Amendment insofar as the field of espionage is concerned," and put forth a series of questions about Communist associations, threatening prosecution upon failure to answer.

If the witness, anticipating this adroitness, declined to state whether or not he was engaged in espionage, McCarthy publicly concluded that he was a spy, as worthy of execution as Julius and Ethel Rosenberg, whose appeals were just then running out.

In certain criminal and Communist investigations, Elmer Davis' comment seemed correct: the privilege against self-incrimination was originally intended for the innocent; currently the guilty were getting the benefit. But it was also true, as Justice Hugo Black observed in the dissent of Rogers v. the United States: "On the one hand [witnesses] risk imprisonment for contempt by asserting the privilege prematurely; on the other hand, they might lose the privilege if they answer a single question. The Court's view makes the protection depend on timing so refined that lawyers, let alone laymen, will have difficulty knowing when to claim it."

There was no real answer to the dilemma provoked by the Fifth Amendment. The best the lawyers could produce were variations of Byzantine refinement. The Diminished Fifth, invented by Carl Foreman's counsel, Sidney Cohn, allowed a witness to deny present Party membership, but neither affirm nor deny his membership in the past. Under the *Augmented* Fifth the witness also denied present Party membership and refused to deny past membership, but deafeningly added that he was not sympathetic with Communism or its aims.

In this confusion, liberals chose to forget that it was *they* who had once cheered Congressional investigations from the bleachers, the grandstands and, on occasion, the dugout. When Justice Hugo Black was a Senator, he had published an approval of Woodrow Wilson's query: "If there is nothing to conceal, then why conceal it?" The *New Republic* of 1939 had editorialized, "Nothing holds the forces of darkness in check like a Senatorial searchlight always in readiness to be turned upon their activities." And John J. McCloy, former High Commissioner in Germany, now chairman of the Chase Manhattan Bank, pilloried the New Deal in a cruel reminder: "If the liberals had been more expressive when the so-called Congressional investigations of the thirties were studiously violating personal rights when business was the target, there would have been less likelihood of excesses in this day and age."

Early in 1953 Lillian Hellman attempted to banish that corrupt history and to impose some sanity on the present. Upon the receipt of a subpoena, she mailed a famous demur to Congressman Wood: "I am not willing . . . to bring bad trouble to people who, in my past association with them, were completely innocent of any talk or any action that was disloyal or subversive. I do not like subversion or disloyalty in any form, and if I had ever seen any, I would have considered it my duty to have reported it to the proper authorities. But to hurt innocent people whom I knew many years ago in order to save myself is, to me, inhuman and indecent and dishonorable. I cannot and will not cut my conscience to fit this year's fashions, even though I long ago came to the conclusion that I was not a political person and could have no comfortable place in any political group."

Wood replied that his Committee could not permit witnesses to set forth the terms under which they would testify. The resultant go-round of playwright and Committee resulted only in more confusion. Hellman was not and never had been a Communist, but her private code and her long association with Dashiell Hammett had made her intractable. Wood asked her, "Can you fix . . . a period . . . during which . . . you have not been a member of the Communist Party? . . . Were you yesterday?"

Hellman: "No, sir."

Wood: "Were you last year at this time?"

Hellman: "No, sir."

Wood: "Were you five years ago at this time?"

At the urging of her attorney, Joseph Rauh, Hellman hesitated. The Supreme Court had recently ruled that "disclosure of a fact waives the privilege as to details." In short, to admit membership or even fellow-travelership (the specifics were hazy) was to waive the privilege of withholding names. Rauh had been kicking Hellman under the table; he wished her to admit nothing. But in the end, when Wood asked, "Were you [a Communist] two years ago from this time?" Hellman gave her final "No, sir." When Wood asked, "Three years ago from this time?" she wearied enough to reply, "I must refuse to answer." It was from this reply that it was incorrectly deduced that Lillian Hellman had left the Communist Party somewhere around 1949.

2

By 1953 the House Un-American Activities Committee, like a no-star restaurant, swept down and anxious for new customers, let it be known that it was under new management. The dishes were the same, the ambience was identical. The waiters had not lost their sullen rudeness, and the bill of fare never varied. But the manager was indeed different. In 1948 Harold H. Velde, a former FBI agent, had sailed to Congress under the infectious slogan: "Get the Reds out of Washington and Washington out of the Red." Now, as the new chairman, Velde expanded his realm to include Hollywood and New York, where his Committee concentrated on still more entertainers. Artie Shaw, clarinetist, band leader, *Red Channels* listee and member of many front groups, described himself as a dupe and wept at his early inanities. In his contrition, Shaw and Congressman Doyle did a little turn worthy of Beckett:

Mr. Doyle: "You feel that the security of your Nation is more important—"

Shaw: "Than any individual."

Doyle: "—than your own personal status?"

Shaw: "Yes. I think it is more important—"

Doyle: "And you are placing—"

Shaw: "—than any individual status."

Doyle: "—the security of your Nation ahead of any embarrassment or loss of income?"

Shaw: "I think the security of the Nation affects millions of people and I don't think that any one person is more important than millions."

Doyle: "Thank you."

Shaw: "That is just about the way it sums up."

Jerome Robbins, the balding, fastidious dancer, choreographer and director, had committed a number of personal indiscretions. The Committee caught up with them and with him in 1953. Robbins had been threatened with loss of network and film assignments, and with worse, unless he proved fully cooperative. In May, with his lawyer R. Lawrence Siegel prompting him, Robbins testified loquaciously, but not altogether truthfully. He had been a rather indifferent member of the Party; he had joined, he insisted, because at the time of his membership the CP was vigorously opposing fascism and anti-Semitism. Now Robbins saw the Party's utter hypocrisy, that it vigorously promoted anti-Semitism where it seemed profitable. Having gone this far, Robbins felt compelled to name the members of his cell, among them Madeline Lee and Edward Chodorov (Lee and Chodorov had not met: Edward Chodorov was never a member of the Party). Other discrepancies were later noted; one member was in the Army overseas at the time Robbins fingered him. Robbins' testimony estranged him, for a time, from members of his own family. But it pleased the Committee mightily, particularly Representative Doyle. Earlier the Congressman had urged Artie Shaw to push patriotism on the bandstand. ("You might take a minute for a chosen word or two.") He instructed Robbins on the same theme. "You are in a wonderful place . . . to perhaps be very vigorous and positive in promoting Americanism in contrast to Communism. Let me suggest to you that you use that great talent which God has blessed you with to put into ballets in some way, to put into music in some way, that interpretation."

Robbins the meek stepped down. Stander the choleric came on, belching fire. To the Party administrators there were revolutionaries and there were rebels. The revolutionary acted in concert: he was no more individual than a zero is in the sum 100,000,000. A rebel is the 1, the soloist in the choir. Lionel Stander was a rebel. His very face could not agree with itself: one eye was gray, one brown. At his most prepossessing, Stander resembled a prince after a witch had finished with him. His vocabulary was aristocratic, but his appearance and deportment were pure gargoyle. The Committeemen, in their ignorance, had no idea that their witness had been just as impudent to the Bolsheviks. John Howard Lawson himself had once considered the actor an outrageous example of how a Communist should *not* act before strangers.

Now Stander became part of another textbook, written by the enemy. His role as negative exemplar, however, remained unchanged. Other leftists traditionally appeared before the probers with austere props: a lawyer and, somewhere in the audience, a concerned wife or friend. Stander entered with two dynamite broads. Other witnesses spoke in taut, modulated voices. Stander, whose normal tone was that of a rasp file on granite, bitched in loud, blasphemous tones. Not for him the haughty indignation or the *Pravda*-esque accusations of Fascism Reborn. He demanded that the television lights be turned off because he appeared on TV only for entertainment or for philanthropic purposes. This road show, he indicated, was neither. The actor had been detoured from the touring company of *Pal Joey*, where he was playing a low comic villain, and he continued to polish his part.

Representative Wood, Counsel Tavenner and Chairman Velde all tried to ride Stander, but it was three men on a horse—strictly farce. The witness, named as a Communist by Marc Lawrence, charged that Lawrence was a psychopath, and supplied the Committee with the names of the informer's shrinks. Stander then offered citations of his patriotism from the Red Cross, the War Bond drive and the Treasury Department; he claimed to have exposed union racketeering even before Westbrook Pegler, and told the Committee of *"real* subversives—a group of ex-Bundists, America Firsters and anti-Semites, people who hate everybody, including Negroes, minority groups and most likely themselves."

When Stander implied that these people were none other than the HUAC, Mr. Velde warned the witness that he might be forced by marshals to leave the room.

Stander modestly lowered his eyes and croaked, "I am deeply shocked, Mr. Chairman." A minute later he growled, "I am not a dupe, or a dope, or a moe, or a shmoe, and everything I did—I was absolutely conscious of what I was doing. . . ." His current appearance, he went on, was due solely to his interest in

the buck; his agent had been told that if Stander would swear
to non-Communism he would have his own TV program and a
salary of $150,000. Every question was deflected with a pratfall.
Even when asked about the presence of his wife at a cell meeting, Stander stood off the invader. Which wife? he asked. Apart
from his throaty impudence, Stander made only one permanent
contribution to the combat against the blacklist. His subpoena,
he said, was tantamount to being banned "because people say,
'What is an actor doing in front of the Un-American Activities
Committee?' "

What, indeed, except to fatten a blacklist, or to make the
hearing a public confessional?

Velde hastily dismissed the dangerous jester and put on Jay
Gorney, composer of "Brother, Can You Spare a Dime?" Con-
sulting occasionally with his counsel, Bella Abzug, Gorney was
almost deferential in his invocation of the Fifth; the *pro forma*
protests were back in style. The Committeemen relaxed. Once
again jurisprudence was academic gray. The fauve had gone.

Outside the courtroom, Stander posed, between blondes, for
autographs and a few more laughs. His hand shook as he lit his
cigarette. It had not been so frivolous after all. Caliban would
not work in an American film for a decade. Before finding
asylum in Europe he was approached by the FBI for information; studio lawyers let it be known that he would be ideal for
the still unpublished article "I Was a Sucker for a Left Hook."
To survive, Stander became a customer's man for a downtown
brokerage house. The intimate fellow-traveler, the railer against
the tide, had found his salvation not in the Fifth Amendment,
but from that implacable, unprejudiced villain—Wall Street.

Not all the witnesses were so hostile as Stander or so rigidly
doctrinaire as Gorney. Karin Kinzel Burrows was happy to give
names. Her husband, Abe, had been almost amnesiac on the
stand; he could not remember dates, associations, friends. Yet
he recalled, in his defense, the moment when Abraham Polonsky

had invited him in for a drink and asked him to get busy in progressive organizations. The comedy writer had answered with indifference; Polonsky had turned away. "I made a note," Burrows told the Congressmen, "that I never got a drink." Mrs. Burrows was less trivial. She had left the Party at the time of Maltz's self-abnegation, repelled at the notion of a believer forced to turn against himself. Then she gave the Committee more than twenty names of colleagues from the time when she was a believer. The Committeemen charitably refrained from asking her about Abe.

Back in 1951 director Robert Rossen had been one of those recalcitrants who claimed Constitutional rights not to cooperate with the Committee—a maneuver that had cost him $100,000 in film contracts. Now that venality could not be charged, Rossen testified that he had been a member of the Party, and named his names and associations. The testimony, like that of so many others, was Caligarian, the history of a somnambulist who, after the thirties, walked through drama, scarcely believing what he heard himself saying. Out trotted the Maltz affair, the Trials— and all the other lethal valleys of the Communist experience. Out, too, came fifty-seven names, all inconsiderable, like letters cut into a statue in a forgotten public square, worn by rain and wind, obscured by guano and time.

Rossen concluded the Committee's hearing in New York. He was thanked profusely by Harold Velde, and the public was informed that the Congressmen now had "other duties to fulfill besides chasing Reds, so to speak."

The other duties included probing of the clergy in what Velde called "the church field"; investigation of the universities and examination of those who would ask clemency for the Rosenbergs, among them Albert Einstein, who urged intellectuals not to testify before the Committee because "this kind of inquisition violates the spirit of the Constitution."

Before totally packing it in, Velde and his associates gleaned some more intelligence. They were amused to learn from loose-lipped cooperators the code words of the enemy. In show-business circles, when a Communist spoke to another Communist about a third person, that person was designated as "terrific"—which meant he was a Red. A good guy meant a fellow-traveler. A bastard designated an active anti-Communist. The Committeemen were also delighted to hear the pleas of several union men, once activists, now close-mouthed, fearful takers of the Fifth who begged the chair not to ask their addresses because, said one, "I have small children and we have been molested by some hoodlums; my wife suffered a nervous breakdown and we have had to move out. We are in a new home now." This plea could, in earlier days, have been put down as Red treacle. But by 1953 patriotism had indeed been appropriated by the lout.

3

The Shirley Templesque plea, "Mommy, is it true you're a Communist?" seemed to have been scripted by the Hollywood Ten in one of their most saccharine anti-fascist melodramas. Nevertheless, it had been articulated with authentic concern by one of Jean Muir's sons who had been badgered in school. Dalton Trumbo's son, surveying his father's plight, loudly announced that when he grew up he was going to become a capitalist, a remark vaguely reminiscent of those children in Czechoslovakia who wished, when they became adults, to be Russians, because Russian soldiers ate three times a day. Albert Maltz's children had endured harassments in Mexico City and the United States. In the East, Sidney Buchman's daughter, Sue, was called the Big Red who went to Little Red [Schoolhouse].

The paroxysms of hysteria shook both terminals. Julius and Ethel Rosenberg's last plea for clemency was denied. In an ecstasy of righteousness, the left held a final, futile rally in

Washington. On the line of demonstrators, Madeline Lee Gilford met Jerome Robbins' sister, Sonya, who had, she said, forbidden her children to talk to their uncle. "If this keeps up," Sonya told Madeline *"you* could be in a concentration camp. We could all wind up in concentration camps. Who knows where this can end?"

In New Mexico, problems were less speculative. Outside Silver City, Herbert Biberman and his crew were finishing their film *Salt of the Earth.* Written in clanking, agitprop prose by Michael Wilson, *Salt of the Earth* explored the difficulties of noble Mexican laborers confronted with vicious bosses. Its financing came, in part, from the old Stalinist International Union of Mine, Mill and Smelter Workers, long since expelled from the CIO. If the movie faithfully resurrected the bromides of the thirties, its enemies also acted like lynch-mob cartoons from the *New Masses.* Local vigilantes riddled the exiles' car with bullets. Several union officials were beaten senseless. The film's star, an untrained Mexican, was deported to her native country before the film's completion.

During the picture-making, Congressman Jackson did more violence to the property on the floor of Congress. The picture, he said, was "being made in the state of New Mexico, not far from the Los Alamos Proving Grounds and, as Mr. Victor Riesel points out in his article, 'Where you try to hide secret weapons, you find concentrations of Communists.' . . . In effect, this picture is a new weapon for Russia . . . the production company of this picture also imported two auto carloads of colored people for the purpose of shooting a scene of mob violence."

Biberman, for whom art and propaganda were forever synonymous, nonetheless had a few ideas of his own. The Negroes were not film agitators, they were crew members. The Congressman, quite understandably, had never heard of black technicians working on a movie.

Neither, apparently, had Roy Brewer, chairman of the Hollywood AFL Council. Still the town's stainless-steel anti-Communist, Brewer resented the very attempts to film *The Salt of the Earth*. Yet, he held his fire. Brewer had lately amended his crusty approach to political wrongos. No longer did he play the ruthless prosecutor. In 1953 he preferred the part of father-confessor, guide to the tortured and lorn; John Huston and José Ferrer had recently been restored by his ministrations.

Huston, recalled Brewer, "thought we were just out to smear people because they were liberals. We were able to show him how the underground had laid down specific procedures to dupe him." The "underground" consisted of the "unfriendly" Howard Koch, Huston's longtime assistant. "Huston was sure the organizing of the Committee for the First Amendment was his own idea," said the union chief, who employed the psychological strategy of the MKVD. "We were able to cast doubt as to that and by reconstructing the meetings to show how the ideas he thought were his had been carefully and shrewdly planted." Ferrer was another happy example of the reconstructed liberal. "He was confronted," said Brewer, "by an intelligent anti-Communist approach and he responded magnificently."

No star was too blonde, no vehicle too frivolous for the union chief with the art of gold. One evening Brewer received an anxious call from Paris. Zsa Zsa Gabor, her Hungarian accent suddenly deprived of its kittenish quality, asked whether she should appear in a new picture directed by Jules Dassin. Brewer advised the star that the choice was entirely up to her. But he thought she should know that Dassin had recently been identified by Frank Tuttle and Edward Dmytryk as a member of the Communist Party, and that the director had not made himself available to Committee subpoena—which was why he was now working in Europe. Zsa Zsa, a quick study, saw the point.

It was with fresh calm and assurance, then, that Brewer could write to Congressman Jackson in re *Salt of the Earth*: "The Hollywood AFL Council assures you that everything which it can do to prevent the showing of *The Salt of the Earth* will be done."

An industry adviser gave Jackson some further details on censorship:

> If the Picture Industry wants to prevent this motion picture from being completed and spread all over the world as a representative product of the United States, then the industry needs only to do the following.
>
> Be alert to the situation.
>
> Investigate thoroughly each applicant for the use of services or equipment.
>
> Refuse to assist the Bibermans . . . in the making of this picture.
>
> Be on guard against work submitted by dummy corporations or third parties.
>
> Appeal to the Congress and the State Department to act immediately to prevent the export of this film to Mexico or anywhere else.
>
> > Sincerely,
> > *Howard Hughes*

During this Hughes conspiracy Biberman made an unfortunate but wholly unexpected discovery: his cutter had been reporting regularly and secretly to the FBI.

1953 was a brisk time for the Bureau, which since 1947 had been granting audiences to frightened performers and writers anxious to clear themselves. Lee J. Cobb found that refusing aid to Alvah Bessie did not constitute sufficient anti-Communism. When employment dwindled, he consultd the FBI, then was granted an audience *in camera* with William Wheeler, investigator for the House Un-American Activities Committee. Cobb was alone; he wished no counsel because he wished to invoke no amendments. The actor unloaded his cargo of barricaders with indecent carelessness, for he knew that his testimony was shortly to be published. Phil Loeb and Sam Jaffe were, said

Cobb, active in a far-left caucus within Actors' Equity, "though I never knew them to be Communists. And I don't mean by mentioning their names to suggest that they were."

Cobb's only new revelation was but one more custard pie to be flung at that thoroughly stained and melancholy target, John Howard Lawson, who had once taken it upon himself to revise Stanislavski. In a West Coast "project" with young actors and writers, the old revolutionary had employed the absolute standards of hindsight. Under Lawson's baton the Russian director's theories were tinctured with Stalin's newest doctrines. "The project failed miserably," recalled Cobb, "because the moment we departed from the text as published by Stanislavski we destroyed the most important aspect of it, and consequently I resigned." Stanislavski altered by the revisionist Lawson, rejected by the disillusioned Cobb, who informed upon his colleagues, most of whom were as disenchanted as the witness. Reflections in a mirror facing a pool; an infinity of betrayals. Thus in 1953 did the Party faithful continue to burn the Party faithful.

At about this time Vincent Hartnett decided to re-enter the neglected field of journalism. His article "Red Fronts in Radio, TV" was published in the always receptive *American Legion Magazine*, this time under his own byline. The piece contained the usual defamatory remarks, finger-wagging polemic and fear for the nation's future. Broadcasting was still in the hands and throats of the Reds, and all—well, almost all—the sponsors and managements were asleep at the mike.

There were, however, a few vigorous and politically reliable companies, and Hartnett was happy to name them. Behind this gesture lay the raw elements of extortion. Hartnett later reconstructed his techniques of English composition: "I told Stuart Peabody, who was in effect Advertising Director of the Borden Company, that I had written [the about-to-be-published] article when he asked if I would serve them as a consultant." This, Hartnett concluded, put him in a "peculiar position as a journalist. . . . Ethically I could not seek to withdraw the article." What, then, was a writer to do?

He was to exceed himself. After the Peabody offer, Hartnett inserted his emendations in italics: *"It is emphasized that Pall Mall and the Borden Company, when alerted by Legionnaires and others to the situation . . . obviously finally took all appropriate measures to correct the situation."* The Borden Company eventually paid the blacklister a $10,000 retainer. Every penny of it was earned in two sentences inserted in the galley proofs: "Judging from the fine talent now being used on *Big Story* and *T-Men*, it seems evident that the sponsors, Borden in particular, have an effective policy not only of providing splendid entertainment but also of making positive contribution to Americanism. For this they deserve the support of all patriotic Americans."

It must not be concluded by these melancholy and fearful performances that the blacklisters and their companions were without mercy, or that the old left was entirely friendless. Certain Congressmen, brought close to money or power, chattered generously, like Geiger counters in the presence of pitchblende. LUCY NO RED, SAYS JACKSON, FANS LOVE HER, DESI, TOO, boomed the autumn headlines. Jackson was Congressman Donald Jackson of California. Lucy was Lucille Ball and Desi was her husband, Desi Arnaz. Their show *I Love Lucy* was then at its apogee: CBS had paid Lucy and Desi eight million dollars for a thirty-month contract. Walter Winchell, irked by Ed Sullivan's intermittent disclosures of Commies in show business, had scooped the world by hinting that Lucille Ball in her early days had been a Red. And as it turned out, Winchell had some admissible evidence. In 1936 the young actress had indeed registered as a Communist in the Los Angeles primary election. True, she had not voted, but the stain remained. Had Lucy remained a batty, lightweight comedienne, she would have been whisked from the air, deprived of reputation, income and future. Performers had been blacklisted for much less, and on shabbier credentials. But Lucy had grown; she and her husband now controlled Desilu, a corporation larger and greedier than the Warner Bros. studio of 1947. The chorine now controlled a big piece of Celluloid City, and Donald Jackson, acutely aware that politics is property, and suddenly anxious for Justice, called a press conference. Playing Daddy Warbucks to Lucy's Little Orphan Annie, he told television audiences that for years the HUAC had been cognizant of Lucille Ball's political gaffe, but had not thought it "proper" to disclose it. He had summoned the press because the rumor-mongers, left unchecked, might do "irreparable damage" to the comedienne. The next day he handed the press Lucy's testimony, given in secret to a member of the California Un-American Activities Committee. It was her grandfather Fred Hunt, she said, who had wanted her to vote Communist. "All through his life he had been a socialist, as far back as Eugene V. Debs, and he was in sympathy with the working man as long as I have known." Fred Hunt's radical agitation seemed limited to exhorting the family maids to ask for salary increases. Lucy and her brother Freddie had registered as Communists, she claimed, merely to do Grandpa a favor. He was stroke-ridden and failing; no one wished to get him exercised. But, Lucy underlined, "I at no time intended to vote that way."

Her husband hastened to her side. "There's no doll more patriotic than this one," he cracked in the quirky Latin tone familiar to fifty million viewers. "There's nothing red about that girl except her hair. And even that isn't legitimate." After those reassurances there was nothing left but the press conference, held around the Arnaz swimming pool. Amidst the beer and ham and cheese sandwiches, Lucy and Desi chatted with reporters. In case anyone was unkind enough to mention Lucy's ancient interest in the Hollywood Ten, four press agents stood by to parry the curious: one from CBS, one from MGM, where Lucy and Desi had just completed a film, one from Philip Morris, sponsor of *I Love Lucy*, and one, of course, from Desilu

Productions. This conference was, despite its tone of strained levity, yet another secular version of the Committee, with the witnesses called upon to malign themselves and their own families. It remained for Desi to summarize the psychology of the moment. The late Fred Hunt, he said, was "a wonderful guy, a lovable guy—the kind of guy who wanted everybody in the world to be happy and have more money. . . . In 1936 it was a kind of a joke, a kind of very light thing. If Grandpa was alive today, we might have to lock him in a back room."

ELEVEN

1

CLEARLY, the scattershot wounding of innocents could not continue. Despite the increasingly close security checks and shrewdly extended lists, there existed no reliable method of protection and prosecution. Into this great, inviting vacuum rushed Aware Inc. In December of 1953 the newly incorporated group announced an action program "monitoring and investigating . . . Communist influences in all the varied aspects of entertainment; distribution of facts on the organizations and individuals employing Communists and fellow-travelers and denying employment to non-Communists."

The president of this vigorous secular body was no embittered upstart, anxious for name or reputation. Godfrey Schmidt, a lawyer of Thomistic wit, had long ago established an anti-Communist position. In 1941, as Deputy Industrial Commissioner of New York, Schmidt had attempted an investigation of subversives. These unclean persons were to be dismissed from positions in the State Labor Department. But Schmidt planned to investigate some four thousand employees, and this was soon deemed prohibitively expensive and time-consuming. The Commissioner's plans were not aided by certain exhumations from his speech before the Catholic Central Verein. To this traditional, devout gathering he had declared democracy

"divinized" in the United States and that "the whims of convictions of 20 percent of the people" had been allowed to
become "the guiding policy of the government, bestriding and
coercing the other 80 percent."

To Schmidt the government must have seemed a haven of
saboteurs totally beyond redemption. He was to find the private
sector far more congenial. A scholar in Constitutional law,
Schmidt lectured at Fordham University and practiced privately
(one of his clients was Francis Cardinal Spellman, who once
found Schmidt useful in a dispute with cemetery workers). And
he seemed to dream periodically of a new investigation, unin-
hibited by the Constitution. By the early 1950's Schmidt had become an adornment of McCarthy rallies, and his vision had
cooled and hardened into an institution.

Schmidt's colleagues at Aware Inc. were a crew of varying
skills and predictable allegiances. Late in 1953 Mrs. Jack Gilford
had attempted to trace the source of her husband's troubles at
NBC. The radio actress had assumed her best secretarial voice
and dialed Lawrence Johnson's private number in Syracuse. She
was, she said, speaking for the President of NBC, Sylvester
"Pat" Weaver. "Weaver?" demanded the grocer over the crack-
ling wire. "*Ned* Weaver?"—and suddenly the buzzard was
flushed. The announcer Ned Weaver had been secretly noting
his colleagues' opinions at meetings of the American Federation
of Television and Radio Artists. Those who appeared in a pink
gel were reported to Syracuse; the Dungey troops took it from
there to the networks. Now, in Aware's atmosphere of militance,
Weaver cast off the role of secret agent. He became an executive
blacklister, first vice president of Aware. Other officials included
Richard Keith, Jean Owens and Vinton Hayworth, all, conven-
iently, members of AFTRA. Schmidt himself was a member of
that union. On twenty-eight programs he had been the children's
storyteller for NBC. Those familiar with his anti-labor bias wondered why Schmidt had bothered to maintain his union dues;
now they knew. Other officers of Aware needed no link with

AFTRA to be useful. Vincent Hartnett supplied his dossiers, newly swollen with damnations. Paul Milton, neglected by Merle Miller, also sat, perennially hopeful, on Aware's board of directors.

Milton, Aware's weedy, timorous middle-manager, was a writer of considerable talent. Unhappily, the talent had nothing to do with writing. Before the inauguration of this greatest and final blacklisting enterprise, he had striven for a career in the arts. According to Milton, the confection of several *Mr. and Mrs. North* radio scripts had secured him a position as scenarist for the hour-long *Treasury Men in Action*. In fact, his ascent was not so elementary. *T-Men* had been fired upon by the blacklisters. To protect itself, it had called upon a bodyguard, the peerless Vincent Hartnett, who was commissioned Clearance Consultant to the show. The staff writer at the time was Sheldon Stark, a personage whom Hartnett and Milton had found "controversial." The *T-Men* producers obediently cut loose the albatross and, several months later, hired another albatross: Paul Milton. The new writer lasted for only one show; he had other flesh to fry.

Abruptly barred from commercial broadcasting, Stark found *his* career a bit more fragile. Through a devious friend he obtained an assignment to write radio scripts for the United Nations. After Stark completed the work, federal authorities denied him payment. He had, it seemed, been named as a subversive before the Senate Internal Security Subcommittee. Stark demanded a confrontation with his accuser. Rather surprisingly, the government arranged the meeting. Milton, suddenly very tentative and unsure, said that Stark was not all bad. Uninformed, perhaps, but certainly no Red. Stark received full clearance and returned to commercial broadcasting. He had lost more than two years of employment.

Milton was quick; there was no need to warn him twice. By 1954 he had learned to distinguish between the use and the abuse of power. For Aware Inc. he was careful only to abuse.

The case of Everett Sloane provides a *précis* of his manner. Since *Citizen Kane,* Sloane's exothalmic performances had been a staple of films and broadcasts. Shortly after the publication of *Red Channels* Sloane found himself mysteriously graylisted, although he had been nothing more subversive than a member of Orson Welles' Mercury Players. Upon investigation he found that it was not his associations that the producers feared. It was his name. On page 136 of *Red Channels* there was a Sloane with a citation condemning the American Legion and the hydrogen bomb. It was *Allan* Sloane who was listed, not Everett, but producers of the fifties could not make subtle distinctions. Everett Sloane, like Sheldon Stark, sought solace from the U.N. "I found out," he recalled, "that if you worked for the U.N. Radio more than twice . . . you were required to obtain the same status as a permanent employee and that included submitting to an FBI check." Sloane obtained copies of a memo from the Secretary of State to the Secretary General. "After a full field investigation," the paper stated, "it has been determined there is no reasonable doubt as to the loyalty of Everett Sloane to the Government of the United States." There was only one officer who thought himself above the Secretary of State: Paul Milton. Sloane sought him. Milton smiled indulgently. "I take this document with a grain of salt. We at Aware have different standards of clearance than the United States Government's agencies. We are a little more stringent. We feel they are a little too lenient."

To what bureau, then, should Sloane hie himself? "Well," Milton advised, with infinite Jamesian qualifications, "I suggest that you let me arrange a meeting for you with Mr. Hartnett, at which meeting perhaps you and he can evolve some statement that you will make that will be satisfactory to Mr. Hartnett. And will also prove satisfactory to, perhaps, the people who are not presently hiring you."

Sloane, a beaky, restless man of intemperate disposition,

refused to resolve this simple equation, and waited out the winter.

There were reasons to expect a general thaw. Many black-listees could sense crocuses beneath the snow in 1954. Senator McCarthy's Napoleonic adventure had taken him too far into America. In the Senate the skids were luxuriously greased; censure beckoned. How long, then, could it be before the binary passions of security and subversion burned themselves out?

The blacklistees failed to understand that McCarthy was *sui generis*. He lampooned candidates ("Alger—I mean Adlai"), he juggled names. He broadened his half-shaven infectious grin and provided the base for a thousand political cartoons. But once condemned, he lost his grip on the pillars and fell alone. The Senator pulled neither the government nor its enemies with him. To the end, he barked at his own medicine show, aided only by shills. Rabbi Benjamin Schultz, long obscured by bigger hysterics, came out from the shadows to stand beside the blooded warrior, and to announce that the U.N. was a cesspool of traitors and Communists. The diminishing crowd, in unre-quited passion for their country, clapped hands in time to the ballad "Nobody Loves McCarthy But the People, and We Just Love Our Joe." But the networks refused to play the song.

And the blacklisters thrived. In fact, 1954, the year of the censure, was their vintage period. By now a poorly prepared *New York Post* series on blacklisting had been reprinted and distributed and passed out of mind, remembered chiefly by Vincent Hartnett, who overheard everything and forgave nothing.

Widening his gyre, Hartnett found that Kim Hunter, along with several other interested parties, had paid for the reprinting and distribution of the *Post* series. The other actors were of mild interest to Aware Inc. But Hunter provided an authentic challenge. Two years before, for her supporting role in A *Street-car Named Desire*, she had won an Academy Award. It would be difficult indeed to hobble such a praised talent. But not impossible. Within two years the master blacklisters had made her almost unemployable. To his client, the American Broadcasting Company, Hartnett had written, "In my opinion you would run a serious risk of adverse public opinion by featuring on your network James Thurber and Kim Hunter." Hartnett experienced a twinge at one of those names and he sought to assuage his pain. "I am aware of Thurber's battle with failing eyesight," he reported. "However, the fact remains that he had a front record during the late thirties and was involved in one front in 1947. Many will defend him as merely a militant libertarian. But it is also a fact that his works have been in great favor in Communist circles."

By 1954 Kim Hunter found herself restricted to a single TV performance—as Ella Logan's substitute on *Janet Dean, Registered Nurse.* Her press agent, Arthur Jacobs, sought to clear his client by employing the traditional sanitation devices: Roy Brewer and the Motion Picture Alliance. But the balance of power had suffered a continental shift. Brewer could only advise Jacobs that "an affidavit would be necessary that would be acceptable to Mr. Hartnett." The agent prepared a statement guaranteeing that his client was "not sympathetic to the Left Cause"; that, like Edward G. Robinson, she had appeared in Arthur Koestler's "violently anti-Communist *Darkness at Noon.*" Did the blacklister have a dossier on Hunter, and would Hartnett allow her to have a peek at it?

Hartnett replied that his files contained numerous front activities of Miss Hunter. To gain access to them would cost the client, say, $200? Here communications frayed. Kim Hunter imprudently became incensed and told the blacklisters what they could do with their dossiers. Hartnett was deeply wounded. "Here's not Miss Hunter but a public relations man," he claimed, "who probably makes five G's a year on this. On some accounts his probable retainer is fifty G's a year, and . . . I think I would be a complete ass if I did it for nothing."

That cranky tone was the subtext of many Hartnett communiqués of the period. The demands on his time and space grew so heavy that he contemplated the abandonment of his home-cum-office uptown; he scarcely had time to reflect any more. His closest associates found him irritable. Lawrence Johnson himself once felt compelled to indicate an error in research. He received a reply couched in middle dudgeon. How was he to know, Hartnett demanded, that the supposedly left-winged actor Marvin Miller was actually a dues-paying member of the Motion Picture Alliance—and that Miller had filed a letter with Roy Brewer? As a matter of fact, the ace investigator claimed, he had "no responsibility to go out looking for these things when an individual has created by his own public activity an unfavorable record."

Worse still, Hartnett was being teased by his clients. Periodically, the American Broadcasting Company sent him names for approval or censure. On one list were Henry James, Owen Wister and Arthur Schnitzler. Perhaps Hartnett perceived two thirds of the insult. The authors of *The American Scene* and *The Virginian* were passed gratis. The writer of *La Ronde* was another matter. It cost ABC $2 to learn that Arthur Schnitzler (1862–1931) had "no record."

By 1954 it must have been clear to Hartnett and to other officers of Aware Inc. that their organization rested neither on legal nor, despite vigorous pretense, on purely philosophical grounds. It was, *au fond*, a public-relations agency engaged in the compelling business of engineering mass consent. With a membership that never exceeded 350, and a very small treasury, Aware concentrated on the power of the missive. Letters to influence government policy, it told its audience, "should not go only to those with whom you agree, but also those you oppose. Your letter may not convert, but it will emphasize that opposition exists."

Letters to influence public-opinion media, the bulletin went on, "should be about 300 words. The *New York Times* prefers letters beginning, 'Your splendid editorial yesterday.' Few papers enjoy publishing letters critical of themselves. Therefore begin your letter if possible with some praise, then develop your point." To radio and television functionaries, plaintiffs were urged to gripe in controlled, reasonable terms. "State your views briefly, with a supporting reason or two," said the bulletin tersely. "Violent letters are dismissed as crackpot."

The Aware membership was saddened by the addendum: "Members earning their livelihood in entertainment communications find it understandably risky to express themselves on entertainment issues. In such cases, friends and relatives may be found willing to write the desired letters." The sleeve of the blacklister had been caught in machinery he had designed.

2

To the wounded observers of the fifties, no personal or professional severance occasioned more comment than the creative divorce of Arthur Miller and Elia Kazan. Shortly after Kazan's great defection, Miller gave Broadway his metaphorical pronouncement on political hysteria, *The Crucible*. Falsifying history where it suited him, Miller presented the seventeenth-century witch-hunts of Salem, Massachusetts, informed by a fifties social conscience. In the drama John and Elizabeth Proctor, a stolid farming couple, are denounced as Devil-worshipers by the adolescent hysteric Abigail Williams. Proctor is willing to confess to false misdeeds, but the prosecutor, Deputy Governor Danforth, is a monster of legal conformism. He is dissatisfied with self-incrimination. Danforth wants names. "I speak my own sins," replies Proctor, in a tone the author was soon to use before the committee. "I cannot judge another. I have no tongue for it." In a line that indicated his old friend and director, Miller placed himself in Proctor's skin: "I have three children—how may I teach them to walk like men in the world, and I sold my friends?"

Danforth: "You have not sold your friends—"

Proctor: "Beguile me not! I blacken all of them when this [confession] is nailed to the church the very day they hang for silence!"

And so John Proctor, the good and silent martyr, hangs. The author, straining for poetic effect, gives a final stage direction: "Drums rattle like bones in the morning air."

It took very few interpretive skills to read the temper of the blacklist into *The Crucible*. But Miller himself did not push contemporaneity. Ticket holders, he said, were free to find within the text any echo they chose. That was their business, not his. Never mind that he had made Abigail a nubile, seductive seventeen-year-old, when at the time of the trials she was actually eleven. Never mind that had his ego projection John Proctor, a God-haunted, righteous man, actually seen devils, he would surely have given Danforth names, addresses and times.

Perhaps it was too much to ask of Miller that he work out his conceit. He wished to be marked on intent, not execution. Only after the *succès d'estime* did Miller's moral confusion become fully noted. He had spoken in contemporary voice in his previous work, but somehow to shout *J'accuse* in the blacklist era he felt the need to assume a costume and a New England accent. Miller's attempt at explication and apology demonstrated the same evasions as his stage manipulations. "The analogy seems to falter," he conceded, "when one considers that while there were no witches then, there are Communists and capitalists now, and in each camp there is certain proof that spies of each side are at work undermining the other. . . . But," he concluded, "I have no doubt that people were communing with and even worshiping the devil in Salem, and if the whole truth could be known in this case, as it is in others, we should discover a regular and conventionalized propitiation of the dark spirit."

At the bottom of *The Crucible*—which was about one inch from the top—lay the central doctrine: informing is cowardly, degenerate, wicked. But what of the man who sees not apparitions but authentic criminals? A robbery, perhaps, or a lynching? Or treason? By not informing, is he a hero, too? Or does he play himself or his society false? The question is a valid one, worthy of the most scrupulous exploration. Instead, it was exploited by the blacklist's celebrated informers, Elia Kazan and Budd Schulberg.

For several years Schulberg had played with the idea of a dockside melodrama. He had prepared one script and taken an option on Malcolm Johnson's Pulitzer Prize exposé of the New York waterfront. But, somehow, the film never got made. Then, one day, he received a letter from Gadge. Something on his mind, Kazan wrote. How about lunch? The author and director met for the first time and began a series of conferences. "We needed," Schulberg was to recall, "a new story, a stronger approach." They found it in the stations of Terry Malloy, failed pug and hired goon of the labor racketeer Johnny Friendly. At first Malloy is merely a tool, auxiliary to murder, placid fellow-traveler with racketeers, solicitous only of Number One. But once a Kazan hero has entered, a pair of blue eyes cannot be far away. Their owner is Edie Doyle, sister of the murdered man. In time, with the assistance of an inalienable waterfront priest, Father Barry, Malloy is inched to the witness stand. He is fully reformed only when his brother Charley, Friendly's shrewd, amoral hatchet man, is himself done in by the racketeer. There are times, Malloy learns, when breaking the gang code of silence is the only moral act, when informing is the sole "American" deed left to the corrupted. *On the Waterfront* never bothered to consider the complexities of sweetheart contracts between unions and shipowners; those owners were as remote from the picture as Arthur Miller. And though there were famous waterfront priests of the period, *Waterfront* gave its cleric an inflated, deafening role far in excess of his dramatic weight.

Still, those who theorized that genuflection to the Committee automatically meant a desertion of principle and a dissolution of talent were given a severe shock. Kazan had not forgotten how to direct; he was the only one who could contain Marlon Brando, releasing crescendos of that feline energy only at discrete moments. His cast of ex-boxers like Abe Simon and Tony Galento, his subordinate players, Eva Marie Saint and Rod Steiger, all supplied a passion that carried Schulberg's dialogue along with scarcely a pause for thought. It was only in retrospect that the film seemed rigged. Karl Malden, giving his customary imitation of a potato, was all knobbly surface as spiritual guide, a role restored to the Church after a brief seizure by the FBI. And the presence of those excellent players Lee J. Cobb and Leif Erickson, both refurbished members of the old left, was more than coincidental.

Nevertheless, the picture worked; it grossed four million dollars, won Brando an Academy Award and resurrected the reputation of its creators. In the process, it illuminated new areas in a period swollen with irony. Miller had, in effect, blacklisted Kazan, whose contributions to *All My Sons* and *Death of a Salesman* were almost as great as their author's. *The Crucible* was directed professionally, but without imagination, by Jed Harris.

Miller's "noble" characters lacked ignition; Schulberg's goons and pseudo-illiterates were presented in all their two dimensions by a master at emotional manipulation. *On the Waterfront* was the more effective play and the shrewder propaganda. In Schulberg's shoddy novelized version, however, the cosmetics cracked and peeled. Gone were Kazan's inflammable scenes, the classic exchanges of Brando and Steiger, the neurotic Leonard Bernstein score and the petroleum and grit of the New York waterfront. In its place was the author's intense self-justification ("and the truth, the raw, ugly, purging truth poured out of Terry . . .") plus a scrap of revelatory matter. In the film Terry gives evidence and triumphs. In the novel his body is discovered, punctured twenty-seven times by an icepick. The informer, apparently, wished death not upon his enemy but upon himself.

The following year Miller returned to the stage with his own waterfront saga, *A View from the Bridge*. Here, again, the essential subject was informing, seen from the far side. Betraying his wife's cousins, informing the immigration authorities of the relative's illegal entry into America, Eddie Carbone is cursed by his niece. She is Italian, but the torrent she releases is Universal Jewish. ("He bites people when they sleep! He comes when nobody's lookin' and poisons decent people. In the garbage he belongs!") Even as Terry Malloy is punctured in the novel, Eddie Carbone is stabbed by the man he exposes.

And *still* the exchange of informer and holdout was not finished. Nine years later Arthur Miller produced *After the Fall*, his *apologia pro sua dolce vita* with Marilyn Monroe, as well as a fast shuffle through his many cards of identity. *After the Fall* reunited Miller and Kazan after ten years of cold separation. Miller had never stated his disagreement publicly; Kazan, in turn, had never openly referred to his split with Miller. But for *After the Fall* a peculiar and unique confrontation occurred. For perhaps the only occasion, Kazan directed himself once-removed. The Kazan of *After the Fall* was a lawyer named Mickey who betrays and ruins his partner, Lou. In a brief exchange Miller had reconstructed the history of a wrecked collaboration:

> MICKEY: Lou, what am I protecting by refusing to answer? The Party? But I despise the Party and have for many years. Just like you. What am I defending? The fact is, I have no solidarity with the people I could name—excepting for you. And not because we were Communists together. But because we were young together. Because we—when we talked it was like some brotherhood opposed to all the world's injustice. Therefore, in the name of that

love, I ought to be true to myself now. The truth, Lou, *my* truth is that I think the Party is a conspiracy. I think we *were* swindled; they took our lust for right and used it for Russian purposes. And I don't think we can go on turning our backs on the truth simply because reactionaries are saying it. What I propose—is that we try to separate our love for one another from this political morass. Come with me and answer the questions.

LOU: Name . . . the names?

MICKEY: Yes. I've talked to all the others in the unit. They've agreed, excepting for Ward and Harry. They cursed me out, but I expected that.

LOU (*dazed*): Let me understand—you are asking my permission to name me? If you do it, Mickey, you are selling me for your own prosperity. If you want to use my name, I will be dismissed. You will ruin me. You will destroy my career. If everyone broke faith there would be no civilization! That is why that committee is the face of the Philistine! And it astounds me that you can speak of truth and justice in relation to that gang of cheap publicity hounds. Not one syllable will they get from me! Not one word from my lips! No—your eleven-room apartment, your automobile, your money are not worth this.

MICKEY (*stiffened*): You can't reduce it all to money, Lou! *That* is false!

LOU (*turning on him*): There is only one truth here. You are terrified! They have bought your soul!

MICKEY (*angry, but contained*): Have you really earned this high moral tone? . . . this . . . (*Lou's wife appears*) perfect integrity? I happen to remember when you first came back from your trip to Russia and I remember who made you throw your first version into the fireplace! I saw you burn a true book and write another that told lies! Because she demanded it, because she terrified you, because she has taken your soul.

And so it ended in a vituperation grown stale, in mock Ibsen and cold Odets, the song but not the singer. In a good play everyone is right. *After the Fall* was only a narcissistic exercise in which everyone seemed incorrect. Yet in that mock-sincere recital was the seedling Good Play. For both Mickey and Lou speak what amounts to a documentary. Betrayal was not invented by the Committee informers; righteousness did not come with the subpoena.

But in 1954 it *could* all be reduced to money and to mutual terror. Kazan, past insult and immune to Congressional investigation, had indeed done it for money. He had paid his dues and resumed his incessant dramatic glorification of the male adolescent. Miller, grown unpopular with certain critics, decided to take some time off from the theater and from politics. But neither the theater nor politics was through with Arthur Miller. His was one of the largest dossiers at Aware Inc. It was not to be wasted.

3

On December 9, 1954, after acrimonious debate, the membership of AFTRA elected a slate of officers satisfactory to Aware Inc. Some, like Vinton Hayworth, were official secular blacklisters. Others, like the radiant radio quizmaster Clayton Collyer, whose voice was always healthy and well-dressed, just came along for the fight. For Collyer there was no proved case of authentic blacklisting. Actors who were unemployed, he said, were simply being temperamental. Time, snow and dust would cover everything. All would be well, he soothed, if the membership would only wait. That was the MC's traditional answer to all problems. The plight of the black actor, perennially unemployable in the fifties, was introduced at one meeting. Wait, replied Collyer, wait and all will be well. "God damn it, I *can't* wait," said a young actor. "I have to make it now, while I've got my hair and my teeth." But Collyer remained bland and implacable, and Sidney Poitier learned that he would have to make it on his own, without union aid.

Still, many members of AFTRA opposed Aware Inc. both before and after the election. They, too, learned the folly of dissent. Immediately after the election an Aware bulletin found its way to the membership, the networks and all interested sponsors. Lee Grant, it said, "studied at the left-wing Actors' Studio and gave a militant speech at a memorial rally for J. Edward Bromberg." Jack Gilford, Martin Balsam, John Randolph, Ruby Dee had "what are considered significant *public records* in connection with the Communist-front apparatus."

Aware was not content with overt attack, although in listing these actors it consigned them to catastrophe. In addition to the bulletin, the organization used a sly, efficient method of terror familiar to those who have read their Poe. During a union debate a short, dapper character actor named Leslie Barrett noticed a man he had never met. The man appeared to be studying him—or was it, Barrett wrote in his diary, merely fancy? "The meeting ended," he noted, "and I left dejected and miserable, the reason being that the tenor of these meetings is fraught with fear, distrust and acrimonious debate. There is disagreement but few if any will speak out. Why? 'Because I have a little list,' so the saying goes, and if your name is listed you do not work. Strange as it may seem, I sensed I was being followed."

Two days later Barrett received a communiqué:

In preparing a book on the Left Theatre, I came across certain information regarding you. A photograph of the 1952 New York May Day Parade shows you marching.

It is always possible that people have in good faith supported certain causes and come to realize that their support was misplaced. Therefore I am writing you to ascertain if there has been any change in your position.

You are under no obligation to reply to this letter, as a matter of fact, I am under no obligation to write to you. However, my aim is to be scrupulously fair and to establish the facts. If I do not hear from you, I must conclude that your marching in the 1952 May Day Parade is still an accurate index of your position and sympathies.

I am enclosing a 3-cent stamp for a reply.

Very truly yours,
Vincent Hartnett

Barrett consulted the officers of AFTRA, who told him for God's sake to answer the letter. Hartnett was not to be ignored and *never* to be crossed. Barrett consulted the FBI; the desk men sanctimoniously assured him that they deplored private citizens who usurped the Bureau's function. Barrett then made a perilous move, scorned by all blacklisters: he called his lawyer. The counselor mailed a careful denial to Hartnett, swearing that his client Leslie Barrett had never marched in any May Day Parade and that the actor had no sympathy for or leanings toward Communism.

Outraged by this third-party intervention, Vincent Hartnett hastily countered:

Dear Mr. Barrett:

To my surprise I received today a letter dated December 13 from Mr. Klein, a lawyer. . . . As things stand at this point, I have not received from you any reply to my December 9th letter. I have no way of establishing that Mr. Klein is authorized to speak for you or that he has accurately transmitted to me your statement.

Parenthetically, is this the same Harvey L. Klein who is listed as having signed Communist Party nominating petitions in 1939–40?

Enclosed is a photograph of a group of marchers in the New York May Day Parade in 1952. The gentleman underneath the left arrow looks like you. Possibly I am mistaken. There may be some other actor in New York who closely resembles you. I have no desire to harass you.

My only desire is to establish the facts. Frankly, I am disappointed up to this point. In my previous experience in similar cases, people who had nothing to hide did not pull a lawyer into the discussion. They simply and candidly denied or affirmed the evidence. I hope you will be equally candid and direct. You will find me most sympathetic and understanding.

So sympathetic that when Barrett furnished him with a letter reaffirming both his and his lawyer's faith in the American way, Hartnett dropped both men from his list. "I appreciate your writing me," he replied. But he could not resist a final dig: "I hope you incurred no expense by the unnecessary move of calling in a lawyer. This only muddied the waters. Frankly, two people in radio and TV who know you thought the man pictured in the May Day Parade photo was you. Research to establish a positive identification of the man is continuing."

Not all of Hartnett's time could be taken in the search for truth. As officer and consultant to Aware Inc., he seemed to feel that the actors who opposed blacklisting—even those with no leftist affiliations—must perforce be aiding the Party. Worse still were those who would not contribute to the organization, or speak for it at union meetings—were not the first people Dante met in hell the neutrals?

In Aware's final bulletin for 1954 the closing paragraph showed the ominous Hartnett touch: "In the opinion of qualified observers the independent anti-blacklisting slate in AFTRA this year demonstrates the need for a full-fledged investigation of the entertainment industry in New York."

By now Representative Francis Walter had gained charge of the HUAC. Walter, a canny Pennsylvania Democrat who had openly criticized Harold Velde, Martin Dies and Joe McCarthy, could resist extremism only so long. He had begun his chairmanship of the Committee with a promise: the era of probes into specific professions was over. But the lure of show business soon proved as irresistible to Walter as it had been to his predecessors. In July of 1955 the Committee answered the fondest wishes of Aware Inc. The Representatives and investigators readied themselves for the last great raid on Broadway.

TWELVE

1

No, SAID THE Screen Writers' Guild contract. In accordance
with the agreement made with the Producers' Association,
Albert Maltz, writer of the first-draft screenplay of *The Robe*,
would not be given screen credit.

2

"The Borden Company in its previous program had so much
trouble with politically unreliable actors and pro-Communist
sympathizers that the agency made up this white list," David
Levy stated the Young and Rubicam position. "If you use it,
you can have the sale [of the weekly melodrama *Appointment
with Adventure*]."

"This list will have to be enlarged," David Susskind told him,
accepting the sale with his unique negative panache. "You will
be forced to enlarge it. You will come to understand that. Incidentally, this list is the most humdrum list of dead-beat, un-
talented actors I have ever seen."

3

Cinema Annex
3210 W. Madison Street
Chicago, Illinois
Gentlemen:
Like other loyal citizens, we of the American Legion have
known from the inception of the making of the motion
picture, *Salt of the Earth*, that it was thoroughly, through
and through, an endeavor on the part of Communistic
elements to produce the greatest Communist propaganda
picture ever developed in the United States of America.
. . . While it is your prerogative to show any picture you
decide to sell to your customers, we, however, do not believe it is becoming the dignity of your house to indicate
cooperation with the Communistic elements of our city
and nation. We trust there is sufficient time available to
replace *Salt of the Earth* with one whose complexion is not
identified with a foreign nation that has the objective of
conquest in accordance with their way of life, regardless of
bloodshed, be it the soldiers on the battlefield or the
women and children unfortunately caught in a war-torn
area.

> I remain
> Sincerely yours,
> *Edward Clamage, Chairman*
> *Anti-Subversive Commission*
> *Dept. of Illinois*

4

Arnold Forster, general counsel for the Anti-Defamation
League of B'nai B'rith, nourished a pragmatic philosophy. In an

ideal world, aspects of moral law could be argued until Dooms-day. But this *was* Doomsday, and methods of salvation had to be scrounged. His was the sorry, necessary task of clearance, the sandblasting of the sooty and vandalized. "If a man is clean and finds his way to me," he revealed privately, "the first thing I do is examine his record. I look particularly to see if it includes charges that he is a member of the Communist Party. Once I am convinced that he is not a Communist, or if he has been a Communist, has had a change of heart, I ask him whether he has talked to the FBI. If he hasn't, I tell him the first thing he must do is go to them and tell them everything he knows. I tell him to say to them, 'I am a patriotic citizen and I want you to ask me any questions you have in mind.'"

After the FBI, Forster led his anxious client through the intricate minuet of restoration. The first bow was to the American Legion. There, James O'Neil, if he was satisfied, waved him on with the reassurance, "I won't put anything in writing, but if anyone is interested have him call me."

Then came George Sokolsky and Victor Riesel from the Hearst Syndicate and Frederick Woltman from Scripps-Howard. "When I've gotten four 'affidavits' from key people like these," Forster confessed, suggesting the last hours of his client John Garfield, "I go to Jack Wren at BBD&O and to the 'security officer' at CBS. I wait a few days, then I telephone Wren. He may say, 'You're crazy. I know fifteen things this guy hasn't explained.' I say to him, 'What are they?' and he says, 'He didn't come clean.' So I send for the guy. He comes in and moans and wails and bangs his head against the wall. 'I have searched my memory,' he will say. 'I have questioned my wife and my agent. There's not a thing I can remember.'

"I call Wren back and he says, 'When your boy is ready to come clean I'll talk to him.' In that case we've reached a dead end. My boy has been cleared but he can't get a job."

Wren was not always so flinty. There were times when he told Forster, "I think you are right about this boy, but what do you want from me? I can't hire him." The listee then hunted for some producer willing to roll the dice and hire a "boy"—for a man in trouble always loses his majority along with his dignity. *If* the actor was lucky and found such a producer, and *if* his show was successful, and *if* no complaints were received by the network, then he was rehabilitated.

"If the attempt backfires and protests come in," Forster conceded, "the guy is through."

Of all the purification rituals, Forster favored the direct Wren-to-CBS approach. The Columbia Broadcasting System, despite its large casement displaying the anti-McCarthy journalism of Edward R. Murrow, was the most easily intimidated of all networks. Its loyalty oath, security officers and splendid relations with Aware Inc. made the network a citadel of Americanism. In 1955 an appearance on a CBS program constituted a visa to the white list.

5

Susan Strasberg (fifteen) was rejected for television appearances by Vincent Hartnett. Her father, Lee, had been listed in Hartnett's File #13 as the director of the Actors' Studio.

6

Harnett to Johnson: "I called Jack Wren about a woman in a crowd scene on the Robert Montgomery show last night."

7

"[This man's] confession," wrote Stewart Alsop, "is likely to initiate a serious investigation of the new post-war profession of the informer, and this could have good results for the political health of the United States." The confessor, it was revealed, had signed affidavits calling himself a liar. He had, it appeared, blacklisted and maligned the innocent for the highest purposes: power and money. "Matusow," reported Murray Kempton, "has done what no respectable person could do; he has shown up the last ten years of respectable anti-Communism."

The respectable anti-Communists, of course, would not allow Kid Nickels to escape with his *mea culpa* intact. With their prodding, federal machinery produced Resolution 131 ordering contempt-of-Congress citations for one Harvey M. Matusow, former aide of Senator McCarthy and Representative McCarran. Jail awaited the stubby, ectomorphic figure. But Harvey's natural ebullience allowed only a few hours for self-pity. Then he bounced back, glad to accept a sentence at Lewisburg Federal State penitentiary for his sins, eager to proclaim an enduring fondness for Joe McCarthy. "I liked him," Matusow was to admit. "He and I had the same little boy in us."

Boys will be boys; despite his affection for the rightists, Harvey abandoned his old pals to write a book, *False Witness*, that exposed the whole foul nest. He banged out the first chapters in Jack Anderson's office on the stationery of the J. Edgar Hoover Foundation, charting his progress from radical to "witness for the persecution," handyman to committees, "expert" on every sort of radical corruption but his own, inventor of Red plots in the Boy Scouts and to the New York public-school system, accuser of churchmen, actors, trade-unionists. In his coda he appeared in a new uniform: sackcloth, as a soul-sick wanderer in the temples of Las Vegas and Reno, unable to choose between a suicide and confession. Four eminent and reputable publishers spurned his ill-formed book, and it issued, at last, from the imprint of the old progressive Angus Cameron, the blacklisted former editor-in-chief of Little Brown, whom Harvey had once denounced as subversive. *False Witness* was an inefficient moral detergent for the author, however, and one afternoon he took the time to wander to Greenwich Village.

There he rang Jack Gilford's bell and offered his hand. "I'm Harvey Matusow," he said in his witness-stand tone of arrogance and insecurity. "I'm sorry." Gilford, for once without *ad lib,* could only extend his own hand in shock and wonder.

8

Dear Larry:

. . . Ben Grauer was bitter to Ned Weaver when the latter asked him to sign a letter for Aware and against condemning it but Grauer has been out of fronts since 1947. I am trying to make up my own mind about him . . . how would your boys feel about Ben Grauer in a show?

Sincerely,
Vincent Hartnett

9

Early in 1955 officers of Aware Inc. gave evidence that they were not wholly impervious to criticism. Most Reds, they knew, were impenitent nihilists. Still, there *were* a few whose souls deserved a second act. The script for that act was published by Aware under the title *The Road Back (Self-Clearance): A Provisional Statement of View on the Problem of the Communist and Communist-Helper in Entertainment Communications Who Seeks to Clear Himself.*

The little pamphlet was headed with an apposite quote: "—that they should have a change of heart and mind—performing deeds fitting this change"—Acts 26:20. This attitude of frigid piety was maintained throughout. The ex-radical must "seriously embark on . . . an intellectual and moral transition . . . it must be a voluntary surrender to the exigencies of reality, of truth, of love." Hatred of Communism, ran the catechistic pastiche, "is like hatred of sin and error: a moral obligation. This does not mean hatred of individual Communists. It means 'informing' in the noble sense of warning, educating, counseling. The sinful informer sells, for money or selfish advantage, the cause he knows to be right."

The road back offered a dozen rungs to decency, from the deep questioning of oneself (number one) to a return to religion (number twelve). Midway was the "voluntary and cooperative interview with the Federal Bureau of Investigation and a written offer to cooperate, as a witness or source of information, with the Committee on Un-American Activities of the House of Representatives, Room 225A, Old House Office Building, Washington 25, D.C."

As a supplemental police force, Aware reiterated its approval of the Stalinist formulae: state trial and public confession. For lagniappe, the pamphlet bombed the underground railway of such clearance specialists as Arnold Forster, Martin Gang and Jack Wren: "A final Comment: No expenses are imposed or necessary. Lawyers, publicity men and fixers usually do more harm than good."

The once faint redolence of duplicity grew unbreathable. Three members of AFTRA's board of directors were also directors of Aware, and, not coincidentally, the lawyer for AFTRA was Henry Jaffe, once the husband of *Red Channels'* most famous victim, Jean Muir. Jaffe had urged his wife to accept settlement rather than combat the blacklisters; he had urged the same on Philip Loeb. His was the voice of calmness, rationality, quietude. As he urged his clients, he quietly became a talent agent high in the favor of NBC executives.

Customarily, broadcasting thrives in an anaerobic environment; the process of secular blacklisting might have persisted as long as the cold war itself, save for Aware's unacknowledged capacity for self-destruction. Discontented with merely winning offices in AFTRA, Aware badgered those whom it had defeated in the union election. This attitude of avenging angel grew repellent to some of its sympathizers and infuriated almost all members to the left of Louis XIV. A few of the angrier dissidents decided to challenge Aware at the next election. In their angry naïveté they believed that they moved in an open society. Accordingly, they met at the Blue Ribbon Restaurant on West 44th Street, where Madeline Gilford made the mistake of reminding the assembly that Vincent Hartnett was a major author of the blacklist, that he first condemned his victims, then charged clients $7.50 a head for making a report on an actor.

Madeline Gilford, still the indomitable bitterball, was a radio actress; she enunciated clearly and well. The words were beautifully captured on Hartnett's bugging device, secreted near the speaker. When Jack Gould, television critic of the *New York Times*, wrote several columns attacking Aware, Hartnett trotted out his little tape-recorder and offered his guest a playback. The blacklister wished to clarify the record; it was typical of these subversives, he complained, to lie and smear. He did *not* charge $7.50 a head for making a report on an actor. As he had iterated time and time again until he was sick of it, the fee was only $5 for a first report. If a client wanted a recheck on the same actor, to make sure that the subject had signed no new petitions, joined no dangerous organizations, then there was an additional charge of only $2. Hartnett did *not* accept fees from artists who courted his counsel. Such advice was provided free of charge.

There was, of course, a *quid pro quo*. The artist would be expected to give the blacklister his version of radical history. Hartnett, who would never recover from his infatuation with radio drama, needed the information for his new publication, *File 13, Vol. 2*. It would be "an encyclopedia of the left theater." His fond hope, he told Gould, was to "clear up" some existing cases of mistaken identity.

Everett Sloane, it appeared, was only the first to be condemned because of a coincidental surname. A scenarist named Louis Pollock had suffered in the same way. Pollock had written six mildly successful films, including *Port Said* and *The Jackie Robinson Story*. In the year of the jackal, 1955, he found that his talent had somehow suffered a precipitous decline. No more of his scripts were purchased for film or television. It was only accidentally that he mentioned his problem to a knowledgeable producer, who later called to ask, mysteriously, if Pollock had been born in Hungary, if he had ever operated a clothing store in California and whether his name wasn't really spelled Pollack. And he was fifty-nine years old, wasn't he? No, the writer returned, he was fifty-five, he had been born in Liverpool, England, and he had never operated any store. "Ah," said the producer delphically, "we have you confused with someone else."

Pollock could not pry more revelations from his informant. He obtained them, instead, from the public library, where the records showed that in the spring of 1954 one Louis Pollack, clothing-store proprietor from San Diego, had taken the Fifth Amendment before the subcommittee of the HUAC. Pollock immediately retained Martin Gang, who wrote to Richard Arens, staff director of the Committee. Arens replied in a letter exuding regret over the confusion and embarrassment. "I very gladly point this out for your benefit or use," he added. By this time Pollock's use to the studios was nugatory.

Hartnett knew of other such cases and clucked dutifully over them. In his book there would be no such atrocities. He would insist on accuracy for his victims, and the truth would set them in chains. Hartnett's policy was attractive to a few union members who, numb with terror, were ready to revive the 1947 hit, properly dubbed by Lillian Hellman "The Judas Goat." But there were not enough stomachs capable of enduring those Hollywood scenes again. The Blue Ribbon militants soon multiplied into a sizable crowd. In March they circulated a petition calling for the union's condemnation of Aware Inc. "Certain members and officials," read the charge, "have openly associated themselves with an outside organization (Aware Inc.) which prints attacks upon AFTRA members and invites a Congressional investigation of the entire entertainment industry."

Aware proved equal to its billing. In May the organization dispatched a defense to union members: "Some individuals may have signed [the petition] in good faith, thinking they were 'protecting' certain other AFTRA members who . . . have been unjustly accused by AWARE of having Communist-front records. *The plain fact* is that members of AFTRA with *notorious* Communist-front records apparently succeeded in getting some unsuspecting AFTRAns to sign the letter with them, so that all of the signers *guilty and innocent alike*, would be in the same boat. Doesn't this technique sound familiar to you? Doesn't it strike you as a 'strange coincidence' that many—too many—members of our profession have suffered in the past through joining Communist fronts at the instigation of the *very same people* who recently roped unsuspecting members into signing . . . ?"

A valid question. Too many members had indeed suffered—all through the offices of Aware. The implication was very clear; new suffering hung from the branches, waiting a meal of fresh dupes.

The threat failed; the blacklisters had misread the entrails. They failed to understand, though the example of 1947 was still clear, that if there was one thing show business hated worse than a Communist it was a Congressman. That blacklisting inspired fear, but whitelisting engendered something worse: jealousy of the privileged. Finally, that while Aware loudly promoted the high animal cunning of the Communist-fronter, its members privately dismissed their opponents as boobs incapable of coherent resistance. Once this miscalculation was made, political defeat was inevitable. It began with a great ventilation of the indecencies and grievances of the past. At a charged AFTRA meeting some traditionally vocal actors exercised their political outrage—along with some performers whom the membership had rarely heard. Leslie Barrett, after initial strain, brought out his diary, with its shadowy and obscene details. His friends followed with similar atrocity stories.

Godfrey Schmidt, the great Constitutional expert, offered the blacklisters' position: "There is a clear intent expressed here in the anti-Aware resolution that another type of activity should be denominated blacklisting. That is to say, to tell the truth about candidates. . . . The truth, ladies and gentlemen: Every single line in [the Aware bulletin] is the unchallengeable truth, the best proof of it that none of you will dare, if you feel aggrieved, bring it to court, as you could. . . ." (One day a federal judge would receive the members as plaintiffs. For now, the AFTRA membership treated the *meeting* as a court.)

In reply to Schmidt's inflexible program, a minor radio actress named Elaine Eldridge testified that she was blacklisted by Aware "because I had accepted two years ago a telephone call which came to me from the National Committee of Arts, Sciences and Professions, asking me if I would be willing to teach on their staff. I said yes, and I went to one meeting at which the program was to be organized and it fell through. I never heard anything further from it. That was two years ago, and today that organization is still not on the Attorney General's list. So I think it is a little presumptuous and perhaps a little premature on the part of Mr. Schmidt to consider all these people as dangerous and menaces to our society."

Lee Grant, whose career had been propelled by her performance as the pathetic shoplifter of *Detective Story*, would suffer an abrupt decline shortly after the meeting. Her appearance at union gatherings would be more frequent than those she made in films or on stage. Still she could not be silent. "I think," she said, "the fact that our board members are sitting with a man, Vincent Hartnett, who is the author of *Red Channels* and helped to put out lists is a shameful, shameful thing and should not be tolerated in our union." The applause grew louder now. Schmidt's discomfort evidently rose a few dols; he came to resemble a man who suddenly makes out the crowd noise and realizes that it is chanting "Kill!" Harold Gary, an actor who looked and sounded as if he was auditioning for the part of a bookie, took a withering look at his tormentor: " . . . he uses the term 'Americanism' . . . I would like to know where Mr. Schmidt learned his Americanism. When I learned about Americanism—and I like to think of myself as a pretty good American—I learned nobody can appoint himself as a self-constituted judge and jury of his fellow man." (Applause.) "I don't know how long you have been an actor, Mr. Schmidt, if you are one, but I want you to know that you're playing with dynamite, and only people who are duly authorized and licensed should be permitted to play with dynamite. . . ."

Gary warmed to the response. "An actor's career is very precariously perched," he went on. "I have been an actor long enough to know that. The least bit of censure, whether justified or unjustified, can ruin him, whether it is on moral, political or other grounds, and I think it is a horrendous thing, a criminal thing, for you to toy with other people's careers that they have given all their lives and emotions and study to. And the point is that not only are they involved, but also their families. This is a very dangerous business."

Aware's protectors were equally outraged. Rex Marshall, a spaniel-faced announcer, growled for the defense. "It seems to me," he said, "that we're indebted to a group that gives its time freely to expose elements that are dangerous to this country and to this union. I don't think you can condemn a vigilante committee for being vigilant. If it is accused of being a lynching committee, I think the accusation should be made properly by the persons who considered themselves in danger of lynching." The partisans were unmoved. Marshall tried to win them with Aware's shiny mirror logic: "Until proper charges have been brought by those accused in the Bulletin we can only assume that the accusations are justified and we should thank the people who are interested enough to give their time to look for our interest."

The acrimony could not be contained in one meeting. But Vincent Hartnett saw no reason for dejection. He wrote his friend Lawrence Johnson:

> Confidentially I had a good telephone conversation this morning with Kim Hunter who just returned to New York from the Bucks County Playhouse. I stressed to Miss Hunter that she *had* to take a public stand against Communism. She assured me that she would do so and if she comes through tomorrow night at the AFTRA meeting as she promised she would do, you will hear the comrades shrieking all the way from New York to Syracuse.
>
> The Kraft situation seems to me to be very much improved, thanks to you know who! Keep up the fight, Larry. You and your associates have done wonders.
>
> Sincerely,
Hartnett

The wonder was performed on schedule. Hunter could not make herself appear in defense of Aware, nor would the merciful blacklister force her to. He asked only for a nice, reciprocal, carefully worded telegram. She delivered it:

> To the membership. For your union to condemn Aware Inc. shouldn't it also bring suit against Aware for libel and defamation of character? Is AFTRA prepared to follow this through to its logical conclusion? And what earthly good do we hope to accomplish for the union or its members by passing this resolution?
>
> I'm neither a member of Aware Inc. nor a friend, nor am I in sympathy with any of its methods, but I urge you all to think very carefully indeed before voting for this resolution. The individuals hurt by Bulletin No. 12 have recourse

to right any wrong that may have been committed, but AFTRA will have no recourse whatsoever if it places itself on record as protesting and aiding the Communist conspiracy, even if this action is taken in the noble desire to aid and protect the innocent.

The wire, the offstage wheedling and the cranky counterpunching speeches were too late. The membership had decided long before the debate that it was time to burn the blacklists and begin again. On May 24, 1955, the attending membership voted 197 to 149 to condemn Aware. The blacklisters confidently moved to poll the *entire* membership, not merely this slanted minority which haunted meetings with its Bolshevik intimacy with *Roberts' Rules of Order*. Aware got its wish—and a more definitive condemnation, 982 to 514.

Schmidt immediately characterized the vote as "meaningless; one that hurt AFTRA more than us." This was more than petulance. The wartime euphemism "they are hurting" means that the enemy is killed or ruined. Aware and its enemies were engaged in a conflict of lethal proportion. "Hurt," in the case of AFTRA, was to have had an identical definition.

Aware began its counterattack with the news that Francis Walter had renounced his even-handedness, that even now he was slouching toward New York with subpoenas and dossiers. The AFTRA membership, having shouted their condemnation, shivered at the echo of their own voices. Suppose this condemnation vote was misinterpreted as pro-Communism? Suppose the investigators were to do to New York what they had done to Hollywood? With judicious haste, the AFTRA board of directors, which included such right thinkers as Clayton Collyer, Rex Marshall and the movies' most aristocratic smoothie, Conrad Nagel, gave the membership a new resolution: "If any member of AFTRA is asked by a duly constituted committee of the Senate or House of Representatives of the United States whether or not he is or ever has been a member of the Communist Party, and said member fails or refuses to answer that question, said member shall be subject to the charge that he is guilty of conduct prejudicial to the welfare of AFTRA. The accused may be investigated and charges may be heard by the board of the local of which the accused is a member. The local board may, in its discretion, fire, censure, suspend or expel the accused from membership. . . . AFTRA believes its members have a solemn duty as citizens to cooperate with the committee in its investigation."

The membership had until August 8 to vote: the HUAC would settle into New York for a brief, virulent stay two weeks later. To help voters understand the meaning of the Fifth Amendment, Aware produced a news supplement listing eight actors as subversives: Lloyd Gough, Elliott Sullivan, Will Lee, Madeleine Lee, Stanley Prager, Art Smith, George Tyne and Albert M. Ottenheimer. All had been previously named by HUAC informers. All were immediately barred from television. It was known that at least five of them were to be summoned to testify at the new hearings. All would undoubtedly invoke the Fifth. How would AFTRA look *then?* The membership got the message. By August 8 they had voted to condemn those members who utilized their Constitutional privileges.

With this new weapon, Walter entered the city reiterating his hope that theatrical employers would remain "traditionally American and withhold judgment until they know what all the facts are." The American Civil Liberties Union, again playing the role of toothless mastiff, made a ritual bark, asking the Committee to restrict its inquiry "strictly to conspiratorial acts."

In the Federal Building on Foley Square, Walter opened the hearings with a long preamble designed to forestall criticism. "For the record," he claimed, "this hearing is not an investigation of the field of entertainment nor of any of the great trade unions which represent actors, actresses and writers, and allied workers in radio, television or the legitimate theatre." By the simple excision of "not" from the above paragraph, listeners could have arrived at the truth.

Indeed, during the proceedings against Aware, Harnett had written in panic to John Dungey: "Those of us who are on the spot and in a position to know the facts realize that Equity is virtually lost, and that we may well lose our solid control of AFTRA." The HUAC's central intent was always to restore union control to the Committee's allies.

Walter had one more reassurance before the first witness testified. "May I make it clear," he said, "that the fact that a lawyer appears before the Committee as counsel for a witness should not be taken as any disparagement of counsel for so doing." As he revealed within a week, Walter's intent could be divined, again, simply by removing the negative from his proclamation.

The Committee's first witness was the dough-faced George Tyne, whose name was not as familiar as his films (A *Walk in the Sun, Sands of Iwo Jima, Decision Before Dawn*). Tyne had been named as a Communist by Lee J. Cobb. Seven times Tyne was asked if he knew Cobb, seven times he dodged. "I am disturbed by anybody," Tyne fumed, "who appears before this committee as a stool pigeon, who curries favor, who tries to get jobs, and money, and gives names." "That is not a response to the question," Walter reminded him, setting the monotone for the proceedings. John Randolph, a beefy, choleric performer with an extremely short fuse, followed Tyne. When the durable Committee counsel, Frank Tavenner, asked him a preliminary question, Randolph inclined toward his lawyer, Leonard Boudin, long a defender of unfriendly witnesses. "Mr. Tavenner," he began, "according to my counsel—" "You answer the questions," interrupted Walter. "I don't care about your attorney's opinion." Randolph had no intention of cooperating with the Committee, and his answers were the customary evasions and Constitutionally guaranteed silences. But he was able, for the first time, to tell the Congressman about the methodology of the blacklisters. Randolph had been condemned by "Mr. Johnson of Syracuse . . . then later by *Counterattack,* and then by Aware Inc. I never knew what the accusations were, or what reasons, but they were anonymous phone calls, and you know the kind of stuff. There were little hate letters and so on and so forth, and not many, but enough to make me quite disturbed about it, and find out that I was being blacklisted on television and I never could find out who did the accusations or anything of that sort and I never had a chance to answer any of that."

Stanley Prager, a comedian whose timing did not desert him on the stand, was then appearing in the musical *The Pajama Game.* He was a born survivor, a round cork of a man who would bob to the top of an ocean or a sewer. His idiom had been the *lingua franca* of the blacklisted: Francis Walter, said Prager, had a lot of shmuck going for him; the Committee was six actors in search of a pogrom. When asked why he did not inform on a few movie associates, Prager replied that he could get more money for his soul back East in musicals.

The jaunty, deprecating manner was not wholly a performance. Prager was a career optimist who entertained the peculiar belief that because he wished harm to no one, no one wished him harm. He could never quite fathom Hartnett's relentless pursuit of subversives, unless it be for the almighty buck, and nobody, Prager felt, needed a dollar that badly. When Walter reminded the actor that the Committee had begun researching his past two years earlier, Prager remarked, "Since then I have been working in New York, so I think this must be a fairly good indication of what kind of threat to the national security I must be." But the time for picadors was past. Prager ended by stating, "History has shown that if you attack this Committee and if you are openly aggressive you are in great jeopardy of losing your job." In fact, Prager thought himself in great jeopardy of losing his part of Prez in *The Pajama Game.* After appearing before the Committee and the cameras, he walked on coals to his dressing room. There he learned that the show's director and producer, George Abbott, desired an interview. Abbott, as Prager once observed, was known to his intimates and probably to his mother as Mr. Abbott. No one called him George, least of all Stanley Prager, already blacklisted from all other phases of entertainment. Now he imagined his final source, theater, taken from him as he approached the director, and thought rather enviously of two blacklisted colleagues, George Keane, who had become a successful insurance agent, and David Fresco, a stalwart in the day-old-bread business.

"Stanley," said Mr. Abbott, "it's time you got a raise."

"He never explained himself," said Prager. "To me or to anyone else. I think he had no use for my politics but even less for those of the Committee, and *no* Star Chamber deputy was going to tell Mr. Abbott whom to hire."

The Committeemen could not follow each actor backstage, and they found, to their distress, that many reluctant witnesses were still earning salaries. Tavenner grilled Sarah Cunningham (Mrs. John Randolph) about a production of *The World of Sholem Aleichem*. This modest collage, produced by the fine movie villain and stage Shylock Morris Carnovsky, had become an honor roll of blacklistees, among them Zero Mostel and Jack Gilford, who could work nowhere else. Cunningham answered only that it was the highlight of her career and took refuge in the Fifth. Her lawyer, Boudin, once again engaged the wrath of Walter—but it was closing time and the chairman refused to be drawn into debate.

The following morning Elliott Sullivan, the light tragedian who had appeared in more than eighty films before being listed in *Red Channels*, saw his career terminated in a series of elliptical exchanges during which he denounced the informers Lee J. Cobb, Martin Berkeley and Jerome Robbins, all of whom had named him as a Communist. Only two scraps of dialogue proved noteworthy.

In *The Big Knife*, Odets' villain, movie producer Stanley

Hoff, attempts to bully a star into signing a contract "with the same pen General MacArthur used to sign the Japanese surrender." Representative Walter similarly attempted to coerce Sullivan into retracting a statement about the impropriety of the HUAC. "Do you suppose," Walter asked, "that this Subcommittee, with its distinguished counsel, who prosecuted Tojo in Japan, would ask a question if he thought it was an improper question?"

The Committeemen also took umbrage at a skit Sullivan had performed at a summer camp. In it, two men slither onstage.

First man: "Want to buy a copy of the Bill of Rights?"

Second man: "How much?"

First man: "Two bucks."

Second man: "I'll take it for a dollar."

The money is passed, then both men reveal themselves as FBI agents and arrest each other. Blackout.

For Mr. Tavenner the crowning insult was not the merchandising of the Bill of Rights, but the selling of it for only a dollar.

The Committee met with stubborn opposition from all witnesses except the sour, disappointed actor George Hall. On the third day of testimony Hall's tenor voice narrated the misadventures of his own year and a half in the Party, condemned the indiscriminate use of the Fifth Amendment, and named as fellow Reds eight individuals—every one of whom had, coincidentally, received a subpoena. Hall's testimony met with profound approbation by the Congressmen. One might almost have felt that they had written it themselves.

Releasing the witness, Walter looked down with enormous benignity. "Your contribution here cannot be appraised," he told Hall. "It may be equal to that of a division of infantry." The Committee's only cooperative interviewee consumed the morning—much to the delight of the next witness, Madeline Gilford. The Committee, she knew, was booked for a limited run. The longer *she* stayed on, the fewer witnesses could be summoned to engrave their names on yet another blacklist. Sam Jaffe stood in the batter's circle waiting to come up if Mrs. Gilford failed to stall. She fussed with her pocketbook, half out of nervousness, peered into the television cameras, looked away and on, fouling all pitches until the umpires called rain. At one point she grew so loquacious that Representative Willis advised his colleagues, "She will run out of words. Let her rant a little bit."

Before she ran out of words the clock ran out of minutes. When she was through, the day was over. Sam Jaffe was saved. Madeline Gilford's counsel was not. His very presence was sand under Walter's skin, and when Mrs. Gilford consulted him once too often the chairman beefed, "If you would pay attention to me instead of carrying on a continuing conversation with your lawyer, maybe you would hear these questions. . . . You have no right to consult with your lawyer. We are extending a privilege, even though we know what the results of such conferences will be."

Boudin exploded, "I don't understand that remark, Mr. Walter, and I resent it, and I would like an apology from you right now."

"I think you protest too loud," said Walter, saving his reason for animosity for another day. "You will get no apology."

But the next day Boudin received the reason for Walter's animus. The witness was the narrow, sad-eyed folk singer and producer Tony Kraber, named by Kazan and Odets. "You addressed me as 'professor' yesterday," Boudin reminded the chairman. "I know you didn't mean it as impertinent. Are you under the impression that I am a professor of law?"

The answer came promptly. "You were a professor at the Jefferson School, the Communist school in New York City, that is why."

"Am I a witness here?"

"No."

"Is it your custom to address counsel that way?"

"I thought I was being—"

"You thought you were being what, Mr. Chairman?"

With a stage-sized cough, Mr. Tavenner separated the combatants and returned to the mutton: "Let us get down to the facts involved here, Mr. Kraber. . . . Elia Kazan testified that he was recruited into a Communist Party organization formed within the Group Theatre by Tony Kraber. . . ."

"Is that the same Kazan," Kraber wanted to know, "that signed the contract for $500,000 the day after he gave names to this Committee? Would you sell your brothers for $500,000?"

Since Kraber would not tell them whether or not he was a Communist, the Committeemen refused to tell him whether they would sell their brothers, and moved on to their only real celebrity, the tenor of the Weavers quartet, the great balladeer and full-throated liberal Pete Seeger. The dossier on Seeger was nearly as large as the combined papers on the Hollywood Ten. His name could be found on dozens of incriminating programs, from rallies for Henry Wallace to that triumph of naïveté, Culture Fights Back, sponsored by the Committee to Defend the Communist leader V. J. Jerome. Seeger, blacklisted since the Weavers' collision with *Counterattack*, retained his open-faced amiability throughout, and for a moment it seemed that the Committeemen, like all Seeger audiences, were to be charmed by his ineluctable grace. Through the thin, winning voice came the echoes of "greener pastures on the other side," and not a trace of defiance could be found in his speech or manner—at first. Then Tavenner handed the witness a photograph of a May Day Parade, taken in 1952, and asked him whether he was the gentleman carrying a placard.

Seeger remarked, "It is like Jesus Christ when asked by Pontius Pilate, 'Are you king of the Jews?' "

"Stop that," demanded Chairman Walter, stricken. He would not allow sacrilege in his court. Business as usual was all he wanted to see.

But business was bad. By the time Seeger was dismissed, the

investigation had dissected only twenty-four individuals, not nearly enough to move the gears of Aware and Vincent Hartnett. However, a device was attached to the transcript of the hearings and, in the end, this proved the blacklisters' most significant tool. The device was called the Cumulative Index, and it listed in alphabetical order every name that had surfaced during the hearings. The curious or malicious researcher could find in the back of the government publication not 24 names but 276. For the index included such evidence as hearsay from a friendly witness, an advertisement for a May Day celebration in the defunct publication PM, and a 1942 program for the Artists Front to Win the War, held in Carnegie Hall in 1942.

Thus Aware Inc. and Vincent Hartnett could charge for a report on the radical backgrounds of Gladys Cooper and Duke Ellington, Charles Laughton and Jane Pickens, Xavier Cugat and Bela Bartók, Pavel Tchelitchew and Zero Mostel.

And yet, with all of this, 1955 was the blacklisters' last vintage year.

Indifference smothers the righteous as well as the sinner, and the gray academic years of the Eisenhower era were beginning to blunt and nullify the paranoid style. Vincent Hartnett's income plummets from this year, and Aware descends from significant force to a collection of cranks, sour Taft fans and disappointed old ladies in bombazine. Only once more will they enjoy the power of wreckers—at the close of the year, when the name Arthur Miller reappears, not in the theater, but in the streets.

In 1955 youth gangs called the Viceroys and the Dragons prowled and controlled sections of Brooklyn. This was not far from Miller's old territory, and he found himself attracted by the dramatic scrimmage of youth and police. He began making rounds with the Youth Board workers and spent nights with the gangs. A social worker remembered the playwright "one night when a gang was out to kill two rival members for re-

venge. Miller drove down in his station wagon and took all the
kids to Coney Island. He didn't say anything, just let the boys
have fun. After the night was over the kids had cooled down."

Soon afterward Miller attended the funeral of a boy who had
died after an overdose of heroin. One of the mourners remembered the first time he had ever seen the bony, stooped figure.
"He came down here one night alone. We were sitting in an
old Chevy drinking beer. We took up a collection for beer and
Miller threw in.

"It turned out he knew a lot about cars and motors. The guys
seemed to take a liking to him. What they liked about him
was that he wasn't on top of them. He sort of sat in the background."

"He wasn't like a stiff that came down one time from a radio
company," another gang member put in. "The stiff was a ques-
tion-and-answer man, always pushing, pushing. Miller never
treated us like we were monkeys in the zoo."

Given these reviews, Miller decided that he had been too
long removed from the creative process. He submitted a twenty-
nine-page treatment of a film about a youth-board worker, to be
played by Frank Sinatra.

Miller and his production company, Combined Artists,
offered the city 5 percent of the net for their cooperation. The
Board of Estimate swiftly approved a contract—and then the
town fell in about their ears.

The *Journal-American* and the *World-Telegram* abruptly
exhumed the old charge of fellow-traveling; at the flap of these
flags, Aware put its head down and charged. Its new bulletin
informed the city that "Miller's public record showed at least
forty-one (41) distinct affiliations with at least twenty-nine
(29) officially cited Communist-front organizations, etc." The
data on Miller listed those organizations, quoted *Daily Worker*
raves for *The Crucible* and *A View from the Bridge,* and placed
an asterisk next to any subversive actor who appeared in Miller's
plays—among them Arthur Kennedy, Fredric March, Van

Heflin and Lee J. Cobb. As Cobb's listing demonstrated, there was no real road back; Kazan himself was in the Miller file with a dreaded star after his name.

The Board of Estimate suddenly entertained second thoughts about Miller and, after sustained attacks by the American Legion and the Catholic War Veterans, voted 11 to 9 to reverse its approval of the film. The Youth Board chairman, Hon. Nathaniel Kaplan, justice of the Domestic Relations Court, issued an official lie after the vote: "We cannot make any decision which would assure us of less than 100 percent cooperation from all the people. We are not passing judgment on Miller's loyalty, nor on his merits as an artist."

Rabbi Benjamin Schultz and George Sokolsky were. On behalf of the American Jewish League Against Communism, they wired their congratulations to the Youth Board. On behalf of Miller, the ACLU asked the city to ignore Aware Inc. under penalty of its displeasure. "Apparently all that is required to cause a city agency to abandon a project intended for the benefit of the whole city," it pouted, "is a loud noise from pressure groups."

But the city did not bend to pressure groups, it was *composed* of pressure groups. The trick was to use the pressure to advance yourself or your cause. Aware had known how; the ACLU had not. Nor had Miller. Pressed for a reply, he composed an epitaph and went home. "The majority of the Youth Board has now decided that this picture shall not be made," said Miller. "So be it. Now let us see whether fanaticism can do what it never could do in the history of the world: let it perform a creative act. Let it take its club in hand and write what it has just destroyed."

It took up the club as instructed. But not to write.

THIRTEEN

1

Communists on the Court. How can the Reds have infiltrated there? The President in chains. Can it have come to this? Nothing intervenes between the Constitution and the libertarians. The studios are defiant, the networks indifferent, the public shaking out its kinks, fear dispelled, walls dissolving, loyalty oaths canceled. Curtains are in tatters, the guards are disarmed. The blacklist is on fire. . . .

Terrible prophecies leaped from the rarebit fantasies of Aware in 1956. Its prim, authority-loving members felt themselves in a world of lapsed standards as the decade flowed downhill. The nation in 1955 was caught in their jaws. Yet, within a year their ambitions were hooted down; within two years it was *they* who were doubling back on their tracks in a futile attempt to lose the hunters. How had it happened? They knew no more than their listees.

2

One of Carl Jung's favorite stories concerned the knight who wailed, "Will these Middle Ages never end?" It is convenient

to think of the blacklisted locked inside the museum of para-
dox, banging on the doors and asking to be let out. And it is
appealing to think of rescuers riding up and opening the gates
with a golden key on such-and-such a date in the year of our
Lord 19—.

But American life in the fifties indulged appetites for chaos,
not order. As one arena stirred, another declared bankruptcy. As
private paranoia diminished, federal panic flourished. In 1956
Vincent Hartnett earned only $17,658. Borden alone had paid
him $10,000 in 1955. Lawrence Johnson, no longer young or
even middle-aged, sold his markets in 1956. He, like many
gerontians, had decided to retire to an old age of puttering—except that, while other old men cultivated their gardens, Johnson
played at Jingo and attacked companies employing Stalin's little
creatures. Without his emporia, however, the grocer was de-
smocked. His influence, by painful degrees, began to ebb.
Money came slowly to Aware Inc. American society was suffering from political cramp, an affliction that occurs when a position is taken by the body for too long a time. Late in 1956 the
Republican Party was enjoying a second lease on the White
House. For too long the GOP had assailed the Democrats for
their moral laxity, their tolerance of Reds and traitors. But now
that Vice President Richard Nixon seemed to be filing for the
next eight-year lease, Republicans wished the pickets to go
away. Talk of subversion would, soon or late, reflect upon the
government. Even now there was dangerous anti-administration
talk when the Republican appointee, Chief Justice Earl Warren, administered extreme unction to the Eisenhower security
program.

Item: Senator Eastland: "The Court seems to be issuing just
one pro-Communist decision after another." Senator Mc-
Carthy: "You're so right." Senator Eastland: "What explanation is there except that some Communist influence is working
within the Court?"

Could it be, the probers wondered, that they had been investigating *the wrong party?* And the knell continued to sound not merely for an epoch but for a sensibility.

Still, the inertia of the blacklist could not suddenly be stopped by the little barriers of jurisprudence. It would be possible for a while yet to dig under walls and to vault over certain legal barriers. No parenthesis can be closed in 1956. The blacklist was fatally stricken in that year, but no victims knew it. If they had, it would have been no more comforting than the Yiddish proverb: "Rich man up, poor man down, it's still not the same."

When Philip Loeb took his own life, his residence was 225 West 86th Street, in the apartment of the night-club comedian and actor Zero Mostel. The following month Mostel appeared before a private session of the Committee in California. He had been touring in the comedy *Lunatics and Lovers* and begged permission to be interviewed on the Coast instead of in New York. "We always try to cooperate in these cases," Representative Doyle assured him—and the wish was granted. For the performance Mostel got himself up as one of those wistful, apolitical clown-tramps in his paintings. Filling his pingpong-ball eyes with moisture, he told the Congressmen that he was called Zero after his financial standing in the community. Zero swung the Fifth Amendment around like a slapstick comedian with a board—always coming within a micrometer of impudence and despair. The comedian was openly belligerent only once, when he insisted on his right to private opinions—and even then he slipped into his guise of animated zeppelin.

"If I appeared [at a leftist rally]," Mostel wanted to know, "what if I did an imitation of a butterfly at rest? There is no crime in making anybody laugh. I don't care if you laugh at me."

"If your interpretation of a butterfly at rest brought any money into the coffers of the Communist Party," said Representative Jackson, "you contributed directly to the propaganda effort of the Communist Party."

"Suppose I had the urge to do the butterfly at rest somewhere?"

"Don't have such an urge to put the butterfly at rest by putting some money in the Communist Party coffers. . . . Put the bug to rest somewhere else next time."

"I suggest," said Representative Jackson, who liked his little joke, "we put this *hearing* butterfly to rest."

"The witness is excused," responded Doyle. "Thank you, Mr. Mostel. Remember what I said to you."

"You remember what I said to you," Mostel returned. Neither man, of course, paid the slightest attention to the other's exit line.

Mostel immediately joined the list of fourteen other performers who made Aware's new roster. Actually, the secular blacklisters had only a passing interest in Zero; he was simply a member of AFTRA, one of fourteen who defied the HUAC. The bulletin was entitled *AWARE Publication 16* and sought, with great enterprise, to ruin not merely Mostel and the thirteen others; its higher aim was to bring down those individuals who had engineered the union's vote of condemnation.

They were a group who called themselves "Middle-of-the-Roaders," candidates who had wrested control of AFTRA from the blacklisters. Middlers, neutrals, non-rightists, as we have seen, were perceived as deeply evil. They would have to be destroyed even before the Communists. Certain parallels to German history did not escape the *Daily Worker*, which loved to spray enemies with the term "fascist" and which described the election of the "Middlers" as one of the cultural highlights of the fifties.

Like the *Worker*, Aware also regarded the Middle-of-the-Roaders through convex lenses. Bulletin 16 went through finger-wagging motions at the Fifth Amendment antics of Mostel, Sullivan, Randolph, Prager and others. But the focus of their awful vengeance was on the Texas raconteur John Henry Faulk,

the Ivy League comedian Orson Bean and the CBS newsman
Charles Collingwood.

The blacklisters could get nothing on Collingwood, whose
past was pure. In a cranky aside, Aware could only ask the new
AFTRA president to "discharge his responsibilities" and remind him of Frank Tavenner's warning that the "New York
hearings left no doubt as to the existence of a Communist Party
faction and the recent election battle within the AFTRA local
further corroborates these findings." Tavenner insisted not only
that there was no blacklist at all, but that, on the contrary,
some of the named individuals had found it *easy* to secure
employment. "It is significant to note," the investigator added
darkly, "that the election of the so-called anti-blacklist candidates in the recent AFTRA election has been greeted enthusiastically by the Communist press."

First Vice President Orson Bean was more vulnerable. He
had been spotted at a rally of the Emergency Civil Liberties
Committee, on behalf of those AFTRA members subpoenaed
by Congress. Vainly, Bean was to recall that Joshua Shelley, one
of the subpoenaed actors, "was hot after an actress for whom I
was also horny. Because of his subpoena he became a martyr in
her eyes and I became consumed with jealousy. The Emergency
Civil Liberties Committee, later to be named by the Attorney
General as a Communist Front, called a protest meeting at
Carnegie Hall at which some of the subpoenaed actors appeared. And Dummy Bean. To impress the girl. While I was
waiting to go on, a leftwing friend spotted me and said, 'What
the hell are you doing here? The place is lousy with FBI guys
taking everybody's name down. Get out.' He didn't understand
about moral convictions: I went on and did one of my routines
from the Ed Sullivan Show, the girl was duly impressed and
that was that."

Or so Bean had hoped. But one morning Ed Sullivan called
to tell the comedian that he was sorry, that any future bookings

were out. "Incidentally," added the columnist in the tradition of the American Legion, "if you tell anyone I said this, I'll have to deny it."

"But I didn't know it was a Communist meeting," Bean protested. "I didn't attack any Committee. I just did one of the dumb routines I've done on your show."

"Well," mumbled Sullivan, "I'll help you when I can." Sullivan knew all about moral convictions; when the hysteria ceased, he was pleased to re-employ Dummy Bean. But not now; not just now.

"Overnight," Bean remembered, "from being the hot young comic at CBS television, I stopped working. Just stopped. I saw actors cross the street to avoid having to say hello to me. The money stopped coming in, the glory was gone and my career as a television comic seemed like a memory."

AFTRA's Second Vice President Faulk was singled out for greater extinction. With citations from the *Daily Worker*, a program of the Independent Citizens Committee of the Arts, Sciences and Professions, volumes of the Bulletins of People's Songs and other equally significant publications, Aware accused the Texas folk talker of hypocrisy, collusion, fellow-traveling and political indecency.

Unlike Collingwood, who was protected by Edward R. Murrow's inviolable fief, and Bean, who could survive in night clubs and on stage—and who would imperceptibly creep like an hour hand from left to right—Faulk had no resources but his CBS talk show. His colleagues gave excellent imitations of men badly frightened by a network. Bean fled from the Middle-of-the-Road slate; announcer Dick Stark, who had been one of Faulk's most rigorous supporters, suddenly saw fit to attack the Middle-of-the-Roaders at a meeting. Thereupon Ed Sullivan wrote an apostrophe to the heroic ex-Marine for his guts. Comedian Cliff Norton, another wanderer on the Middle of the Road, also attacked his former beliefs, but Sullivan had only so many inches in his column for good works.

Privately, the AFTRA lawyer Henry Jaffe counseled Faulk. There *was* a way out, he suggested. Faulk could call Francis Walter and tell him that he wanted to press charges against any AFTRA member who had been identified as a Communist. Jaffe would find some local informers who had aided the Committee in the past. They would gladly help Faulk by testifying once more; it was a tested and trouble-free method, Jaffe said. All Faulk needed was a temporary suspension of soul. Jaffe seemed astonished at the MC's polite refusal, and unsurprised when Faulk started down the short road to bankruptcy.

Libby's Frozen Foods was among the first accounts to leave Faulk's CBS program; this was followed by a number of other fine American products, including Rheingold Beer and Hoffman Beverages. During these defections Hartnett was making more intuitive leaps into the Stalinist mentality. Dissatisfied with Aware's inability to think big, the free-lance investigator attempted a structure of totalitarian sweep: he engaged the sympathies of the New York Police Department. In some thirty instances, conversations with a Lieutenant Thomas Crain furnished Hartnett with information about artists employed in broadcasting and the theater. In return, Hartnett swapped stories from his files, particularly anecdotes about the Middle-of-the-Road slate and its vulnerable functionary, John Henry Faulk. Theoretically, this cooperation could, in time, lead to the blacklisters' dominant fantasy: instant information retrieval and total power would elevate the pioneer anti-Communists to official status, with large offices, greater moral and economic suasion and—who knew?—perhaps, in time, uniforms.

The dream evaporated overnight. Simultaneously, several newspaper critics began to speak with clarity and indiscretion. John Crosby, radio critic for the *Herald Tribune,* called Aware a "little wolf-pack of vigilantes." In the *New York Times,* Jack Gould peppered Hartnett with a series of damning allegations. The target replied hotly, "Mr. Gould wrote that 'a commercial cloud was cast over the anti-Communism of AWARE by the confirmation of Vincent Hartnett, a director of the organization, that he was professionally engaged in reviewing the political background of artists.' This argument has as much merit as the argument that a commercial cloud is cast over the American Medical Association because one of its directors happens also to be engaged in the practice of medicine." The longing to be regarded, with his little blacklist, as something like a professional with his little black bag was pathetic in its grossness. It seemed almost rude for Gould to employ logic in his reply: "To my knowledge, the AMA does not encourage an individual physician to make a business of passing on a colleague's eligibility to practice."

But this was mere backchat. Two more important tendencies crystallized in 1956, both of them in their way fatal to the blacklist. These, coupled with Aware's exaggerations and outright falsifications about John Henry Faulk, were to exhaust and destroy the plague, more than a decade after it had been introduced.

In January the House Un-American Activities Committee announced that a "Communist-supported campaign against 'so-called' blacklisting . . . completely falsified the true hiring policies applied to entertainers." That, in fact, the networks "continue to use the talents of Communist Party members because of inadequate information and investigative facilities."

On the surface this seemed overkill. The voices of criticism were still lonely soloists in a few newspapers, endangering no blacklister worth the name. But the HUAC announcement was not an appraisal. It was an anticipation, an advance critique of an imminent report by the Ford Foundation's Fund for the Republic—under the editorship of John Cogley, former editor of the liberal Catholic weekly *Commonweal*. In an irony beyond the Committee's comprehension, the report was a small part of the Foundation's research into the nature and dimensions of Communism in America. Blacklisting in show business, said Fund Director Robert Hutchins, "is an area in which there are many flagrant cases in persons of undoubted competence who have lost their positions because of charges, often unfounded, about their political opinions. It is also *an area in which the nature and scope of Communist infiltration can be studied.*"*

Tirelessly, Cogley conducted interviews, dug back into forgotten files, read faded union transcripts and yellowing newspaper clips. Hutchins had a personal disdain for such research; he called it "fact-grubbing." Such grubbing was meat, drink, dessert and coffee for Cogley and his assistant, the brilliant, quirky young socialist Michael Harrington. Cogley was the first to admit his limited political sophistication—that was why he had hired his assistant. "Harrington needed a job," Cogley explained. "He was eating at the *Catholic Worker*. He was very bright and he knew more about the Communist Party than I did; he knew his way around the ideological world better than I."

Together, the two researcher-writers and a small staff worked for almost two years before they published the two-volume *Report on Blacklisting.* The report carefully delineated the character and the methods of censorship in movies (Volume I) and radio-TV (Volume II). It contained brisk histories of the Hollywood unions and their battle with Communist infiltration and reactionary censure. It gave thumbnail descriptions of Johnson and Hartnett (whom Harrington would later recall as "a prototype of the spoiled priest"), described some of Aware's methods, and provided biographies of blacklistees, blacklisters and clearance specialists. The report had but one failing: like Merle Miller's sources five years back, Cogley's were still so frightened that they would speak only under the tent of anonymity. Page after page contained unattributed quotes, references to "a public relations man," "an actor," "a radio-TV director," "a leading actress." Sometimes the cover was pathetically, almost

* Italics mine. S.K.

deliberately, easy to pierce. The leading actress was Uta Hagen, never called by the Committee, continually blacklisted despite affidavits swearing her fealty to the United States. The report's pseudonymous "Miss B." was Jocelyn Brando, Marlon's sister, signer of petitions for Willie McGee, a Negro railroaded in Mississippi; sponsor of the Waldorf Peace Conference; starlet of a few promising pictures, and now in an alcoholic slump, counterweight to her brother's great and sudden elevation. Blacklisters, however, were uncloaked or barely cosmetized; clearance experts like Arnold Forster and James O'Neil were quite perceptible to the initiated.

The Cogley report had used up time, talent and $127,000. It had proved beyond scruple that there was indeed an institution called blacklisting, that artists had been barred from work, and that the HUAC had been responsible for the decline in motion pictures dealing intelligently with social issues. That was all the Committee and its friends needed to hear. Karl E. Mundt told the Senate that the report gave "aid and comfort to Communists in this country and abroad." Chairman Walter, riled, decided to subpoena Cogley to appear July 10 at a closed hearing. Though Walter had not bothered to read the report at all, and though Congressman Doyle had read only "four or five pages," the chairman announced that he would attempt to discern "what the purposes of the Fund and Mr. Cogley truly are." The Hearst papers hotly denounced the study as "further conclusive evidence of the anti-anti-Communist slant" of the Fund for the Republic. (As it happened, the editorial writer himself had not read the Cogely volumes. "I read a news story, a clipping about it, and I got a note from Mr. Hearst suggesting an editorial," he explained; Mr. Hearst had not read it either.)

On July 10, 1957, John Cogley pushed past reporters and entered the Committee room. He was accompanied by a young Minnesota Congressman, Eugene McCarthy, who threw his arm around Cogley's shoulder in a gesture of support. It was the last one the editor was to receive; the agency officials and broadcasting executives remained silent forever.

Walter began his "Investigation of So-Called 'Blacklisting' in the Entertainment Industry" by siccing Committee Staff Director Richard Arens on the witness. Arens opened with a quote from Vincent Hartnett's favorite publication, the *Tablet*, asserting that the liberal Catholic publication *Commonweal* was not Catholic at all; so much for Cogley's shield of religious affiliation. Then followed the subordinate charges. "Did you at any place in your treatise," Arens wanted to know, "list the Communist-front record of Larry Adler and of Paul Draper which is as long as two arms?" The second charge accused Cogley's assistants of pro-Red bias. One assistant was Michael Harrington, perhaps the Socialist Party's most difficult and intelligent member. "You, of course, are aware of the fact," Arens lectured Cogley, "that Lenin, the key philosopher of Communism, had said socialism is only one transition toward Communism." Had the listener shut his eyes to the newer fashions in attire and address, he could have sworn himself back with old Joe Starnes battling against the Federal Theatre's Christopher Marlowe and the incursions of the New Deal.

Another of Arens' prime targets was Dr. Maria Jahoda, who had made a little study of anti-Communists in broadcasting. "Did you know," asked Arens, "that she was admitted into the United States only in 1945?" Showing just the slightest impatience, Cogley replied that Miss Jahoda "had a pronounced accent. I presumed it was not too long ago."

Cogley's third assistant, Paul Jacobs, was attacked because he, like James Wechsler, had belonged to the Young Communist League twenty years before. Since that time he had been a soldier in the labor-union battles against Stalinists. But once a Red, always a Red, the Committee maintained. For the HUAC, no inoculation against the Leninist virus could ever take; the Fund for the Republic was clearly no more than a generously funded and padded cell.

Cogley, in another admission of strain, had the temerity to ask why he had been subpoenaed. Walter told him: "We called you for the purpose of ascertaining what your sources were in order to determine whether or not your conclusions were the conclusions we would have reached had we embarked on this sort of project." Translation: Blacklisting does not exist and we will blacklist anyone who says it does.

Cogley was as implacable as a stone. Investigators who wanted the names of those anonyms in the report were told that the witness had no intention of cooperating. They replied that there were federal punishments awaiting Cogley if he failed to cooperate. He answered by repeating his refusal to part with his notebooks.

The next day Arnold Forster appeared. The Committee hoped to use his testimony as a bucket of tar on the report. Forster expressed his gratitude to men like George Sokolsky, Victor Riesel, Jack Wren and Fred Woltman, "to whom we [in the Anti-Defamation League] had gone innumerable times to solicit their opinions." But he insisted that the ADL had actually cleared only eight artists, not the report's "more than a dozen." Walter leaped to thank the witness. "You have confirmed the suspicion that this Committee has had right along, namely, that this report isn't worth the paper it is printed on. . . . I do not think there is a blacklist. I cannot find evidence of it." Forster protested that there *was* denial of employment, that, in fact, "it was a dreadful thing." Walter brushed him off with an indulgent smile and summoned Frederick Woltman, star of the *World-Telegram*. The columnist thought the process of rehabilitation was most worthy. "Anybody who breaks with the Communists ought to get a job," he said. As to the study, it was dangerous. "As a result of this report," he said, "I am sure the guys who are mentioned in there are going to spend less time helping to rehabilitate people . . . because they were put in a reprehensible light for something which a person like Robert Hutchins [the Fund's Director] should applaud."

James O'Neil, eleven-year member of the American Legion's National Americanism Commission, was then summoned to the stand. He boasted that the American Legion had made "a major contribution in helping to reestablish a climate of employment for the innocent, the stupid and the repentant guilty in the entertainment industry, principally in Hollywood." George Sokolsky wrote the Committee that his heart condition would not permit him to appear in person, but he wished a statement to be inserted in the record. The study, he wanted the world to know, "suffered from inadequate research, from either an unwillingness or an inability to get all the facts, from a double standard of morals." Sokolsky admitted that he was a minor and casual clearance expert, modestly assuming "the burdens of a private citizen judging the political trustworthiness of other private citizens." But it was, he insisted, an act of pure charity, and, indeed, the columnist had never accepted money for his work.

As to the number he and his friends had aided: "My rough estimate runs about 200 men and women who are today working in the motion-picture industry who could not work before because of the record they had established of Communist or pseudo-Communist associations. Rather than being a blacklisted effort, this was an effort in rehabilitation."

The Committee saved its friendliest witnesses for dessert. Vincent Hartnett, talking in confident staccato, immediately excoriated the report that had described him as "the most widely criticized man in the movie-TV industry." The study was, he declared, "dangerous slanting," and its author "either woefully ignorant or he is a rogue." To Hartnett, the fifties remained the country's reddest decade. Take the contemporary subversion on the public airwaves: "You will still find," he asserted, "script after script in which the policeman shoots an innocent teen-ager, not the bad teen-ager. It is always the innocent. The wrong man is identified and sent to jail. An honest official abroad is suspected of being a Communist agent and the man who points the finger at him is always a fanatic, disgruntled."

Hartnett further simplified the crisis: "In other words, if you could believe television, our courts are incapable of convicting the right man, our witnesses are incapable of making a positive identification, our juries are incapable of coming in with the right finding, private citizens are incapable of making a right evaluation."

Roy Brewer followed Hartnett with yet another attack upon the report as a "complete falsification." He, Arens and Representative Scherer—who had, he admitted, merely "scanned" the Cogley report—noticed similarities between it and articles in the *Daily Worker*.

Paul Milton added *his* condemnation. When Walter called the study "gobbledegook," Milton told him "that is somewhat an insult to gobbledegook, sir," and gave the Aware position on Commies. Godfrey Schmidt came on and called the report "the Communist line," and Frank McNamara, former editor of *Counterattack*, added that "the Party high command would be delighted to have every week a document like this come out, because this fronts for a line that seems to me has been increasing."

That evening, with a crisp, gloating tone, Fulton Lewis, Jr., told his Mutual Network audience: "Perhaps our reportorial work over this microphone . . . is beginning to bear fruit. A Congressional committee looks into one of these phony studies and finds it to be exactly what I have reported to you . . . an ill-disguised and somewhat clumsy propaganda effort to brainwash the American public against the loyalty security program, against investigations into Communism and Communist-front activities, and to persuade the public that the Communist conspiracy is a political party like the Republican or Democratic party and should be accepted on the same basis."

The comedian Stanley Prager remembered that broadcast as part of an elaborate fantasy. The trouble was that no one could determine whose dream it was. "In 1958," he said, "the committee was living on the other side of the mirror shaking with paranoia, insisting that no blacklist existed, constantly looking under the bed for subversives and finding nothing but dustballs. And then calling the dustballs subversive."

But occasionally Prager thought it was *he* who lived in a fictive world. "Who would believe," he asked, "that Nathaniel Frey, who had appeared in shows with me, and shared jokes and dinners with me, would cross 44th Street to avoid running into me, because then he would have had to say hello, or shake hands, and somebody might have seen him, and then he, too, might be out of work." This fear-snobbery was a commonplace of the time. Madeline Gilford found that, as she walked down Bank Street, radio actresses who used to bend over her baby carriage now preferred to inspect the curb. Orson Bean was horrified to learn that even the doorman at CBS snubbed him.

The victims of the Terror in Paris found that all trembling and restriction ceased upon arrest. In jail, condemned without trial, they found their tongues loosened and their minds flooded with something very like relief. They were all damned together; they could speak freely for the first time. Similarly, the blacklistees, once condemned, no longer needed to be careful. For the first time they could really conspire.

On the 26th of June 1956 they were given their chance. The sensational author of *My Life in Court*, the man who prompted the *New York Post* to headline the end of the Elizabeth Taylor–Eddie Fisher marriage: WANTS NIZER, IT'S ALL OVER, the Napoleon of the courtroom, Louis Nizer himself was going to take the case of a blacklistee to the courts. The victim was the amiable, now almost forgotten raconteur, John Henry Faulk. The MC had needed money to pay Nizer's expenses and Edward R. Murrow had advanced him $7,500. "I am investing this money in America," he told Faulk. "This is a very important suit. I don't know whether even you realize how important it is." And Carl Sandburg had sent word: "Whatever's the matter with America, John ain't." Very reassuring, the bankroll and the flattery. But Faulk's case needed something more: evidence.

Madeline Lee Gilford assembled three shopping bags full of case histories; Garry Moore, who had never been blacklisted but who remembered excising an aerialist because he had the same name as a tainted college professor, aided the prosecution; David Susskind, the canny bargain-hunter who had been pleased to hire the blacklisted at an 80-percent discount, nonetheless offered incriminating details about Young and Rubicam and other moral abdicators. Tony Randall, Charles Collingwood and Everett Sloane also served as pallbearers for the burden of proof.

The defense was in every sense aware of these enemies. Hartnett, still playing his favorite role of radio counter-spy, again contacted Kenneth Roberts, the unwilling candidate for fink back in 1950. In 1949, said the investigator, Roberts had attended a Communist Party Theatre Group meeting at the Royalton Hotel. The announcer promptly wrote his tormentor: "Your letters to me represent a clear implication of threat and intimidation unless I admit to something of which I am not guilty, and throw myself at your mercy."

So it was not to be the Moscow Trials *redevivus*. The whisperers now spoke in audible tones. Even the ad men, traditionally the most cautious and cowering, spoke up. An executive named Thomas Murray recalled a bruise administered by one of Lawrence Johnson's blunt instruments—a threatening call. It was a disgrace, the ex-grocer had argued, that Murray's client, the Pabst Brewing Company, was using a Communist like John Henry Faulk to advertise its products. "How would you like it," he inquired, "if your client were to receive a letter from an American Legion post?"

Murray remembered his answer. "I said I was a veteran myself and that I couldn't believe that the American Legion would lend itself to what I considered to be an obvious black-mail attempt."

That the American Legion *would* be a party to extortion, hysteria and simple corruption was beside the point. Murray was that anomaly of the fifties and that sport of the advertising industry, an outraged citizen. To Johnson he had looked like a man in spats and derby, a type of citizen resolutely out of fashion.

There was worse news for the blacklisters—in some ways the saddest revelation of all: the black market was enjoying a vigorous boom. Men who could not write under their own names had chosen other identities—and other people to whom they could attribute their work. "Blacklist, shmacklist, as long as they're all working," Billy Wilder cracked.

Lester Cole and Dalton Trumbo, as we have seen, employed their wives' names until the alert was sounded. The novelist Eliot Asinov was blacklisted because he was: (1) married to Jocelyn Brando, and (2) had signed a petition at Yankee Stadium asking for Negroes to be admitted to major-league baseball. Asinov's blacklisting came late. Before he fell, he acted as a front for Walter Bernstein, lending his name to Bernstein's scripts. When CBS decided Asinov himself was too subversive for employment, an ad man named Julian Koenig fronted for the front.

Millard Lampell sent in scripts under a pseudonym. Once, when his work needed revision, the producers demanded the non-existent writer's presence. They were informed that he was vacationing in France. They settled, instead, for a cheap, fast blacklistee: Millard Lampell.

Late in the decade two notable pictures were released. One, an Amazon adventure, was voted by the aestheticians on the *Harvard Lampoon* as the world's worst film. The other, *The Brave One*, written by Robert Rich, won an Academy Award in 1957 as the year's best original script. When the Oscar was presented, reporters were naturally anxious to obtain a little bio on Mr. Rich. The redoubtable King Brothers, producers of *The Brave One*, claimed that they were also anxious to find him. Frank, the quiet King, told the Hollywood press, "He's in Europe somewhere. I'm looking for him now. He's around thirty-four and he wears a goatee." King might have added that Rich had freckles and a sword. For there was no Robert Rich; there never had been. There was only Dalton Trumbo. He had also written the Amazon adventure film—under the pseudonym Theodore Flaxman. The dogged and indefatigable craftsman, the writer to order, the man Hollywood banished but could not do without, did not acknowledge his Oscar and watched, amused, as claims of authorship were filed on behalf of the late Robert Flaherty, Orson Welles, Jesse Lasky, Jr., Willis O'Brien and Paul Rader.

At the same time, *The Friendly Persuasion* was released without a writer's credit. The scenarist was the blacklisted Michael Wilson. Critics and audiences warmed to the film, and before the Motion Picture Academy could turn around, Wilson seemed an unstoppable candidate for Oscar nomination. (He had won one for *A Place in the Sun*.) With the moral inconstancy that is their hallmark, the Academy suddenly ruled that blacklisted writers were ineligible for awards.

Then yet another film by blacklistees achieved disproportionate success: *The Bridge on the River Kwai*, adapted from the Pierre Boulle novel. This time the grosses were beyond socko; the Academy had no choice but to grant it a nomination. On Oscar night the prize for Best Screenplay from Another Medium went to Pierre Boulle. M. Boulle was unfortunately unable to accept his award in person. But perhaps it was just as well. He was not fluent in English and the acceptance speech might have underlined the open secret: the script had been written by Michael Wilson and Carl Foreman.

From London, Foreman put in a claim of authorship. It was obvious, he said, that he was the scenarist. In all of his scripts he sneaked in three names: Weaver, Grogan and Baker. They were his signature, like Alfred Hitchcock's pawky cameo appearances in *his* films. The interested (or obsessed) detective could indeed find "Baker" in other Foreman projects. In *High Noon* he was a town coward, in *The Men* a drunken paraplegic, in *Champion* a fighter with a porcelain jaw. The next day, however, Foreman issued a strange denial. He had not written the screenplay, he said. At the offices of Sam Spiegel the author's peculiar behavior was quietly explained. Foreman, once denied a passport when John Foster Dulles interested himself in the case, had found England hospitable. But now he wished to work again in his own country. Discreet feelers had been sent out; the HUAC now seemed indifferent to the case. At the Spiegel office, Foreman's associate admitted that the old hazard, "controversy," lay at the base of Foreman's retraction. "It's like getting a divorce," he said. "You just want to get it—give her whatever she wants, the house, everything."

3

Among their numerous resemblances the United States and the stegosaurus share the two-brain phenomenon. The great mesozoic dinosaur was too large to be ruled entirely by his head. So nature happily provided him with an auxiliary nerve center at the base of his spine. In the United States the true brain was, and is, in the Northeast. The supplementary brain tended (and still tends) to wander, sometimes to the Midwest, sometimes as far south as Texas, sometimes, in the case of the blacklist, to California. There, at the terminus of the nation's spine, the ganglia had not received the message of change. There, the Russo-American conflict still existed in all its inane fury. There, loyalty oaths were still enforced. There, station KHJ-TV ran the old movie *Tom, Dick and Harry* in a slightly shortened version. Paul Jarrico's name had been removed from the credits. "The public," observed Jarrico, "is not to be protected from my work—however beguiling and subversive it may be. The public is only to be protected from my name."

But at the brain there was a pronounced difference in style and attitude. In mid-1957 John Cogley was again roused by the HUAC, which greeted him with a new subpoena. It still wished to inspect the documents gathered during his research for the blacklisting report.

Cogley responded tartly. "No one we interviewed or corresponded with," he wrote, "had any idea that what he said or wrote would be turned over to a Governmental body. Were I to supply you with the material you demand, I would feel that I had betrayed these people. . . . I will not supply you with the documents you demand. In stating this, I know that I may be asking for a great deal of trouble. There may be a high price to pay. Please God, I will be ready to pay it."

To ensure the security of his sources, Cogley gathered his documents, retired to his apartment in Brooklyn and fed them into his fireplace. All the damning confessions and accusations, all the valuable names, fled up the chimney. The potential blacklist became soot and swirled through New York as airborne garbage. Please God, there was no price to pay. The new hearings were postponed, then discontinued.

As Stanley Prager had it, "By 1958 you could sense a difference in the agencies and networks. They used to tell me they couldn't use me because I was too short. At the beginning of the year they whispered that they couldn't use me because I was blacklisted. In the middle of the year they told me how much they hated the blacklist. By Christmas they were willing to be seen talking with me on the street." To hire him—or his fellows—was, of course, another matter. In 1958, the needy Zero Mostel agreed to do a club date in the Catskills. He had intended to trot out his *shticks* from the days of the *boîtes*. But when he arrived at the resort, he found that the manager had reduced the rate from $300 to $150. Raging, emptying tumblers of Scotch, Mostel eventually reeled onstage and delivered his entire act in Yiddish, pouring torrents of abuse upon his audience. With transcendent obtuseness, his audience applauded enthusiastically; they had interpreted the routine as insult comedy.

By now Arthur Miller, Pete Seeger, George Tyne and other members of the non-cooperative had been cited for contempt, only to have the citations thrown out by higher courts. A theatrical impresario named Joseph Papirofsky, better known as Joe Papp, director of the green, exuberant New York Shakespeare Festival, had been hauled before the Committee to intimate that he had left the Party long ago. When the young director argued against the notion of a blacklist, investigator Arens countered with the tired jawbreaker, "Do you think it is wrong to disassociate from public media of expression in this country people who are secret members of a conspiracy which has as its avowed objective the overthrow of this Government by force and violence?" Papp replied, "I just think it is wrong to deny anybody employment because of their political beliefs," and this time the witness was free to return to Central Park. There the patron saint of cement, Robert Moses, criticized Papp's productions because the fans of free Shakespeare were trampling on the grass. (The Bard did rather more poorly at the festival at Stratford, Connecticut. There, when a lowly stage manager took the Fifth and was retained, five trustees resigned in protest.)

In May 1958, Aware Inc. held a festival entitled "Unite and Fight!—A Citizens' Rally in Support of the FBI, the Senate Internal Security Subcommittee and the House Committee on Un-American Activities." Rabbi Benjamin Schultz gave the invocation; Fulton Lewis III entertained at the organ. The old faces were there: O'Neil of the American Legion, Roy Cohn of the hallowed McCarthy subcommittee, Arens of the current House Committee, William F. Buckley, Jr., of the *National Review*, Hartnett of Hartnett. By now Aware had begun to

attract some very unsavory types who liked to spread hate literature; the directors found it necessary to add a line at the bottom
of the program: "Aware Inc. and Cooperating Organizations
are not responsible for any literature distributed outside the
auditorium." There were mighty few showfolk left on Aware's
letterhead of affiliations. Ward Bond of the Alliance still maintained his allegiance. So did comedy scenarist Morrie Ryskind.
And Herbert Philbrick, ex-FBI man, considered a tertiary creative type now that a TV series had been made from his best-
seller, *I Was a Communist for the FBI*. This handful exhausted
Aware's glamour. The rally heard the presentation "This Is the
Enemy" with sullen reaction. There were not enough attendants
for sustained applause. Even though admission was only a dollar,
the rally could not draw flies. Aware had struck bottom. At the
meeting Hartnett, never the most relaxed of speakers, appeared
tenser than usual. Perhaps it was because he had been instructed
to appear for his official Examination Before Trial in the case of
Faulk v. Aware.

It was during this exam that the state of the blacklist was
strikingly embodied in a scrap of testimony. At Nizer's office
Hartnett and his attorney, Godfrey Schmidt, displayed a lac-
quer of benignity and confidence. Hartnett puffed a large cigar
and answered questions pleasantly until Nizer began uncovering
some wormy disclosures from the early fifties. "Mr. Nizer,"
Hartnett suddenly snapped, "I would remind you that I'm not
on the witness stand and you're not a district attorney." Nizer,
whose forensic style could be turned on like a spigot, quietly
informed the court reporter that what he was about to say was
on the record. Then he fed Hartnett his own recipe: chilled
indignation. "Do I understand, sir, you presume to instruct me
in the conduct of this examination? How dare you impudently
speak of district attorneys and witnesses? You, sir, you who have
sat as judge, jury, prosecuting attorney and executioner on the
lives and careers of hundreds of loyal, innocent victims! You,
sir, who have drawn the noose of starvation around the neck of

that innocent man sitting there, seeking to starve his children and destroy his reputation? You dare, sir, instruct me in the conduct of this case?"

Faulk, like some maimed survivor from the Terror watching Robespierre in bonds, witnessed Vincent Hartnett *in extremis*. Faulk remembered the talent consultant "trying to puff his cigar and sticking it, instead, in his ear." Schmidt could not help his client. Hartnett was beyond legal aid, beyond prudence. Nizer pressed for a confession, for an admission of malediction. He got it. As regards the plaintiff, Hartnett suddenly admitted, "I was sold a barrel of false information." The researcher extraordinaire, the man with the computer brain, "the walking encyclopedia of subversives," as Matusow had called him, had blown it. Faulk v. Aware Inc. would continue to the court, but technically the blacklist was approaching its final cardiac arrest.

Even now, however, Aware Inc. refused to close down. Shortly after Hartnett's confession another rally was held, this time to welcome the Un-American Activities Committee at the Sheraton McAlpin Hotel. The title of this get-together was Cocktails Against Communism, and it featured Arens and Dolores Scotti, the Committee's local broomstick rider. There were perhaps a hundred people in attendance—at the same $1 per. Don Appel, Committee investigator, complained to his audience that fifteen of the persons he sought had gone underground. As the evidence soon proved, the charges against these few had no more substance than the Communist fronts that had once attracted them.

Take, for example, the witness of Dalton Trumbo, an authority on Hollywood Communism. He was one of the few Hollywood writers who had joined the Communist Party twice, 1943–48 and 1954–57. By mid-1958 he estimated the total Old Red membership as five. In New York there can have been few more. The Committee's hands were empty. Aware's treasury was as bare. Its membership now seemed to consist largely of those blue-haired ladies commemorated in *The New Yorker* cartoon, knitting the sampler: "Impeach Earl Warren." The name Marsha Hunt was maligned by one member. "I think you're wrong," said another. "I know her very well, and you can trust her." The old names had disintegrated like old nitrate stock, but a few fans still liked to be close to show biz. To knock or to boost a star was still to drop her name. Aware was the last to know that Hollywood was dead. Murray Kempton, who attended Cocktails Against Communism, wrote a slightly premature obit: "It is all up with them. Their back is broken. Still we are condemned to stand and watch them as they wriggle on until sundown."

Touched by no one knew what memories and guilts, anxiously spelling his liberalism in block capitals, Stanley Kramer hired a blacklisted writer in 1958. His name was Nedrick Young, once a hostile witness and now forced to hide under the pseudonym Nathan E. Douglas. With his collaborator, the whitelisted Harold Jacob Smith, Young wrote the script for *The Defiant Ones*, an uplifting blockbuster about race relations, written and directed in Bodoni Bold. It featured a black convict (Sidney Poitier) chained to a white one (Tony Curtis), and exhibited the typical Kramer prejudice against substance. In a period of ostentatious social conscience the film became a smash, propelled Poitier from feature roles to authentic star, and made Kramer and United Artists considerably richer. It also defied the blacklist in a cheerful, devious manner, apparent to the Academy but unknown to audiences. In the opening of *The Defiant Ones* a truck is transporting a group of convicts in a harsh, driving storm. As the windshield wipers bang across the windshield, the credit "Written by Nathan E. Douglas, Harold Jacob Smith" is superimposed over the faces of two truck drivers. The driver on the left is Young. The gesture was typically Krameresque, professing a warm liberality to the cognoscenti, and continuing the straight-faced, cooperative attitude should the American Legion be looking on. It *was* looking on, and it threatened to make noise if the Academy rescinded its prohibitions against subversive artists. But by 1958 the Academy felt that it could cross the street without the aid of Eagle Scouts.

With a great wrench, the industry rescinded the stricture that it suddenly found "unworkable and impractical." After a heated debate, the Academy courageously voted to leave blacklisting solely to the producers. "The proper functioning of the Academy," it announced, "is only to honor achievement." The words earned stories in every major newspaper. Their editorials strikingly echoed *Time* Magazine's story headed BLACKLIST FADE-OUT. ("In effect it was the formal end of the Hollywood blacklist. For barred writers the informal end came long ago. At least 15 percent of current Hollywood films are reportedly written by blacklist members.")

In 1959 Ward Bond agreed in a gruff lament: "They're all working now, all these Fifth Amendment Communists, and I don't think that anything I say about it will make much difference. There's no point at issue. We've just lost the fight and it's as simple as that. I think the fight might be resumed some day in the future. I don't know. It's going to take a tremendous change in public opinion, and I don't see how it's going to come about with the courts acting the way they have."

Otto Preminger promptly told the world that he had hired Dalton Trumbo to write *Exodus*; Paramount openly distributed the film *Chance Meeting*, written by blacklistees Millard Lampell and Ben Barzman and directed by the subversive refugee Joseph Losey.

The American Legion had not heard the news, and continued its Americanism policies. When Kramer openly hired Nedrick Young to do the script of *Inherit the Wind*, the Legion's commander, Martin B. McKneally, released an official bull: "The American Legion will not cooperate with Mr. Kramer or anyone else in a conspiracy of silence."

Benjamin Kahane of Columbia hastened to reassure the

Legion that the blacklist was still in effect. Only 4 of the 224 persons named as subversives by the Legion back in 1955 were still working, he said. But the implacable patriots renewed their "war of information," protesting "the hiring of Soviet-indoctrinated artists." But this time when they gave a war nobody came. So severely had the right eroded that in March of 1960 George Sokolsky devoted a column to Stanley Kramer and the depreciation of property values in Hollywood. "A man is entitled to take the Fifth," he said in a final, weary summation of the battle's end. "But I am entitled to distrust such a man. He is right and I am right. If that distrust keeps me away from the box office, that is my business. If he is a sincere man, he will not care. He will proclaim his ideals throughout the land. If he is insincere, he will weep about a blacklist. Ward Bond, whose success is phenomenal in *Wagon Train*, was for years black-listed* for being a conservative, reactionary, flag-flying 110 per-cent American. Did he cry about it?"

End of column. End of epoch. Sok had abandoned his aggressive stance and assumed the role of defender of the political victims. The mind was dizzied; the plague was indeed weakening. Even so, it was not quite finished. Succor for the blacklisters was to come from two sources, familiar and peculiar. In 1960 Nedrick Young, along with John Howard Lawson, Albert Maltz, Lester Cole and others, sued MGM, Columbia and other major studios, charging conspiracy to maintain a blacklist in direct violation of the anti-trust laws. Shortly afterward, in an independent suit, Herbert Biberman started the legal machinery necessary to sue producers' associations and

---

* A partial list of the post–1947 credits of Ward Bond (1905–1960):
Fort Apache (1948); *Unconquered* (1948); *Tap Roots* (1948); *Three Godfathers* (1949); *Singing Guns* (1950); *Wagonmaster* (1950); *The Great Missouri Raid* (1951); *Only the Valiant* (1951); *Hellgate* (1952); *The Moonlighter* (1953); *Hondo* (1954); *Johnny Guitar* (1954); *A Man Alone* (1955); *The Searchers* (1956); *Dakota Incident* (1956); *Pillars of the Sky* (1956); *The Halliday Brand* (1957); *Alias Jessie James* (1959); *Rio Bravo* (1959). At the time of his death he was the wagon master on the long-running TV series *Wagon Train*.

distributors for conspiracies against the film *Salt of the Earth*. The courts proved hostile; the Supreme Court failed to hear the Young suit. The Biberman complaint ended when a jury decided on the basis of evidence that no conspiracy existed against *Salt of the Earth*.

The *unfamiliar* enemy appeared the week of Sokolsky's plea for social justice for Ward Bond. Frank Sinatra, spunky, wealthy, theoretically beyond the reach of the old blacklisters, re-enacted the old Gary Cooper–Carl Foreman playlet in two scenes. First, he told the Legion to go to hell by announcing that he had hired the dreaded Albert Maltz to write a screen adaptation of William Bradford Huie's *The Execution of Private Slovik*. Response was immediate and loud. Not only had Sinatra approved one of the original Hollywood Ten (in whose short *The House I Live In* he had appeared c. 1949) but he had also chosen a book whose subject was the victimization of the only World War II soldier to be given the death sentence for desertion. Sinatra sought to silence his critics in a large ad in *Variety*: "As the producer of the film I and I alone will be responsible for it. I accept that responsibility. I ask only that judgment be deferred until the picture is seen."

But that was not all he was asking. Sinatra had allied himself with a young politician's drive for the Presidential nomination. "I make movies," he continued in *Variety*. "I do not ask the advice of Senator Kennedy on whom I should hire. Senator Kennedy does not ask me how he should vote in the Senate."

Two weeks later Sinatra reversed himself. He had been under intolerable pressures, many of them, Maltz suspected, from the Senator's father, Joseph Kennedy. "In view of the reaction of my family, my friends and the American public," Sinatra said, "I have instructed my attorneys to make a settlement with Mr. Maltz and to inform him that he will not write the screenplay for *The Execution of Private Slovik*. I had thought that the major consideration was whether or not the resulting script would be in the best interests of the United States. . . . But the American public has indicated it feels the morality of hiring Albert Maltz is the more crucial matter and I will have to accept this majority opinion."

No survey, no poll was taken of public opinion; Sinatra had no way of knowing what a popular opinion was. On the other hand, one man, properly placed, constituted a majority. Perhaps it would be better, as Sinatra's friends had said, to give now and gain later. To get Jack the Presidency, and then see a true climate of free opinion return to America. Better to concede on this and win the election. Consider the alternative: What if Nixon were to gain the White House?

FOURTEEN

1

TRAGEDY IS FARCE MISTIMED, its characters caught by movements that should have freed them. (What if the husband had not peeked behind the door? What if the policeman had been late?)

Lawrence Johnson never considered himself a figure of tragedy, or even sadness. His country had rewarded him and, as he saw it, he was simply returning the favor. And it had come to this—ingratitude, mockery, fear. He had not dared to go to the Faulk trial because of a recurrent illness, but he was informed that the opposition's lawyer was like a man possessed. Louis Nizer spoke, one reporter said, "with that ring of somebody's indignation at outrageous injustice which can be rectified only by somebody else's million dollars." Once, back in 1947, the stars had arranged themselves on the right side. Today they were all in malign conjunction. Everett Sloane, Tony Randall, Kim Hunter, Charles Collingwood, David Susskind were playing cameo roles in the dismantling of Aware Inc. Vincent had been particularly bad on the stand. Nizer had found—God knew where—that Hartnett had entered upon his books the item "Santa Claus: $2," thereby blacklisting an actor who assumed the red suit one Christmas. He could imagine what Nizer would do with *that*. Worse, Hartnett had pointed to a

281

woman in the courtroom and identified her as Mrs. John Henry Faulk, whereupon the woman rose and identified herself as Mrs. Evelyn Sofer. The onlookers no longer suppressed their amazement: the laughter was open and Judge Geller had had to warn them several times. Nizer had raised the hoods and revealed the vigilantes. He seemed to know of everything and everyone: Harvey Matusow, Lieutenant Crain, Francis Neuser, John Dungey. Jack Wren, of BBD&O, had come to the stand not as an old friend but as a seething new opponent. His duty, he had testified, was "to protect our clients against Vincent Hartnett, who wrote poison-pen letters behind our backs accusing us of loading our shows with Communists."

The old man felt sick just thinking about the trial, nauseated all the time. Doctors for the prosecution refused to believe him. Only Johnson's own physician, Dr. Warder Ayer of Syracuse, understood the cardiac spasms, the tricks of the esophagus. But *no one* quite understood the feelings of a well-meaning soul turned into a fugitive. In the *New York Post* Murray Kempton called him Sick-call Larry. "It is rather odd," the columnist wrote, "that a man like Lawrence Johnson would not lust to face the enemies of his country; there is something pathetic in this image of him wandering from doctor to doctor, hoping for an exemption . . . he, the senior officer of an unspeakable crew. One might at least expect of him that he would stand up and answer 'here' at its last formation. Vincent Hartnett sits and takes it, and all Johnson could do was to look for a doctor to certify that, in the face of his enemies, there was danger that he might throw up."

Derision. Laughter. Mockery for a patriot of seventy-three years. He had driven up to this place in Bronxville, this Town and Country Motel, seeking to be far away, yet too curious to hide in a bed in Syracuse. He seemed unsure of the time. These fugue states had come on him with increasing frequency in old age. How could he explain to doctors the pain, the fear of accusers whom he had never seen, who wished to embarrass,

humiliate and destroy him? Who could comprehend such catastrophic impulses? Those people who said they suffered when
Aware pursued them, what did *they* know of real fear? It was
late. The pajamas hung loose, the mind dissolved in panic. At
seventy-three a man had earned the right to lie down. The
barbiturates allowed no further light. The water tasted of
chlorine. He lay back, waiting.

2

On July 28, 1962, a man identified as Lawrence Johnson,
defendant in the John Henry Faulk trial, was found dead in
the Town and Country Motel. The information came during
Nizer's summation and was withheld from the jurors. The next
day they awarded Faulk $3,500,000—the largest judgment ever
returned in a libel suit.

The sum was ultimately reduced by the courts; even then the
defendants struck a series of poses demonstrating the emptiness
of their pockets. But the shock value of the verdict remained.
Morality was—and is—a foreign concept to networks, agencies
and film studios. And libel was one of those terms taken care of
by the guys downstairs in Legal. Money, on the other hand,
was—and is—always understood in its basic, excremental terms.
In 1962 the blacklist had at last proved unprofitable. The show
that had been playing to standees could not continue on
twofers. After a run of fifteen years it would have to be folded.
History had overtaken it.

Yet if the nation was done with the blacklist, irony was not.
Hartnett and Aware Inc. continued their appeals to the
Supreme Court. There the counselors petitioned for *certiorari*.
There was, they felt, a Constitutional question, a debate raised
by the First Amendment, used so long ago—can it have been in
this century?—by those angry and bitter men in Hollywood.
The appeal was denied 7 to 2. The blacklisters' only friends in

Court were the dreaded libertarians Black and Douglas. And still there was a punchline to come. Their futile new petition to the Supreme Court maintained that the libel law was derived from English ecclesiastical law. It violated, they said, that part of the Constitution which provided for the separation of church and state. So the crypto-clerics had come to this: an unambiguous case of Scripture quoting the Devil for its own purpose.

3

Despite its ignominious finish, few un-American institutions have proved as durable and effective as the blacklist. Its direct destruction of performers was perhaps never as complete as its practitioners hoped or advertised. In its best year, 1955, Adrian Scott made a scrupulous survey of the Hollywood listees. He counted 106 writers, 36 actors and 11 directors. These, plus a small group of technicians, comprised a total of 214 workmen. Add another several hundred in television, radio, advertising and the total remains a fraction of the industries—the best fraction, it may be argued, but a minority all the same. The real damage extended far beyond the damned. It was done to the subject matter of films for almost two decades—years when American society underwent severe and profound changes, unrecorded—or dishonestly distorted—by films. Television was worse afflicted. In 1963 the CBS program *The Defenders* stoutly presented Ernest Kinoy's drama of an actor blacklisted in the fifties. Up to the week of its presentation, John Randolph was blacklisted by the network. He was released only upon the insistence of the author. The network could see no hypocrisy in its policies. The blacklist also shadowed those whom it could not possibly reach. During the period of the right-wing dissolution, William Faulkner, A. B. Guthrie, Ernest Hemingway, William Saroyan, John Steinbeck, Thornton Wilder and Tennessee Williams each received a letter. It reminded them that motion pictures, policed and censored by federal authority, had become "official art."

"Will you," asked Dalton Trumbo, "as an American writer whose work has been transferred to the screen—perhaps by some of those same persons in whose behalf I make this request—send me a statement condemning the blacklist? And will you permit me to release your statement to the press . . . in still another effort to destroy this hateful business before it overwhelms us altogether?"

Not one of the authors replied. Some were afraid. Others were protected by the general anesthesia of the fifties. Still others experienced a synaptic affliction best described by Millard Lampell: "You knew what you wanted to write, but something happened between the brain and the fingers: the worst censorship of all—self-censorship."

The blacklisted had been damned wholesale; they emerged single-file, blinking in the light. Like most prisoners of war, they disliked talking about the past. When they did recollect, they tended to throw a golden gel on the lost years. "Maybe the blacklist was a good thing," Zero Mostel confided to a listener. "If I'd kept on making lousy movies I might be the most hackneyed, tired old actor you ever saw today. This way I returned to painting. And I got a chance to do James Joyce and Sholem Aleichem."

Stanley Prager likened his colleagues to a submarine crew. "Now that it's over," he said, "we romanticize it. One guy got rich selling insurance; another switched successfully to business. I myself became a director. Once a kid asked me whether I was bitter about the blacklist. I said, 'Why should I be? What would I have been if I had been allowed to continue in the movies? A Jewish Jack Oakie? A funny friend of the hero? This way I started a whole new career.' And then suddenly I listened to myself. It was a con. But it was something I *had* to say. Nobody can recall those lost years, those lost people, without some kind of emotional raincoat."

A few of the writers came back all the way. When Millard Lampell won an Emmy he told the crowd, "I think I should tell you I was blacklisted"—and brought the house down. Tears came to the eyes of producers who had blacklisted him. Now they stood beating their palms in appreciation; what the hell, remorse was what the crowd was buying. Abe Polonsky, Waldo Salt, Ring Lardner, Jr., returned to films and were greeted with the appropriate lamentations and cheers. There was a special poignance in Albert Maltz' gift of royalties to the beleaguered Russian, Aleksandr Solzhenitsyn. "Life," wrote the old blacklistee, "is not a puppet performance."

The newspapers omitted references to Sam Moore, the writer of the forties radio series *The Great Gildersleeve* and one of the highest-paid writers of the period. He had become a maker of industrial films, as obscure in the East as Alvah Bessie was in the West. In San Francisco, as a technician for the *hungry i* night club, Bessie resembled an old Kipling pensioner with a grizzled headful of memories and grudges. Once, between shows at the night club, Woody Allen found himself walking down the street with Bessie. "Suddenly," the comedian said, "he ran into some turncoat from the past. The man recognized Alvah, wanted to shake his hand, you know, forgive and forget, and suddenly Bessie was climbing all over him, pummeling him until someone separated the men. Remember at this time he was over sixty. But he was still tough, and still absolutely unforgiving."

Some of the actors, now middle-aged, returned as fresh faces and hot properties who could not sit down between jobs. They were as resentful as Bessie, but far more reserved. Howard Da Silva, Jack Gilford, John Randolph, Will Geer became subjects for interviews and panel shows, but they were reluctant to dwell for long on the blacklist era. "If I can't explain it to myself," asked Gilford, "how can I explain it to strangers?" No columns, no hours were ever devoted to Canada Lee, Philip Loeb, Jean

Muir, Ireene Wicker, Mady Christians. Show business, like the army, is concerned with survivors, not casualties.

Of all the blacklisters, not one was to remain in public view. They were night creatures of insubstantial composition. The light of social alteration scattered them forever. Harvey Matusow was last seen in London, still the overweight hustler—this time of the rock culture—and insisting that during his blacklisting years he had really been a double agent. In January 1950, he claimed, before offering his services to the FBI and Aware Inc. as an informer, he had written a sworn, notarized statement and placed it with his father. It stated, said Matusow, that the undersigned was really doing "investigative reporting" for a one-man campaign to subvert the right. "I say this document exists," Harvey told an interviewer in 1972. "Take it or leave it; it's up to you. I'm not going to get involved in the pedantic cross-examination of trivia." The poisoning of a culture, the ruination of careers and minds—it was all trivia now.

Vincent Hartnett, free-lance investigator, retired to a home in a Westchester suburb, where he teaches private school in utter obscurity, still sending small checks to John Henry Faulk in partial payment for a wrecked life. Aware Inc. shut down its files; they were no longer of interest even to the FBI. The old vigilantes still hold important business positions, but none exhibits any interest in political life. Where it is convenient, they too distort memory for convenience and, perhaps, sanity. David Miller, long the house lawyer for Young and Rubicam, recently refused to be interviewed on the subject of the fifties. "Young and Rubicam," he maintained, in direct contradiction to all the evidence, "led the fight to stop the blacklist." Thus did the Party line go dead at both terminals.

Anecdota survived the epoch. Blacklistees still love to recount Zero Mostel's greeting to Kazan at a backstage encounter: "Hello, Looselips." Guests at Producer Hal Prince's New Year's Eve party remember Jerome Robbins empurpling like an eggplant when Madeline Gilford raised her glass to him and shouted, "1953 can kiss my ass!"

But this gandy dancing on the grave was painfully small workmen's compensation. The blacklisted for the most part lost their lives; the blacklisters for the most part escaped with dollars and reputation intact. As for those who cooperated, who gave names and references, who helped the inquisition continue—they had only the sentence of that most overrated court, the personal conscience. None of them was the type to wear sandwich boards reading *Mea Culpa*. For a while they felt excruciating remorse, and now and then, at some chance encounter, a cooperative witness would receive a belt from a man like Bessie who had the temerity to remember.

Almost two decades after Elia Kazan's fearless exposé of Elia Kazan, Norman Mailer and the columnist Pete Hamill were challenged by the editors of *Ramparts* when they saw the writers drinking with Gadge. Mailer accused them of "moralism." Hamill later wrote: "I don't know very much about Kazan, although I'm reasonably familiar with the bullshit he committed in the 1950s. The thing is whether that kind of thing can forever damn a man, or whether a writer can afford not to learn something else about the guy's character."

It was Lillian Hellman, typically, who was able to characterize the entire epoch in an aside. At a party she found herself uncomfortably close to some people who had jettisoned their old associations and furnished the Committee with names in 1947. The playwright's face, whose lines were never difficult to read, distressed her hostess. "For God's sake, Lillian," she said, "it's all over. Forgive."

"And this is what it comes to," Hellman replied. "Nobody believed anything."

Such spiritual anesthesia seems foreign to contemporary society, where protest and dissent now seem cloned from the artistic spirit. The pluralistic, roiling seventies, we are told, are reminiscent not of birth but rebirth, the thirties redevivus. In that case, in *any* case, complacency is extremely ill-advised.

Albert Camus had the first words in this chronicle. It is appropriate that he have the last. At the end of *The Plague,* Dr. Rieux "knew what those jubilant crowds did not know but could have learned from books: that the plague bacillus never dies or disappears for good; that it can lie dormant for years and years in furniture and linen-chests; that it bides its time in bedrooms, cellars, trunks and bookshelves; and that perhaps the day would come when, for the bane and the enlightening of men, it would rouse up its rats again and send them forth to die in a happy city."

Farce is tragedy out for a good time; the rats make funny sounds as they gnaw at the walls.

A Selected Bibliography

The casual researcher may wonder whether the blacklist ever existed. Many libraries carry no listings at all under the title, and even the *Reader's Guide to Periodical Literature* missed a score of articles written for small-circulation magazines.

I found the bulk of my information in several hundred interviews, in the unparalleled *Time-Life* newspaper-clip files which, in other decades, managed to cull items from nine major New York newspapers, plus the *Daily Worker*, the *Washington Post* and such vanished periodicals as the *New York Compass* and *PM*. These, of course, are unavailable to the general reader. But there are several books of almost equal value. Some are out of print; all are available through the services of interested (and relentless) librarians.

WRITERS ON THE LEFT by Daniel Aaron (Avon Books). A detailed, scrupulous analysis of the impact of Marxism on writers as varied as John Howard Lawson and F. Scott Fitzgerald. "Forbearance— good word" was the bedrock of Fitzgerald's philosophy, quoted with approval and fine understanding in this indispensable work.

THE FERVENT YEARS by Harold Clurman (Hill & Wang Dramabook). The stirrings, ripening and dissolution of the Group Theatre, a thirties organization that behaved *en masse* as Clurman did singly: "I really only knew what I was about through my actions." Here the great blemished figures of Elia Kazan and Clifford Odets can be seen before their sad capitulations. Equipped with hindsight, the historian can perceive the many tiny personal and historic steps leading to the confessional.

HOLLYWOOD ON TRIAL by Gordon Kahn (Boni & Gaer). The first hard-cover book on the trial of the Hollywood Ten. Kahn could hardly be objective; those were his friends on "trial" and he himself was later blacklisted. Nonetheless, the book invents no melodrama or horror—it simply reports what transpired. Kahn has a fine eye and ear for the accents of the Congressmen and their proud, totally confused targets. Kahn also reports some revealing quotes from angry Hollywood liberals of the period including Cornel Wilde, Gregory Peck, Burt Lancaster, Frank Sinatra, Gene Kelly and others who soon managed to quiet their sense of outrage.

INQUISITION IN EDEN by Alvah Bessie (Macmillan). This is the definitive case history of a screenwriter who made the epochal journey from the New York left to the Hollywood vacuum. Bessie is not much of a historian, but as a refined and furious gossip columnist he shows the methods and manners of the industry for which "politics" had no meaning unless it was preceded by the word "office."

PART OF OUR TIME by Murray Kempton (Simon and Schuster). Although Kempton has openly regretted certain rather censorious portions of this book, *Part of Our Time* has attained the status of a classic memoir. The author's appraisals of the veteran red-hunter J. B. Matthews, his perhaps too cold-eyed view of the Hollywood Communists, and his history of the proletarian novelists are vital to any student of the blacklist—or, indeed, of the thirties.

SALT OF THE EARTH by Herbert Biberman (Beacon Press). The story of an intractable, outraged old radical and his refusal to bend to his time. Biberman's interrupted attempts to produce a labor melodrama in fifties America reads like the trials of a writer trying to produce an honest piece of craftsmanship in Russia of the same period.

THIRTY YEARS OF TREASON by Eric Bentley (Viking). A very serviceable scissors job done by a discerning critic who decided, inexplicably, simply to tidy up and republish the HUAC testimony of a great many show people. Commentary is avoided and the dialogue tends to hang in the air like flies. Still, Committee transcripts are hard to find and Bentley's book can save librarians and researchers a good deal of trouble. His afterword, however, is rambling and intemperate—a disservice to the old left for the service (and the flattery) of the new.

THE JUDGES AND THE JUDGED by Merle Miller (Doubleday). This is the first book about the blacklist in television and suffers from that common and honorable affliction, protection of sources. Miller, one of the few talented writers to have served the ACLU in the crucial forties and fifties, acted as his own reporter and researcher, spoke to almost all the important blacklisters and to many of the afflicted performers. For his pains he was mocked by several terrified ACLU board members and the book was swiftly discredited. *The Judges and the Judged* is a chapter that the ACLU has seen fit to hide and a book that deserves a wider readership.

ADDITIONAL DIALOGUE by Dalton Trumbo (M. Evans and Co.). Hollywood's man of crank letters sends his messages to producers, blacklistees, gas-station owners, agents—anyone, it appears, who has a mailbox. Trumbo's canny, revealing correspondence shows how he was able to survive the blacklist by operating pseudonymously, wheedling favors and badgering his creditors before they dunned him. The book also shows the importance of economics to the old Hollywood radical: nearly every page mentions money with reverence.

FALSE WITNESS by Harvey Matusow (Cameron & Kahn). A mean-spirited little apology by an amateur forger who took in Joseph McCarthy, the secular blacklisters, the Boy Scouts and everyone else who would listen to him. His repellent retraction shows the moral state of a decade that made Matusow a celebrity twice: first as a right-wing expert on American Communism, and then as a guilty liberal.

REPORT ON BLACKLISTING by John Cogley (The Fund for the Republic). The stolid, basic study of the origins and operations of the blacklist. These volumes (one is devoted to the movies, the other to radio-TV) also rely on unattributed quotes and overprotected sources. But their research is sound and their conclusions are unassailable. The Cogley report also includes a study of the blacklisted *right*—an effort never attempted by any of the professional anti-Communists.

FREEDOM AND THE FOUNDATION by Thomas C. Reeves (Knopf). A sharp, neglected analysis of the repercussions of the Cogley report in Washington, where, with exceeding haste, the HUAC summoned Cogley and tried mightily to discredit him, his findings and the Foundation itself.

ONLY VICTIMS by Robert Vaughan (Putnam). A Ph.D. thesis described in an introduction by Senator George McGovern as "a sobering book in today's context." Sober it is, book it is not. Devoid of any connective tissue, *Only Victims* colorlessly recounts the adventures of the HUAC in the arena of show business. Its few acute phrases come from other books—notably Walter Goodman's *The Committee*—and it never gets around to discussing the methodology of the secular blacklisters, a group which, in the end, proved more formidable than Congress.

FEAR ON TRIAL by John Henry Faulk (Simon and Schuster). The journey of a blacklistee from celebrity to obscurity—a descent prompted by a few paragraphs in a mimeographed bulletin. The fear is well defined and harrowingly presented, but the trial is better done in THE JURY RETURNS by Louis Nizer (Simon and Schuster). In crisp forensic style, Nizer unmasks the opposition and shows the blacklisters to be cowards and bunglers undone by their own shabby testimonies.

BOOKS OF RELATED INTEREST

The Golden Web by Erik Barnouw (Oxford University Press).
Hello, Hollywood by Allen Rivkin and Laura Kerr (Doubleday).
The 50-Year Decline and Fall of Hollywood by Ezra Goodman (Simon and Schuster).
Brecht by Martin Esslin (Atheneum).
The Face on the Cutting Room Floor by Murray Schumach (Morrow).
Prime Time: The Life of Edward R. Murrow by Alexander Kendrick (Little, Brown).
Clifford Odets, Playwright by Gerald Weales (Bobbs-Merrill).
Wanderer by Sterling Hayden (Knopf).
The Committee by Walter Goodman (Farrar, Straus & Giroux).

Index

STEFAN KANFER

Stefan Kanfer is the first by-lined film critic in the history of Time *magazine, where he is an Associate Editor. In addition to regular appearances in that publication, he has contributed fiction, cartoons and articles on entertainment, literature, politics and Ping-Pong (another obsession) to a variety of periodicals including* Harper's, Discovery, The New Yorker, The Atlantic Monthly, Playbill, The New York Times Magazine, Life *and* Esquire. *He has been a guest lecturer at several universities and was a writer-in-residence at the City University of New York.*